The Determinants of Currency Crises

A Political-Economy Approach

Björn Rother
D188

palgrave
macmillan

First published 2009 by
PALGRAVE MACMILLAN

Palgrave Macmillan in the UK is an imprint of Macmillan Publishers Limited, registered in England, company number 785998, of Houndmills, Basingstoke, Hampshire RG21 6XS.

Palgrave Macmillan in the US is a division of St Martin's Press LLC, 175 Fifth Avenue, New York, NY 10010.

Palgrave Macmillan is the global academic imprint of the above companies and has companies and representatives throughout the world.

ISBN-13: 978–0–230–22181–9 hardback
ISBN-10: 0–230–22181–5 hardback

This book is printed on paper suitable for recycling and made from fully managed and sustained forest sources. Logging, pulping and manufacturing processes are expected to conform to the environmental regulations of the country of origin.

A catalogue record for this book is available from the British Library.

A catalog record for this book is available from the Library of Congress.

10 9 8 7 6 5 4 3 2 1
18 17 16 15 14 13 12 11 10 09

Printed and bound in Great Britain by
CPI Antony Rowe, Chippenham and Eastbourne

Contents

List of Tables

List of Figures

Acknowledgments

Seven years is a long time, too long to do justice to all those who helped me at the various stages of this project with advice and moral support. That said, some teachers, colleagues, and friends deserve to be singled out. First of all, I am highly indebted to my two advisors and academic teachers at the Free University of Berlin, Prof. Carl-Ludwig Holtfrerich and Prof. Michael Bolle, who were always ready to offer valuable guidance, and from whom I learned a lot. I am also extremely grateful to Michael Neugart and Jacques Le Cacheux for their advice; to my colleagues at McKinsey and the International Monetary Fund (IMF), including Chad Steinberg and Hans Weisfeld, for many interesting discussions on currency crises; to Cynthia Cindric who proof read the manuscript; and to Sean Culhane at the IMF and Taiba Batool at Palgrave MacMillan for helping me with the production process.

Moreover, the project would not have been possible without the incredible support of my parents and parents-in-law, to whom I am truly grateful. Most importantly, however, I want to express my deepest appreciation for the unweathering support of my family, to Friederike, Helena (yes, 'the' book is finally completed), Ferdinand, and Carlotta, who never lost faith in spite of the countless weekends, evenings, and vacation days in which daddy was hiding away in his little study.

1
Introduction

There are strong reasons to believe that political factors can play a role in the occurrence of currency crises. Policy makers deciding on exchange rate issues strive for their political survival in the face of political competition; base their actions on ideological preferences and the influence of special-interest groups; and should pay attention to the institutional structure in which they operate. Of course, all these considerations should be of particular relevance when the political system comes under extreme pressure, as tends to be the case in episodes of heightened currency instability. Such times of crisis typically involve difficult trade-offs between painful macroeconomic adjustment in support of the exchange rate regime in place and the often severe political, social, and economic consequences of a sudden and sharp currency depreciation.

Indeed, one does not need to go far back in history to find spectacular cases where political factors apparently contributed to triggering episodes of intense instability in foreign exchange markets. For example, in 1994, Mexico's Peso came under pressure after the leading candidate for the presidential election was shot. Likewise, on 20 February 2001, the Turkish Lira crashed after two days of publicized conflict between the Prime Minister and the President that revealed the poor cohesiveness of the governing coalition. Hardly one year thereafter, Argentina's convertibility regime was abandoned when key decision-makers within the macroeconomic policy community proved unable to agree on the fiscal reforms necessary to provide credible backing for the currency board in the face of widespread popular unrest.

Against this backdrop, and at a time when many emerging market countries are liberalizing their capital account regimes to better attract international capital flows but in so doing also increase their vulnerability to sudden shifts in investor sentiment,[1] it appears imperative to understand better the linkage between politics, the process by which governments are chosen and constrained through their constituents (see Frieden, 1997), and currency crises. In particular, an enhanced capacity to spot political vulnerabilities could help improve the design of exchange rate regimes and macroeconomic stabilization programs and make them more 'crisis-proof.'[2]

Recourse to the existing economic literature on currency crises can only offer limited guidance in this endeavor, as most of the mainstream models ignore the potential explicatory power of political determinants.[3] This is particularly true for the family of first-generation currency crisis models, which, building on the seminal work of Krugman (1979) and Flood and Garber (1984), treat the politics of economic policy making as a black box and portray governments as mechanically following a rigid policy rule that is blind to changes in political or economic conditions over time.[4]

While the government's decision regarding the optimal path for the exchange rate takes center-stage in second-generation crisis models, the political context in which this decision is embedded typically does not receive much attention in the models' structure, perhaps in the name of parsimony.[5] The political dimension is typically confined to a preference parameter in the policy maker's decision function, which indicates the importance given to the objective of a stable exchange rate and thus stable prices relative to competing macroeconomic objectives; given this parameter that is assumed to be time-invariant, a deterioration in economic fundamentals and/or private sector expectations may make the cost of defending the currency peg prohibitively expensive and hence trigger a speculative attack.

The narrow focus on economic and financial fundamentals is also reflected in most of the econometric work on currency crises. In the large cross-country panel regressions that dominate the field, factors including a high ratio of broad money to central bank reserves, a significant degree of real exchange rate overvaluation, and an excessive reliance on short-term external debt have been found to be relatively good predictors of currency crises.[6] At the same time, however, most studies shy away from looking behind these symptoms of looming crisis and do not investigate systematically the political and institutional context in which such economic vulnerabilities tend to build.[7]

By contrast, work in economic history and political science has been more receptive to the idea that developments in foreign exchange markets can be influenced by politics. In both fields, researchers emphasize that the problem of how a country creates the necessary belief in its commitment to a fixed exchange rate is not one that could be solely answered by reference to a more or less parsimonious set of economic fundamentals, but depends also on the specific political and institutional context.[8] In the perspective of these researchers, the credibility of economic policies, defined as the likelihood that an announced course of action would actually be carried out, does indeed depend on more than technical capacity as embodied, for example, in a sufficiently high level of central bank reserves or a favorable state of the economy. In particular, the assessment of a peg's stability would need to include an analysis of factors such as the ideological preferences of the incumbent government, the electoral calender, the objectives and strength of interest groups, and the institutional environment in which the policy makers operate (see Broz and Frieden, 2006).[9]

However, the studies in economic history and political science often suffer from the weaknesses inherent to the case study methodology. To begin with, many of the propositions regarding the causal relationship between political factors and currency crises are not clearly specified, which complicates the development of hypotheses that are suitable for empirical testing. Moreover, as Eichengreen (1998, p. 1012) says in well-crafted terms,

> [c]ase studies are useful for illustrating the practical applicability of abstract reasoning, but they are crude instruments for discriminating among alternative hypotheses and rating their relative explanatory power. Because individual cases, in their richness, are complex, they can always be interpreted in terms of several alternative analytical approaches. And because explanatory variables are correlated, interpretations in terms of one that omit all reference to others will suffer from omitted variables bias and run the risk of spurious correlation.

All these issues make it difficult to draw strong and generalizable conclusions on the link between politics and currency crises from these literatures alone.

Against this background, this study sets out to examine the link between politics and currency crises in an eclectic approach that blends methodologies and insights from all three academic disciplines. The various elements of the analysis are tied together by a unified underlying theme: the task at hand is to deliver an assessment on whether it would pay to look at politics to understand better the phenomenon of currency crises. In other words, I am looking for evidence to prove that political factors, in a systematic way, can have an effect on the likelihood of currency crises. This effect should be independent of economic and other structural determinants so that the inclusion of political factors in an explanatory framework offers an avenue toward more accurate prediction, hopefully without excessive additional complexity.

To limit the scope of this project, I will confine the analysis of the political conditions that could affect either the willingness or the ability of a government to deliver on its promise to maintain stable exchange rates to the realm of domestic politics. This choice appears to be justified because of the fact that, ultimately, politicians are held accountable at the national level and should therefore be expected to act accordingly, rather than in response to incentives at the international level (for supporting views, see Gourevitch, 1996; Putnam, 1988).

I will begin with an analysis of four prominent historical cases, in which a deterioration in the political environment has apparently played a significant role in the break of a currency crisis. Next, I will discuss how a standard model of the economic literature on currency crises can be extended to provide a richer political-economy flavor of this mathematically rigorous strand of work. Finally, the explanatory power of various hypotheses on the link between political factors and currency crises will be tested in an econometric study, which relies on a large cross-country data set.

By analyzing the developments that led to the British and French decisions to suspend gold convertibility in the 1930s, the Turkish crisis in February 2001, and the violent end of Argentina's currency board in January 2002, Chapter 2 seeks to shed some light on potential sources of political instability, and on the channels through which an unfavorable political environment may induce heightened volatility in foreign exchange markets. The four cases have been selected because they offer a rich testing ground for these considerations, including the potential role played by a high degree of ideological polarization in the political system, election-induced uncertainty over future policy preferences, fragile coalition governments, unstable parliamentary majorities, and conflicts of interest among different branches of government.

Chapter 3 will then seek to build upon a standard second-generation currency crisis model to introduce a variety of political-economy extensions, which facilitate a rigorous discussion of the channels through which changes in political conditions may affect the stability of exchange rate regimes. First, drawing on an approach developed by Meon and Rizzo (2002), the discussion will focus on how an upcoming election period could increase uncertainty over the strength of a government's exchange rate commitment, particularly if the prospects for its re-election are slim. Second, a new model will show how a self-interested fiscal policy maker may enjoy *de facto* veto power over exchange rate outcomes, as it can determine the tax take on the economy's output in such a way as to force the central bank into reneging on its exchange rate commitment. Performing several numerical simulations, I will demonstrate that intra-governmental conflict over the direction of exchange rate policy is particularly likely to emerge in situations where the fiscal authority has a strong preference for public spending (and thus high taxes) and does not share the central bank's strong aversion to inflation. Finally, and again based on a new model, the analysis will examine how lobbying activities can affect exchange rate outcomes via a fiscal policy channel.

After the theoretical discussion, Chapter 4 will turn to empirical testing. Using a large set of political indicators from a diverse sample of 69 countries over the 1975–97 period, I will progress from a presentation of descriptive statistics to the estimation of a broad array of logit models to determine the extent to which we should have confidence in the claim that the inclusion of political variables could make a difference in crisis prediction, compared with models that are solely based on economic fundamentals. The study distinguishes itself from other work that has recently been done in the field (see Section 4.2) through its conservative design that is explicitly aimed at a thorough testing of the results. In particular, each political variable needs to compete for statistical significance with other political and economic measures, while extensive robustness tests are performed with regard to the country and time coverage of the data. Moreover, I control for temporal dependence and autocorrelation in the data as well as for the influence of a country's per capita income level. The empirical analysis will conclude with a closer look at the behavior of currency markets around election dates, and at the impact of the composition of the legislature on the crisis risk faced by left-leaning governments.

Chapter 5 summarizes the results and offers some perspective on what to take away from the study.

I hope that this approach will enable us to accumulate sufficient evidence to provide the reader with some assurance that the association of specific political patterns with financial turbulence is more than just coincidental, consistent with Mancur Olson's claim saying that 'if, when we wake in the morning, we are surprised to see a patch or two of white outside, there could perhaps be uncertainty about the cause, but if every twig and piece of ground is freshly white, we know it snowed last night' (see Olson, 1982, p. 16).

2
Some Clues from History

2.1 Introduction

This chapter reviews four prominent cases of currency crises in some detail to identify the types of political conditions that tend to be associated with currency crises. Specifically, in discussing the political economy of the British and French decisions to break the link to gold in the 1930s, the Turkish crisis over 2000–01, and the decay of the Argentine convertibility regime prior to 2002, I hope to shed some light on potential sources of political instability and on the channels through which an unfavorable political environment may induce heightened volatility in foreign exchange markets. This discussion is intended to prepare the ground for developing more formal hypotheses on the link between political factors and the outbreak of currency crises discussed in Chapter 3, before proceeding with more thorough statistical testing based on a large country panel.

In all the four country cases considered, economic developments followed an almost text book-like path that, in hindsight, appears to have inevitably led to a severe currency crisis and the decision to end the prevailing exchange rate regime. All four countries pegged their national currencies to a stable foreign money or gold as a means to end periods of hyperinflation and widespread macroeconomic instability; in all cases, after initial successes in curbing inflation, the real exchange rate began to appreciate due to persistent demand pressures. This resulted in a deterioration of the external current account balance, which, in turn, increased the economies' dependence on a continued inflow of external financing. In all cases except Turkey, external imbalances were accompanied by recessionary dynamics at home, typically as a consequence of adverse external shocks and the rising level of real interest rates required to induce investors to stay once economic fundamentals worsened.

As a first line of defense, governments typically sought to respond to growing economic disequilibria through fiscal policy tightening and, in Argentina and Turkey, efforts to accelerate the implementation of their structural reform agenda. Once these initiatives proved insufficient to restore market confidence, the authorities attempted to stabilize expectations by mounting a more or less determined interest rate defense of the currency, which, except for the case of Argentina, could not be sustained for more than a couple of days or weeks.[10]

While all these dynamics are well documented elsewhere,[11] the case studies in this chapter take one step back and discuss why Argentina, France, Great Britain, and Turkey apparently were unable or unwilling to implement policy adjustments of sufficient strength to sustain their currency pegs in a context of building economic pressure. In particular, by analyzing the politics of macroeconomic policy, I will strive to identify patterns of political conditions that appear to be causally related to the failure of the four country cases to defend successfully their fixed exchange rate regimes; in other words, the search is on for the political determinants of currency crises.

The cases of interwar Britain and France as well as those of contemporary Argentina and Turkey have been selected because they offer a rich testing ground for such political-economy considerations. As we will see, they are sufficiently diverse to highlight the role of a variety of different political factors that appear to have limited the scope for a successful defense of the fixed exchange rate regime in place.

More generally, within the respective episodes considered, all of the countries were weak democracies in the sense that key democratic institutions had not yet matured. In interwar Britain and France, the political systems had to cope with the recent rise of mass politics driven by the emergence of powerful labor unions and the corresponding left-leaning parties in society and parliament.

Seven decades later, in Argentina and Turkey, the transition from autocratic rule was still relatively recent. As a result, shifts in voter sentiment were both sharp and frequent, and the authorities always needed to be careful not to alienate key constituencies in society that might have had the potential to destabilize the political system. While political conditions should be less volatile in mature democracies, the selected cases have the advantage of revealing more clearly the kind of political dysfunctions that affect investor sentiment.

2.2 Ending gold convertibility in the 1930s

This section will make the case that profound changes in the domestic political economy of Great Britain and France made it impossible to sustain the rigid link to gold over the longer term when economic conditions worsened dramatically with the onset of the Great Depression.[12] In particular, once unemployment figures reached intolerable levels, governments accountable to strong labor unions, but vested with fragile political majorities, found it increasingly difficult to allow the traditional adjustment mechanisms to work their way through the economies to correct external disequilibria.[13]

Britain and other European countries made the decision to reinstate gold convertibility in the mid-1920s, with the objective of ending the painful post-war experience of inflation and exchange rate instability.[14] Policy makers hoped that the renewed link to gold would contribute to repeating the success of the classical gold standard, which had facilitated the strong growth of cross-border trade and investment and enjoyed a high degree of investor confidence, as evidenced in mostly stabilizing short-term private capital flows.[15]

However, the early hopes were soon to be bitterly disappointed. After a short period of relative currency stability, a tightening of monetary policy in the United States and the onset of the Great Depression caused increasing strains in the system. In many European countries, current account revenues weakened precipitously while long-term credit from U.S. sources dried up, exacerbating these countries' balance-of-payments problems stemming from chronically overvalued real exchange rates. At the same time, recessionary conditions at home, which caused already high unemployment levels to rise further, made it very difficult for many governments to adjust to the continuous drain on gold by an additional tightening of fiscal policies and increases in interest rates.[16]

These adverse dynamics led to a weakening of investor confidence and ultimately to the suspension of convertibility, first by Austria and Germany and then by Britain in September 1931.[17] Other countries followed, including the United States, which took the dollar off gold in early 1933 after calls for a revaluation to increase prices for tradable-goods producers gathered strength. Given its painful experience with hyperinflation in the early 1920s, France held on to gold for a bit longer, but finally gave in to speculative pressures in October 1936.

Many scholars interpret the unraveling of the gold-exchange standard in the 1930s as the first clear manifestation in international monetary history that an exchange rate regime based on a free flow of capital could not be maintained when policy makers were no longer prepared to use monetary policy in a merely passive way to help adjust to external imbalances.[18] This view was made prominent by Nurkse (1944, p. 229) in his report to the League of Nations in 1944, stating that

> [e]xperience [of the interwar years] has shown that stability of exchange rates can no longer be achieved by domestic income adjustments if these involve depression and unemployment. Nor can it be achieved if such income adjustment involves a general inflation of prices which the country concerned is not prepared to endure. It is therefore only as a consequence of internal stability, above all in the major countries, that there can be any hope of securing a satisfactory degree of exchange stability as well. [...] There was a growing tendency during the inter-war period to make international monetary policy conform to domestic social and economic policy and not the other way round.

But the question then becomes why it is that governments found it so difficult to adjust to balance-of-payments disequilibria compared with the time of the classical gold standard. From a political-economy perspective, the profound changes in the domestic political landscape in many gold countries provide a key part of the answer.[19] Indeed, many of the historical accounts looking at the sociological and political underpinnings of the classical gold standard stress that before World War I, domestic political interests were strongly aligned with gold convertibility.[20] This is particularly true for Great Britain, where societal groups with a strong stake in stable money (the landed aristocracy, holders of government bonds, and the dynamic financial sector) could decide the political conflict over exchange rate policy that arose after the Napoleonic Wars in their favor (see Broz, 2000). Other countries, like France and Germany, did not commit to the gold standard with the same intensity, but found it beneficial to support its continued operation at times of crisis through the extension of liquidity support out of their gold reserves, in particular to the Bank of England.

However, the war experience led to the destruction of key institutions of nineteenth-century society in many European countries. In particular, it catalyzed the emancipation of strong labor movements across the continent and, through the extension of the electoral franchise, helped their political counterparts, the new labor parties, find their way into parliaments and cabinets.[21] The political empowerment of the left was accompanied by a growing recognition in contemporary economic thinking that the state could, and, from the perspective of many observers, should play an important role in determining domestic output, and hence employment levels, through the appropriate use of demand-management policies.[22] As Eichengreen and Jeanne (2000, p. 18) say, '. . . clearly, World War I was a watershed dividing the central bank autonomy of the nineteenth century from the more politicized monetary policy environment of the interwar years.'

Together, these developments led to a situation where governments, for the first time, had to consider whether or not the implementation of deflationary measures would undermine their political capital. Once they hesitated, market participants moved against the currency.

In the summer of 1931, when the loss of the Bank of England's gold reserves intensified after a series of Austrian and German bank defaults and the freezing of British long-term credits in Central Europe (see Oye, 1985), the incumbent Labor government under Ramsey MacDonald initially sought to counter the pressure through a series of fiscal adjustment measures. However, its minority position in parliament and an unwillingness to cut deeply into social programs, including unemployment benefits, on which its political constituency relied, prevented the adoption of a policy package that would calm down the markets.[23] In late August, the cabinet resigned and was replaced by a National Coalition government from elements of the Labor, Conservative, and Liberal Parties under the continued leadership of Prime Minister MacDonald, but this administration fared no better than its predecessor in delivering the required adjustment in the face of widespread popular protests (see Eichengreen, 2003).

Given the political deadlock over fiscal policy changes, responsibility for defending the exchange rate thus shifted to the Bank of England. However, when the sterling crisis struck London in July 1931, the central bank hesitated to raise its discount rate, for fear of the impact on the real economy. When it finally decided to increase the rate, it did so by a modest increase of 2 percentage points to only 4.5 percent. This reluctant effort was not enough to reassure the markets. As pointed out by Eichengreen and Jeanne (2000), the Bank of England was aware of the fact that it was no longer independent of domestic conditions and, in the face of high unemployment levels, did not want to use its policy instrument to the full effect.

Finally, amidst continued outflows of gold, the National Coalition government suspended gold convertibility on 19 September 1931. In doing so, policy makers removed the contentious issue from the political agenda prior to the October parliamentary elections, providing all major parties with an opportunity to abjure responsibility for the decision.[24]

In the case of France, political support for the suspension of gold convertibility gathered strength more slowly, even after the British devaluation in 1931 caused the competitive position of internationally oriented French businesses to worsen significantly. This reluctance to question the Franc's link to gold was a consequence of the country's experience with hyperinflation in the early 1920s, which dramatically surfaced the distributional conflicts existing within French society, but also a result of the marginalization of the urban working class represented in the Communist party—the only political group that consistently advocated a fundamental reorientation of economic policy—within the French political system of the early 1930s (see Simmons, 1994).[25]

That said, the high degree of government turnover made it difficult to implement a coherent macroeconomic policy response to the chronic overvaluation of the Franc Pointcaré. Between January 1931 and June 1936, a multitude of coalition governments led by a succession of 15 prime ministers sought to adopt fiscal adjustment measures of sufficient size to reverse the price pressure on French exports and stabilize the build-up of public debt, but achieved very little. Responsibility for this policy failure lay in the fragmented party system that resulted from the proportional electoral system. In particular, the proportional system favored the representation of narrowly defined special interests and, as a result, made it impossible to form stable parliamentary majorities that would support fiscal consolidation.[26] Economic decision making was further complicated by the 1933 decision of the Socialist party, a key power broker in the interwar political system, to no longer participate in any coalition that would seek a reduction of public sector wages, and by the growing threat from the extreme right of the political spectrum.

The political deadlock was resolved only after the June 1936 elections brought a comfortable majority for the Popular Front government, which comprised members of the Socialists and the Radical-Socialist party, but was also tolerated by the Communists. In response to intense strike activity soon after the election, the newly elected cabinet set out to implement worker-friendly and expansionary policies, including a public works program, a rise in minimum wages, the introduction of the 44-hour workweek, and a three-week annual holiday with pay. It also ruled out further deflationary measures (see Eichengreen and Temin, 1997). However, out of a fear of voter retaliation, the official goal of French policy as late as the summer of 1936 remained to defend and maintain gold convertibility, and the Bank of France continued to respond to gold losses by raising its discount rate (see Eichengreen, 1985). It was only when gold reserves neared exhaustion and the high interest rates became too much of a burden on the economy that the Popular Front government finally decided to end the link to gold in the context of the Tripartite agreement with the United States and Great Britain (see Oye, 1985).

2.3 Coalition bickering in Turkey, 2000–2001

The experience with the Turkish crisis in 2001 provides a good recent case study on how politicking within a coalition government can greatly weaken the credibility of an exchange rate-based macroeconomic stabilization program, even if the coalition enjoys a comfortable majority in parliament.[27] In particular, this example shows that coalitions comprised of parties with very heterogenous constituencies can find it difficult to progress with economic reforms and to retain investor confidence once the initial gains of a disinflation program are realized and the focus shifts toward the politically more challenging issues of deep structural reforms.

The Turkish government coalition committed to an exchange rate-based disinflation program in December 1999, which was supported by a Stand-By Arrangement of the International Monetary Fund (IMF). The program had three key components aimed at reducing the chronic fiscal imbalances that led to unsustainable inflation dynamics: a commitment to defend the Turkish Lira inside a small crawling band around a central parity vis-à-vis a currency basket comprising the U.S. dollar and the Euro, a strong effort of fiscal consolidation to improve the primary fiscal balance of the consolidated public sector by almost 7 percent of GDP to reach a surplus of 3.7 percent of GDP in 2000, and structural reforms aimed at limiting the role of the public sector in the economy that would contribute to increasing the economy's efficiency and render the fiscal adjustment sustainable.[28]

Supported by favorable market sentiment after Turkey's acceptance as a candidate for European membership, the program got off to an impressive start. In particular, a downward revision of inflationary expectations and sizable capital inflows translated into a substantial reduction in interest rates. This helped real GDP to grow at a higher-than-expected rate of 6.3 percent in 2000, and the debt burden of the public sector fell by almost 3 percent of GDP (see Table 2.1). Moreover, over the course of 2000, the quarterly fiscal targets on the public sector's primary balance were easily met.

In part as a result of the program's early success in revitalizing the economy, however, economic vulnerabilities started to build in the second half of 2000. In particular, strong growth in domestic demand led to a sharp increase in imports, mostly for consumption goods,

Table 2.1 Turkey: Key Macroeconomic Indicators, 1998–2002

	1998	**1999**	**2000**	**2001**	**2002**
			Annual percentage changes		
Real GDP growth rate	3.8	−6.1	6.3	−9.5	7.9
CPI inflation (eop)	69.7	68.8	39.0	68.5	29.7
Real exchange rate (+ appreciation)	3.9	5.6	15.5	−21.2	5.0
Avg. nominal T-bill rate	115.7	106.2	38.0	99.1	63.5
			In percent of GDP		
Public sector primary balance	−0.9	−1.9	3.0	5.5	4.1
Public sector borrowing requirement	15.4	24.2	18.9	21.1	12.0
Public sector net debt	43.7	61.0	58.3	93.9	78.8
External current account balance	1.0	−0.7	−4.9	2.4	−0.8
Short-term external debt-to-reserves	161.9	160.7	199.6	164.7	115.4

Sources: International Monetary Fund (2001, 2002, 2005).

while the residual inflation differential vis-à-vis the anchor countries, in conjunction with an appreciation of the U.S. dollar, weighed on export performance. These trends caused the current account balance to deteriorate sharply to a deficit of 4.9 percent of GDP in 2000, from a position close to balance in 1999.

For the financing of this deficit, the Turkish economy relied heavily on short-term debt-creating inflows. As a result, the Turkish economy, and financial sector balance sheets in particular, became exposed to roll over risk and currency mismatches. This pattern was particularly pronounced in the case of many, mostly smaller, private banks, which have relied strongly on external short-term credit lines to fund their purchases of government paper.[29] Overall, the stock of short-term debt plus maturing medium- and long-term debt at end-2000 rose to twice the level of the central bank's foreign exchange reserves.

The growing reliance on short-term external debt contracts for refinancing purposes rendered the performance of the Turkish economy heavily dependent on the continuation of favorable investor sentiment (see also Alper, 2001), which, in light of the mounting current account deficit, depended on a further strengthening of the fiscal position to reduce aggregate demand pressures. At the same time, however, disagreements within the coalition government over critical aspects of the economic program surfaced and revealed the coalition's lukewarm commitment to fiscal consolidation (see Alper and Onis, 2002a; Onis, 2007). In turn, the pickup in publicized coalition infighting led to a continuous weakening of political support for the coalition parties.[30] As a result of these developments, investor confidence in the authorities' economic program started to weaken from about August 2000, as evidenced by the fall in the EMBI bond price index (Figure 2.1).

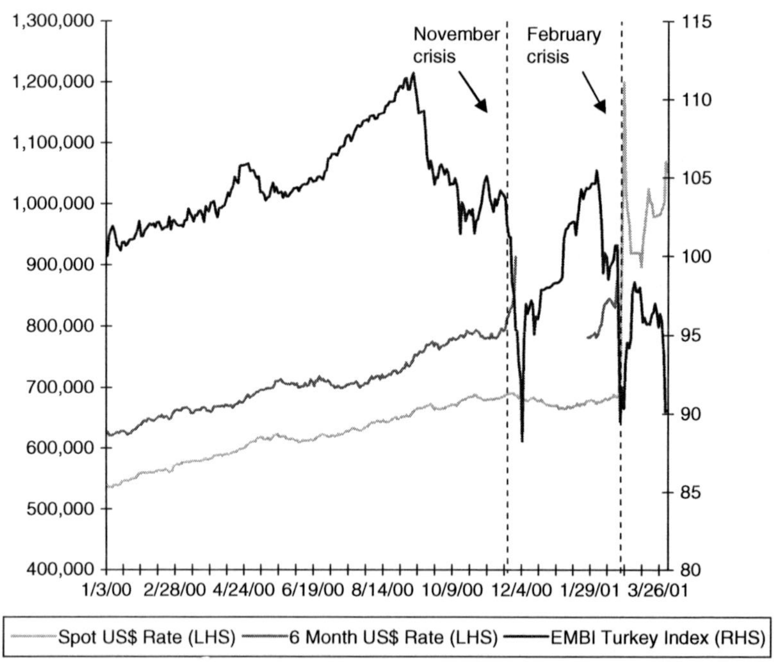

Figure 2.1 Turkey: Exchange Rate Expectations, 01/2000–04/2001
Source: Bloomberg; for EMBI Index, 3 January 2000 = 100.

Chief among the reasons for the perceived weakening of the coalition's commitment to the program were the incompatibility of ideological positions among the three parties as well as their sharply diverging constituencies. The two dominant coalition parties, Prime Minister Ecevit's Democratic Left Party and the far-right Nationalist Action Party, were violent opponents in the past and represented two very different segments of the Turkish electorate: the former party catered to the urban and secular left, while the latter was deeply rooted in poorer rural areas, mostly in Central Anatolia, and was open to some Islamic influence. On the other hand, the two parties shared a strong anti-corruption stance, and both depended on constituencies that were largely comprised of those segments of society that did not benefit directly from economic modernization and thus showed reluctance to implement further market-based reforms.

By contrast, the third coalition partner, the center-right Motherland Party, had its constituency mainly among the affluent urban strata that were the key beneficiaries of the initiatives taken since the 1980s to modernize and open the Turkish economy. Interests close to this party also figured prominently as suspects in corruption investigations.[31] Furthermore, from the outside, the cohesion of the coalition was constantly challenged by the looming threat of a parliamentary by-election if the Constitutional Court banned the Virtue party, which became an increasingly probable event (see 'Turkey's Real Crisis,' *The Economist*, 16 May 2001).

Disagreement among coalition parties appeared over the pace of efforts to restructure the banking sector, which for many years suffered from excessive risk taking, abuse by owners, a weak regulatory and supervisory framework, and large quasi-fiscal losses of the state-owned banks (see International Monetary Fund, 2002). In particular, while the government initially made swift progress in setting-up the new independent Banking Regulation and Supervision Agency (BRSA) as a key component of the IMF-supported program, conflicts within the coalition considerably weakened the government's resolve once politically sensitive decisions needed to be made. These decisions included the choice of the agency's board members and whether the BRSA should replace the Council of Ministers in its politically important role of licensing new banks (see Alper and Onis, 2002b). In addition, conflicts extended to the appropriate pace of banking-related corruption investigations implicating several government ministers, as well as the strategy for restructuring the state banks, which traditionally served as a key instrument of rent distribution to the agricultural and the small-enterprise sectors—constituencies that were particularly close to the National Action Party.[32]

Already concerned about the state of the domestic banking sector, foreign investors panicked when the BRSA actually launched a high-profile criminal investigation into ten failed private banks under government administration in November 2000. In the event, the large-scale liquidation of Turkish assets combined with the repatriation of external funds led bond prices to decline sharply and exerted pressure on the Lira exchange rate.[33] Smaller banking institutions were particularly hard hit by the fallout from the turbulence, as they had to liquidate their asset positions at a loss once domestic first-tier institutions and international banks cut their credit lines on which they relied for funding purposes (see 'Turkey and the IMF: take ten billion,' *The Economist*, 7 December 2000). Overnight interest rates climbed temporarily to extreme levels, before a large IMF rescue package led pressures to temporarily abate in early December.

After the November crisis, market participants became very concerned about the likely impact of the costs associated with the restructuring of the banking sector on the public debt-to-GDP ratio.[34] Hence, to restore market confidence, the governing coalition would have needed to demonstrate a strong commitment to deepen fiscal consolidation and to proceed with structural reforms, including in the politically sensitive area of privatization on which investor expectations were particularly focused. Instead, coalition politics prevented strong progress on either of the two fronts.

Given the rural electoral basis of the National Action Party, party leaders were reluctant to progress with the elimination of subsidies in the agricultural sector, which mostly took the form of price-support schemes for selected crops, as well as with initiatives to improve efficiency in some state-controlled sectors such as the tobacco industry (see Onis, 2003).[35] Moreover, contrary to the spirit of their announced economic program, the coalition government approved legislation to facilitate the late payment of tax arrears.

The implementation of the privatization agenda also proved to be protracted. In particular, the absence of meaningful progress with several high-profile cases, including Turk Telecom and Turkish Airlines, caused the privatization revenue for the year 2000 to turn out more than 50 percent below its target of US$7.5 billion. But even after the authorities renewed their commitment to the privatization agenda in the December 2000 Letter of Intent agreed with the IMF, the sale of a 33.5 percent stake in Turk Telecom continued to be fraught with delays. In addition, a series of obstacles emerged in passing an Electricity Market Law to establish an independent regulatory body tasked with preparing the privatization of electricity generation and distribution (see International Monetary Fund, 2001). While it is difficult to attribute the slow progress in this area to any individual cause, there is reason to believe that the preferences of many stakeholders in the Democratic Left Party and the National Action Party contributed to these slippages: a significant part of these parties' personnel remained attached to a strong role for the state in the economy, opposed the domination of strategic Turkish industries by foreign investors, and feared the impact of privatization-related employment losses on the vote of public sector employees (see Onis, 2000, 2003).

In this fragile political environment, the final blow to the Turkish peg was delivered on 19 February 2001, when Prime Minister Ecevit and President Sezer clashed over the slow pace of corruption investigations targeted at the country's ailing state-bank sector. Minutes after the dispute became known, which led for the first time in Turkish history to the suspension of a meeting of the National Security Council, investors began to close their positions denominated in Turkish Lira.[36] After having initially resisted the capital outflows through a freeze in domestic liquidity, leading interest rates to shoot up to levels of more than 140 percent in annualized terms, the government decided to give up the Lira's defense and float the currency on 22 February 2001. Hence, the nominal anchor of the disinflation program was abandoned only 14 months after its adoption.

2.4 Meltdown in Argentina, 1991–2002

The ten years that lie between the inauguration of the Argentine convertibility regime in 1991 and its demise in January 2002 show how gradual changes in the domestic political environment can contribute to undermining the sustainability of a currency peg. In particular, the discussion will reveal that over time, policy makers at the federal level, regardless of their political orientation, lost their ability to organize stable majorities in support of the fiscal adjustment and structural measures needed to buttress the hard currency peg. In the words of Corrales (2002), Argentina met the 'state-without-a-party condition' when popular support for convertibility, and, as a result, investor confidence, weakened, the proliferation of obstructing actors within the political process rendered it impossible to govern effectively.

Initially, the convertibility regime was very successful in ending a long period of macroeconomic instability. As a result of linking the Peso to the U.S. dollar at par and severely constraining autonomous money creation by the central bank, inflation came down to the single digits from hyper-inflationary levels in the late 1980s and remained low through the end of the convertibility regime. Benefiting from the improved macroeconomic outlook and a series of structural reforms, output grew at an average annual rate of almost six percent during the 1991–98 period. Moreover, compared with the experience of other emerging market countries, Argentina weathered relatively well the shock waves that hit international financial markets in the context of the Mexican crisis of 1995 and the Asian crisis of 1997–98. Indeed, during 1992–99, Argentina received more than US$100 billion in net capital inflows, almost one-third of annualized GDP, of which more than US$40 billion came in the form of longer-term foreign direct investment.[37]

The political risks associated with the radical shift from a state-led development strategy to a market-friendly regime were mitigated through the creation of a new economic policy coalition within and close to the Peronist party. In particular, after taking office in 1989, President Menem succeeded in gaining support among internationally oriented business interests. Partially, this was a function of a congruence of interests, as this sector championed a stable exchange rate and structural reforms aimed at improving the environment for doing business. But the rapprochement between the Peronist party and large corporations was also facilitated by the latters' participation in profitable investment opportunities in the context of privatization and an increased reliance on business-friendly technocrats for economic policy making, which both facilitated a less confrontational and more direct style of interaction than in the past (see Starr, 1997).

Furthermore, to prevent unified labor opposition to the reforms accompanying the introduction of convertibility, the Peronist government was able to capitalize on its traditionally close links to organized labor as well as on frictions in the labor union movement. Workers in the more competitive and modern sectors of the economy were won over for the change in economic strategy, and the pace of structural reforms in the labor market was deliberately kept slow: apart from efforts to introduce fixed-term and temporary work arrangements, deep labor market reforms that could have significantly increased the flexibility of employment conditions were continuously postponed or blocked by the Peronist faction of Congress.[38]

At the same time, in anticipation of growing dissatisfaction among the urban population that would initially be hardest hit by the reorientation of economic policies, the administration sought to ensure continued electoral support by cultivating its links to the Peronist party organization in the economically backward, but politically potent 'interior' provinces.[39] This strategy was largely achieved through sparing the provinces the same degree of fiscal adjustment as that implemented at the federal government level, while offering important Ministries to powerful regional interests. Moreover, its success was facilitated by the fact that most of the privatization initiatives that resulted in significant job losses were geographically concentrated in Argentina's wealthy, urban centers (see Calvo and Gibson, 2000; Gibson, 1997).

Together, these skillful efforts of coalition building ensured the political survival of the administration in the early years of the convertibility regime, even when, as expected, some segments of the traditional Peronist base showed vigorous opposition to the authorities' fiscal tightening and structural reforms. Once inflation stabilized at low levels, political support for the Peronists grew further as strong economic performance induced some segments of the urban middle class to join the reform coalition. This latter trend was facilitated by significant campaign-financing contributions from large enterprises, which substituted for the partial loss of the labor union's mobilization capacity.[40]

However, heightening economic vulnerabilities in conjunction with the re-emergence of distributional conflict caused the reform coalition to erode over time. In particular, competitiveness pressures built when the real exchange rate appreciated due to remaining inflation differentials vis-à-vis trading partner countries.[41] This led the external current account to deteriorate from virtual balance in 1991 to a deficit of 4.3 percent of GDP in 1994, and almost 5 percent of GDP in 1998. To address this growing vulnerability that made the country increasingly dependent on continuing capital inflows and thus favorable investor sentiment, the authorities sought an agreement with the provinces to implement more fiscal consolidation on that level, an extension of the scope for fixed-term and temporary work arrangements, and an increase in a variety of taxes.

Combined with corruption allegations and the firing of Domingo Cavallo, the Minister of Finance who designed the convertibility regime, these measures led to growing discontent within elements of the initial reform coalition and sharply falling approval ratings. When these translated into the loss of the Peronist majority in the lower chamber of Congress in October 1997, the administration was deprived of its parliamentary majority as a basis for economic policy making (see Starr, 1997; Wise, 2000). Moreover, economic considerations were increasingly subordinated to President Menem's quest to seek a third term, which resulted in a spending race between the federal government and leading Peronist governors contesting his move. As a result, fiscal policy became more expansive and structural reform efforts petered out (see Corrales, 2002).[42]

In this fragile political environment, the deterioration in macroeconomic performance gathered pace after the sharp devaluation of the Brazilian Real in January 1999 and the simultaneous appreciation of the U.S. dollar vis-à-vis the currencies of Argentina's other major trading partners (Figure 2.2). Output declined by 3.4 percent in 1999 and by a further 0.8 percent in 2000, disinflation turned into deflation, and unemployment increased from 12.5 percent in the second half of 1998 to 15 percent in 2000. Moreover, the increased fiscal outlays and a growing risk premium on Argentine debt caused fiscal balances to deteriorate. As a result, the public debt-to-GDP ratio increased by ten percentage points within only two years to reach a level of 51 percent of GDP at end-2000. Given that the

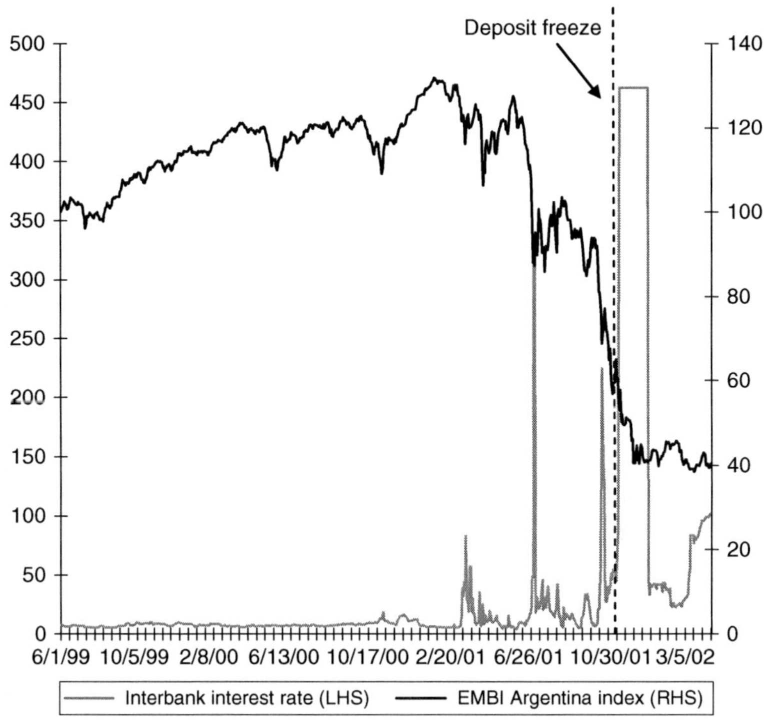

Figure 2.2 Argentina: Market Expectations, 01/2001–05/2002
Source: Bloomberg; for EMBI Index, 1 June 1999 = 100.

market for domestic paper was limited, most of the debt was denominated in foreign currency and thus carried significant currency risk (Table 2.2).[43]

When the new center-left administration under President de la Rua assumed power in the October 1999 elections, optimism returned temporarily. Since the winning Allianza was not beholden to the same interests as the Peronists, voters hoped that it would have more freedom to fight corruption and fund new social programs.[44] At the same time, soaring debt ratios turned further fiscal adjustment into a top priority for the government, much to the disappointment of its electoral constituency.

Table 2.2 Argentina: Key Macroeconomic Indicators, 1996–2001

	1996	1997	1998	1999	2000	2001
	Annual percentage changes					
Real GDP growth rate	5.5	8.1	3.8	−3.4	−0.8	−4.4
CPI inflation (eop)	0.1	0.3	0.7	−1.8	−0.7	−1.5
Money market interest rate	6.23	6.63	6.81	6.99	8.15	24.90
Real exchange rate (+appr.)	0.3	7.7	−3.0	4.1	4.1	−0.1
	In percent of GDP					
Federal gov. fiscal balance	−1.93	−1.46	−1.36	−1.68	−2.39	−3.24
Provincial gov. fiscal balance	−0.44	−0.04	−0.65	−1.45	−1.16	−2.32
Public sector debt	39.1	37.7	40.9	47.6	50.9	62.2
External debt	40.6	42.7	47.5	51.2	51.6	52.2
Ext. current account balance	−2.5	−4.2	−4.9	−4.2	−3.1	−1.7

Source: International Monetary Fund, Independent Evaluation Office (2004).

Unfortunately, however, the new economic team faced political constraints in economic policy making that, on some dimensions, were even more severe than those that had plagued the outgoing Menem administration. Similar to his predecessor, the new Minister of Finance José Luis Machinea had to face a divided Congress in which the opposition party controlled the Senate (see Corrales, 2002). But in addition, the scope for new policy initiatives was severely limited by intra-coalition struggles over economic policy objectives and the Peronist control over two-thirds of the powerful provinces, a situation that rendered the chances for agreeing with the subnational level of government on further fiscal consolidation very slim.

Reflecting these political difficulties, the early initiatives of the de la Rua administration to improve fiscal balances translated into only modest packages, less than two percent of GDP, as the various proposals met the resistance of other cabinet ministers and needed to stop short of cutting the revenue transfers to the opposition-controlled regions (see Machinea, 2003). Coalition infighting over additional expenditure measures and other policy proposals persisted over much of 2000, before the internal bickering reached a climax in early October with the resignation of Vice President Carlos Alvarez—who was also the head of the junior partner in the coalition government, FREPASO—in protest over the slow pace of corruption investigations associated with the passing through Congress of a new labor law.[45]

After this event, the Allianza coalition operated under a constant threat of dissolution and market confidence in the convertibility regime took a temporary hit (see Figure 2.2). The pressure on the prices of Argentine assets, exacerbated through a series of external shocks including an increase in U.S. dollar interest rates and the Turkish crisis, was only alleviated when the authorities agreed with the IMF on a large financing package in January 2001, which promised an increase in the public sector primary surplus to 1.5 percent of GDP, from about 0.5 percent of GDP in 2000. But the recovery in market sentiment did not last; investor concerns soon resurfaced in response to the authorities' failure to meet their fiscal targets for the first quarter of 2001, and the resignation of two Ministers of Finance within a twenty-day period in early March 2001 (see Machinea, 2003).

In this desperate situation, at the end of March 2001, Domingo Cavallo was reappointed Minister of Finance. Helped by congressional emergency powers and strong political backing, he set out to defend the convertibility regime through a more heterodox approach instead of further fiscal tightening. Specifically, he introduced a variety of measures to soften the rigid peg of the Peso to the U.S. dollar and provide more room for domestic liquidity creation, including a reduction of reserve requirements, the replacement of the U.S. dollar peg with a basket once the Euro rose to parity against the U.S. dollar, and the adoption of a separate and more favorable exchange rate for trade transactions. Furthermore, Minister Cavallo secured enough investor support to implement a large debt swap operation that reduced immediate liquidity pressures for the federal government.

But when it became clear that markets remained unimpressed by these measures, the economic team reverted to orthodox adjustment and sought to implement a zero fiscal deficit rule. This program, which received strong backing from the Presidency, relied on several tough budget cuts including, for example, a reduction in central government salaries and pensions by 13 percent over a three-month period. At the same time, however, high and growing debt service costs, as well as delays in reaching an agreement with the provinces on a new revenue-sharing rule, soon made the requirement to balance the budget on a monthly basis almost impossible to meet. It is thus not surprising that market expectations stabilized only for a short period of time.

The final stage of the Argentine crisis opened with the congressional mid-term elections on 14 October 2001, which plainly revealed that the incumbent government had no more political support.[46] As a result, confidence in the authorities' continued commitment to the convertibility regime and its ability to keep its promise to exchange any amount of Pesos for U.S. dollars at par diminished precipitously.[47]

This meltdown in confidence triggered a large run on private sector deposits during 28 November and 30 November, which the administration counteracted by the imposition of a wide range of controls on banking and foreign exchange transactions, including a weekly limit on withdrawals from individual bank accounts. After this harsh response from the government, the country's major labor unions held two days of nationwide strikes that soon turned into large-scale street protests and social unrest, while the opposition-controlled Chamber of Deputies repealed the emergency powers granted to the administration. Faced with this hopeless situation, both Minister Cavallo and President de la Rua resigned on 20 December 2001, before their successors declared a unilateral debt moratorium on 23 December 2001 and the end of convertibility on 3 January 2002 (see Daseking, Ghosh, Lane, and Thomas, 2004).[48]

2.5 Emerging political patterns

The four case studies analyzed in this chapter offer important insights on the type of domestic political conditions that can destabilize a government, and on how the resulting political instability may be linked to the emergence of a currency crisis. In particular, the experiences of interwar Britain and France, as well as Argentina and Turkey throughout the 1990s and early 2000s, suggest that a variety of political factors could render policy adjustment in response to growing economic vulnerabilities difficult to accomplish. This could be due either to these factors' impact on the incumbents' willingness to pay the political and economic costs associated with a defense of the home currency, or their effect on a government's ability to organize and sustain the political support required for such measures.

Interestingly, the evidence suggests that it does not take extreme political events to immobilize governments in the face of growing pressure on foreign exchange markets. While all of the case studies involve weak democratic systems characterized by a high degree of political volatility compared to more mature democracies, none of them featured pathological events such as wars, revolutions, or coups.[49] Rather, the discussion of the four cases points to the importance of relatively common political conditions for investor sentiment and consequently currency stability, which could be relevant for most democratic countries. At some risk of oversimplification, these factors can be grouped into four broad categories.

First, the administration's partisan nature can be expected to affect the strength of its commitment to defending a currency peg in a crisis situation. In particular, in both Great Britain and France, left-leaning governments revealed an unwillingness to pursue sufficiently strong fiscal adjustment at any cost when it involved sacrificing key entitlement programs for their working-class constituencies. Given this preference in the context of a deteriorating economic environment characterized by high levels of unemployment, it became almost unavoidable that convertibility ultimately had to be sacrificed, even if the decision was a painful one to make.[50]

That said, the Turkish case shows that the unwillingness of a party to pursue further adjustment does not necessarily need to be grounded in its left-leaning nature.[51] Indeed, the Democratic Left Party of Prime Minister Ecevit appears to have been more supportive of the reinforced policy package of December 2000 than the extreme-right Nationalist Action Party, which, inter alia, continued its attempts to protect the party's strong agricultural constituency from painful budget cuts (see Onis, 2003).[52]

Second, elections matter as they affect the time horizon of policy makers. In three out of the four country cases considered, the decision to exit the fixed exchange rate regime was taken either shortly before or shortly after a major national ballot. In Great Britain, the National Coalition government suspended gold convertibility one month prior to the October 1931 parliamentary elections. Policy makers hoped that this painful decision would put closure on the politically poisonous issue of whether to remain on gold before the parties entered the final phase of the election campaign.

By contrast, in Argentina and France, the elections occurred a few months prior to the end of the convertibility regime. In Argentina, the results of the October 2001 mid-term elections made it clear that the ruling Allianza of President de la Rua had lost most of its political backing in the electorate. More broadly, many voters used the occasion to demonstrate their general dissatisfaction with the political system, with more than 20 percent of the vote being invalid. Hence, the probability of the authorities' continued political survival deteriorated sharply. In France, the 1936 elections catapulted a Popular Front government to power and, commanding 63 percent of the parliamentary seats, provided it with a strong mandate for reflationary and worker-friendly policies. Hence, in that case, the elections led to a profound shift in economic policy priorities, which proved to be incompatible with a continued defense of the gold parity when the various measures were implemented.

Third, governments appear to be receptive to lobbying from powerful interest groups, particularly in countries where organized labor is strong. In the two interwar cases and in Argentina, labor unions emerged as a permanent political threat to the incumbent governments that tried to adopt and implement painful adjustment packages. In the event, the unions' activities proved to be highly successful. In Britain, strike activity impinged on the efforts of the National Coalition government to agree on further austerity measures in the summer of 1931. In France, labor unions used their mobilization capacity to force the newly elected Popular Front government into swiftly adopting labor-friendly policies, which ultimately made it impossible to retain the link to gold. In Argentina, where strike activity had been common at least since the second part of the 1990s (see International Monetary Fund, Independent Evaluation Office, 2004), the national strike of December 2001, which turned into widespread civil unrest, arguably delivered the final blow to the authorities' political legitimacy.[53] Interestingly, organized labor did not play a comparably strong role in the case of Turkey, a fact that may be explained through the continuous decline in union power as a result of the structural reforms and liberalization efforts undertaken since the 1980s (see Alper and Onis, 2002a).

Finally, even if the key economic policy makers remain strongly committed to the continuation of the currency peg and are not voted out of office, the institutional configuration of a political system can produce political deadlock. Such obstacles to decision making can come in different forms. In the cases of Turkey and Argentina's de la Rua administration, disagreements over economic policy issues surfaced among coalition partners with the effect of watering down the initially proposed adjustment measures and delaying their implementation. By contrast, in the cases of Argentina, Great Britain, and France, it was the absence of stable parliamentary majorities for the incumbent that diminished the scope for effective policy making in the face of crisis.[54] Finally, given a high degree of fiscal decentralization, the Argentinean authorities were forced to seek agreement on reducing aggregate fiscal spending with the provinces, a task that often proved to be difficult in the presence of diverging political incentives.

Hence, regardless of the specific origin of the various veto players whose consent is needed to decide on a change in economic policies, the experience of the four countries suggests that a breakdown of cooperation among key political actors has the potential to greatly diminish the authorities' ability to bring about the changes in economic policies that are required to maintain a currency peg.[55] Moreover, given that political conflict tends to be played out in the open, the proliferation of veto players with conflicting economic policy preferences carries a significant potential to destabilize market sentiment.

The discussion in this chapter suggests that politics can matter for a country's vulnerability to currency crises. At the same time, it is clear that the case study methodology alone, in particular when based on a small sample size, cannot lend itself well to establishing solid explanations. As always in the social sciences, 'everything else is typically not held equal,' relationships of cause and effect are hard to disentangle among the array of observed correlations, and endogeneity, the question of whether bad politics cause currency crises or the other way round, can become an issue.

We should clearly have more confidence in the validity of the results presented above when these are supported by hypotheses derived from a strong body of theory, and when we see repeated evidence of these correlation patterns in a larger sample of cases.

I will take up these challenges in the two following chapters, first by taking a closer look at the theory of currency crisis and the scope for enriching existing models with some of the political-economy aspects identified above, and then by testing the resulting hypotheses in a large cross-country sample.

3

Political-Economy Crisis Models

3.1 Introduction

By eliminating distractive noise, good economic models help us understand relationships of cause and effect in the analysis of empirical phenomena. At the same time, they should not abstract from reality to such an extent as to render their theoretical predictions trivial, and therefore more or less irrelevant for the explanation of observable outcomes. This challenge can sometimes be daunting. In particular, through largely neglecting the political dimension of currency crises, the main strands of the theoretical literature risk losing a potentially important channel for explaining the collapse of currency pegs when times get tough. This omission appears misplaced, given that professional currency investors tend to devote significant resources to analyzing the impact of political conditions on exchange rate stability;[56] it also leaves too much room for attributing currency crises to exogenous factors beyond the scope of the models, such as arbitrary shifts in expectations.

Against this background, this chapter sets out to develop several extensions of a standard second-generation currency crisis model that emphasize the importance of the political and institutional context of macroeconomic policy. In doing so, the models can contribute to deepening our understanding of the vulnerabilities underlying exchange rate commitments and the channels through which the various fundamentals driving crisis dynamics interact. The guiding theme underlying this exercise is that exchange rate stability—most likely, but not necessarily, in the form of a promise to defend a currency peg—depends on the preferences of key political actors with regard to difficult policy trade-offs. In turn, these trade-offs are conditioned by electoral incentives, the institutional framework for macroeconomic policy making, and interest group pressure.

To limit the technical discussion to the necessary minimum, a standard second-generation crisis model serves as a shared basis for the various political-economy extensions. Section 3.2 provides a short discussion of this model, focusing in particular on the basic credibility problem of fixed exchange rates and the two most common commitment strategies used by researchers to address it: the imposition of a pecuniary punishment for breaking the commitment and, in a multi-period setting, the reputation of the monetary policy maker.[57] Following standard practice in economic theory, I assume throughout the chapter that exchange rate decisions are taken by the central bank rather than another branch of government.[58]

Having laid out the analytical basis, the chapter then proceeds to examine the impact of three broad categories of political factors on exchange rate stability. First, the discussion will focus on how an upcoming election period could increase uncertainty over the strength of the current administration's continuing commitment to the currency peg. As will be seen, the outlook for the incumbent's re-election can play a key role in this regard. But the credibility of the commitment is also affected by factors including the authorities' intertemporal preferences and the length of an executive term (Section 3.3).

Secondly, in Section 3.4, the focus will shift to the role of a fiscal policy maker in the explanation of currency crises. Based on a new model, I will argue that in some situations, this branch of government enjoys *de facto* veto power over exchange rate outcomes, consistent with the experience in recent crisis episodes in Argentina and Turkey. The analysis will then focus on identifying situations in which a rational fiscal policy maker would make use of its privileged position to force an exit from the currency peg upon the central bank, even if the latter remains committed to its defense. I will also show that the veto player model—in a setting in which the fiscal authority's spending target contains a stochastic element—can accommodate multiple equilibria and thus the potential for self-fulfilling currency crises.

Finally, the discussion will focus on the impact of interest groups on exchange rate outcomes. Specifically, a model will be developed to demonstrate how a labor union, which is concerned with workers' employment prospects in addition to their real wages, could have an incentive to offer financial contributions to a fiscal policy maker in exchange for a lower level of taxation. Such lobbying activity could indirectly affect the optimal exchange rate decision of the central bank, and thus introduce an additional element of volatility arising from a political source (Section 3.5).

3.2 A basic second-generation model

The decision to exit from a currency peg at times of crisis should reflect optimizing behavior on the part of the monetary policy maker.[59] Specifically, in such a situation, the costs associated with a further defense of the fixed exchange rate should clearly outweigh the respective benefits, independently of technical considerations such as whether the level of central bank reserves would be sufficient to meet the demand in the foreign exchange market (see Obstfeld and Rogoff, 1995). This insight is the starting point for all second-generation crisis models, a particular version of which will provide the basis for the various theoretical developments introduced later in this chapter.

In this strand of reasoning, the fragility of fixed exchange rate regimes stems from the fact that their desirability, from the monetary policy maker's point of view, depends on the specific situation at hand and may change over time. Crucially, there is typically an incentive for the central bank to renege on its promise to maintain a currency peg as an anchor for monetary policy once agents' expectations converged on believing this promise, at least in the absence of a commitment device that would punish the monetary policy maker for misleading the private sector. But even if such a punishment mechanism existed, the commitment to defend a fixed exchange rate 'cout que cout' is not credible: if the state of the world turns out to be sufficiently bad, then the punishment will typically not be severe enough to prevent an exit from the peg. Fixed exchange rate regimes should thus always be seen as a potentially fragile framework for monetary policy making.

In the following technical discussion, I will first establish the basic credibility problem of a fixed exchange rate regime in spite of its potentially benign effect on society's welfare. Then, the focus will shift toward two types of commitment devices that could help improving the chances for a peg's survival under adverse economic conditions.

3.2.1 The credibility problem of currency pegs

In the technical discussion throughout this chapter, I rely on a small open economy model in which purchasing power parity is assumed to hold. Using lower-case letters to denote logarithms (logs), the economy's output is determined from the supply side as

$$y = \epsilon - \epsilon^e - \tau - \mu. \tag{3.1}$$

As output is normalized, $y = 0$ represents the output level which would prevail in the absence of any monetary or fiscal policy interference (see Appendix A for a microeconomic foundation of the output equation). The central bank influences firms' production level via its control over the nominal exchange rate. Whenever the monetary authority succeed in implementing a depreciation of the exchange rate ϵ in excess of private agents' expectations ϵ^e, period production increases due to the associated decline in real wages. ϵ^e is embodied in the private sector's wage contracts, which are signed at the beginning of the period and assumed to remain binding throughout. Given that the exchange rate is defined as the price of a foreign currency unit in terms of the home currency, $\epsilon > 0$ implies a depreciation of the local money relative to the foreign money in the period under review.

Output is also affected negatively through distortionary taxation. Following Alesina and Tabellini (1987), I assume that the fiscal policy maker taxes away a share τ of firms' output in every period to fund public expenditures. Finally, the period's production level reflects the realization of a supply shock μ, which has a mathematical expectation of $E[\mu] = 0$.

The central bank sets the depreciation rate for the (nominal) exchange rate on the basis of a policy loss function that seeks to minimize its disutility. Specifically, in implementing its policy instrument ϵ, the bank strives to find an optimal solution to[60]

$$L^c = \frac{1}{2}\alpha_{cb}\epsilon^2 + \frac{1}{2}(y - \tilde{y})^2. \tag{3.2}$$

This decision rule trades off the losses caused by a positive depreciation rate $\epsilon > 0$ (and hence positive domestic inflation) against the costs associated with a deviation of realized output from a target level $\tilde{y}$.[61] Following standard practice, the function is quadratic in the loss terms as the central bank's disutility should increase with the distance between variable realizations and their target levels.

The weight that the central bank attaches to the exchange rate objective relative to output stabilization is captured through $\alpha_c > 0$. A tough central bank with a strong preference for exchange rate stability would be associated with a high parameter value. In case the central bank enjoys little independence from the incumbent administration, the parameter could also serve as a proxy for the partisan nature of the ruling coalition government. For example, authors including Simmons (1994) and Garrett (1998) have argued that left-leaning parties that traditionally place more emphasis on employment and income distribution than conservative parties should be expected to have a lower tolerance for bearing the costs associated with a currency peg in the face of adverse economic conditions. If this were true, then one could expect a systematic correlation between the ideological orientation of an administration and the level of α_c: left-leaning governments should be characterized by a lower α_c than their more conservative counterparts.

Finally, private agents hold rational expectations and there are no information asymmetries in the economy.[62] This implies that economic agents are aware of the economy's structure and the policy maker's decision function, and take this information into account when forming their depreciation expectation ϵ^e. Hence, agents make no systematic errors in forecasting ϵ, which implies

$$\epsilon^e = E[\epsilon]. \tag{3.3}$$

The sequence of events is as follows. First, nominal wage contracts are signed through agents whose decisions reflect their information about the prevailing level of taxation, the output target of the central bank, and the degree of the institution's inflation-aversion. The shock μ occurs only after contracts have been signed for the period. Finally, the central bank chooses the rate of exchange rate depreciation, before output is produced. The dynamic structure of the decision-making process reflects two key features of macroeconomic policy making: while wage contracts are typically rigid in the short run, monetary (or exchange rate) policy can react swiftly to changes in economic conditions such as those captured by the shock variable.

The model's equilibrium solution can be derived by backward induction. This implies finding first the optimal strategy for the central bank that makes its decision at the end of the sequence based on knowledge about everyone else's behavior. Then, one has to work backwards toward the beginning of the 'policy game.'

To understand both the attractiveness and the fragility of a fixed exchange rate regime in this framework, we need to compare the welfare results from defending the exchange rate rule with those associated with a discretionary setting of exchange rate policy.

In the latter case, the central bank is not constrained by any rule in determining its optimal behavior. Other than under fixed exchange rates, where no depreciation would be tolerated against the foreign anchor currency, implying $\epsilon = 0$, it would determine the optimal rate of exchange rate depreciation ϵ by minimizing its loss function as presented in Equation 3.2. Technically, this would require ϵ to be a solution to the differential

$$\frac{\partial L_c^d}{\partial \epsilon} = \alpha_c \epsilon + (y - \tilde{y}) \frac{\partial y}{\partial \epsilon} = 0,$$

which, after substituting Equation 3.1 into this expression, can be determined as

$$\epsilon = \frac{1}{1 + \alpha_c}(\epsilon^e + \tau + \mu + \tilde{y}). \tag{3.4}$$

In equilibrium, private agents anticipate this depreciation rate correctly. Noting that the mathematical expectation of the shock variable is $E(\mu) = 0$, private sector depreciation expectations should thus converge toward

$$\epsilon^e = \frac{1}{\alpha_c}(\tau + \tilde{y}). \tag{3.5}$$

Inserting this expectations term in the central bank's decision function yields

$$\epsilon^d = \frac{1}{\alpha_c}(\tau + \tilde{y}) + \frac{1}{1 + \alpha_c}\mu \tag{3.6}$$

as the period's depreciation rate for the scenario characterized by a discretionary setting of exchange rates (associated equilibrium outcomes carry a ^{d} superscript). Clearly, this expression could only be consistent with a stable exchange rate when the central bank does not pay any attention to its output objective—α_c would need to approach infinity.

The central bank's exchange rate choice implies a production level of

$$y^d = -\tau - \frac{\alpha_c}{1+\alpha_c}\mu, \tag{3.7}$$

and a policy loss for the institution of

$$L_c^d = \frac{1}{2}\frac{1+\alpha_c}{\alpha_c}\left(\tau + \tilde{y} + \frac{\alpha}{1+\alpha}\mu\right)^2. \tag{3.8}$$

Equations 3.6 and 3.7 show that this equilibrium would typically not be very attractive from society's point of view. It entails a costly inflationary bias to monetary policy with no mean gain in output over the level that reflects prevailing tax distortions. Exchange rate policy could only have a stimulating effect when the economy is hit by a negative exogenous supply shock that the private sector did not anticipate at the time of determining nominal wages.

By contrast, the adoption of a fixed exchange rate regime can eliminate the inflationary bias in monetary policy making through committing the central bank to $\epsilon = 0$. If the private sector believes in the stability of the peg, depreciation expectations should converge toward $\epsilon^e = 0$. Output would thus amount to

$$y^f = -\tau - \mu, \tag{3.9}$$

and the central bank's policy loss would become

$$L_c^f = \frac{1}{2}(\tau + \mu + \tilde{y})^2. \tag{3.10}$$

Comparing Equations 3.10 and 3.8 reveals the benign effect that a currency peg could have on society's welfare: if private agents perceive the regime to be credible, the policy loss under a currency peg should, on average, be strictly smaller than in the absence of an exchange rate rule. Only a sufficiently sized supply shock μ, which, however, has a mathematical expectation of zero, could cause a discrete policy framework to deliver a higher utility level for society than a peg.

This result has been very influential with policy makers since the early 1990s. It delivers a theoretical justification for rules-based approaches to monetary policy making, involving either a delegation of decision making to an independent central bank or, particularly, in the presence of weak domestic institutions, the adoption of a low-inflation currency as a monetary anchor to which the domestic money would be more or less rigidly tied. Many exchange rate-based stabilization programs in emerging market countries have closely followed the second approach, using a (temporary) commitment to a fixed exchange rate as an easily observable external anchor for domestic money growth.[63]

There is, however, a problem with this benign equilibrium entailing low-depreciation expectations and exchange rate stability: due to the central bank's incentive structure and the sequential nature of decision making, there is scope for cheating. As the exchange rate is set *after* private agents form their depreciation expectations, the monetary authority would always be better off reneging on its promise to defend the peg and engineer a surprise depreciation aimed at boosting output. In the words of dynamic game theory, a promise to peg the currency may be an *ex ante*, but not an *ex post* optimal strategy for the central bank.

The monetary authority's policy loss associated with cheating can be derived formally as

$$L_c^b = \frac{1}{2}\frac{\alpha_c}{1+\alpha_c}(\tau + \mu + \tilde{y})^2, \tag{3.11}$$

with the corresponding output level of[64]

$$y^b = \frac{1}{1+\alpha_c}(\tilde{y} - \alpha_c(\tau + \mu)). \tag{3.12}$$

By comparing this loss level with the one under pegging as specified in Equation 3.10, one can identify the magnitude of the incentive to cheat (I_c) that is underlying the credibility problem of fixed exchange rate commitments as

$$I_c = L_c^f - L_c^b = \frac{1}{2}\frac{1}{1+\alpha_c}(\tau + \mu + \tilde{y})^2. \tag{3.13}$$

Equation 3.13 reveals that as long as the central bank cares about output in addition to price stability, the central bank will always be strictly better off exercising its depreciation option than delivering on its promise to maintain the currency peg, even if agents had full trust in the institution's commitment.[65]

3.2.2 Two types of commitment devices

According to the logic set out above, rational agents should never put too much faith in an exchange rate commitment announced by a monetary policy maker. This is a highly unpleasant result, as a currency peg represents a transparent rule for monetary policy that would be welfare enhancing in most situations.

To overcome the basic credibility problem impinging on the stability of fixed exchange rates, economic theory suggests two types of commitment technologies: the imposition of a cost on the central bank when it chooses to abandon the peg, and the policy maker's reputation.[66] By altering the incentives that policy makers face, these devices help to make the results of the theoretical discussion more compatible with the empirical evidence that, apparently, many countries do favor fixed exchange rate regimes over floating rates. At the same time, as will become clear in a moment, the commitment technologies do not provide complete insurance against a surprise depreciation of the currency.

Many second-generation models follow the approach of imposing a fixed cost on the central bank for cheating, given that they typically focus on only one period.[67] This cost could represent a loss of political capital associated with the signal of incompetence that a broken promise sends out. In the extreme, it could be a proxy for the inconvenience associated with losing office, consistent with Richard Cooper's famous finding that the Ministers of Finance in developing countries tend to leave office shortly after exchange rate devaluations (Cooper, 1971). To implement the approach on a technical level, the central bank's loss function, already familiar from Equation 3.2, needs to be slightly modified to include an exogenously set cost term $C(\epsilon)$:

$$L_c = \frac{1}{2}\alpha_c \epsilon^2 + \frac{1}{2}(y - \tilde{y})^2 + C(\epsilon). \tag{3.14}$$

The period realization of C is assumed to depend on the authorities' exchange rate decision. Specifically,

$$C(\epsilon) = \begin{cases} 0 & \text{if } \epsilon = 0, \\ \bar{c} & \text{if } \epsilon > 0. \end{cases}$$

As long as the peg is maintained, implying $\epsilon = 0$, the central bank does not incur any inconvenience from the additional cost term in its decision function. However, once the policy maker exits from the regime with a view to stimulate output, the cost term becomes a positive constant and affects the bank's welfare. Of course, the higher the cost that society sets for breaking the exchange rate commitment, the more crisis-proof the peg should become.

Using this modified decision function and assuming exogenous expectations, the policy loss accruing to the central bank in case of reneging on its exchange rate promise changes to

$$L_c^d = \frac{1}{2}\frac{\alpha_c}{(1 + \alpha_c)}(\epsilon^e + \tau + \mu + \tilde{y})^2 + \bar{c}, \tag{3.15}$$

compared with the loss of

$$L_c^f = \frac{1}{2}(\epsilon^e + \tau + \mu + \tilde{y})^2 \tag{3.16}$$

associated with a continuation of the peg (see Equation 3.10).

As a result, the modified incentive to cheat for the central bank becomes

$$I_c = L_c^f - L_c^d = \frac{1}{2}\frac{1}{(1 + \alpha_c)}(\epsilon^e + \tau + \mu + \tilde{y})^2 - \bar{c}. \tag{3.17}$$

Rearranging this expression and solving for $\bar{c}$ yields the threshold level for the cost term that ensures the maintenance of the currency peg as

$$\bar{c} \geq c^* = \frac{1}{2}\frac{1}{(1 + \alpha_c)}(\epsilon^e + \tau + \mu + \tilde{y})^2. \tag{3.18}$$

As long as this inequality holds, the central bank has no incentive to break its commitment to the fixed exchange rate regime. However, in case it does not hold, a rationally acting central bank can be expected to surprise the private sector with a depreciation of the exchange rate—despite its prior commitment not to do so.

The structure of the central bank's decision rule clearly reveals the state contingency of the currency peg: there is always a level of sufficiently poor fundamentals for which the fixed exchange rate would come under pressure. Put differently, the central bank's exchange rate promise always contains an escape clause that can be activated in exceptionally bad circumstances.[68] In particular, Equation 3.18 shows that the previously determined threshold level $\bar{c}$ might just not be high enough to keep the central bank from devaluing its currency in case a sufficiently large supply shock hits the economy. This can be clarified by rearranging Equation 3.18 with a view to identify the minimum shock size required for exiting the peg as[69]

$$\mu_d = \sqrt{2(1+\alpha_{cb})C} - \epsilon^e - \tilde{y} + k. \tag{3.19}$$

In sum, imposing an institutional fix on the monetary policy maker can help improve the stability of a fixed exchange rate, but would fail to ensure its survival in sufficiently bad times.

The second solution to the credibility problem, the perceived cost to the policy maker's reputation, shares these key properties, albeit due to different reasons. In this case, the commitment to a currency peg gains credibility because the interaction between the central bank and the private sector is extended to a multi-period game.

Specifically, assuming an extended time horizon covering multiple periods, the authorities would need to weigh the immediate gains of surprise depreciation against the future losses that such a strategy entails. Depending on the punishment strategy that the private sector implements after having been caught on the wrong foot, the future losses associated with ending the peg could be sufficiently large to prevent the central bank from breaking its commitment in the first place. Such an approach is typically a much better approximation of reality than the one-period interaction studied before, as it lends itself well to incorporating agents' learning strategies based on the observed action of others. That said, this advantage comes at the cost of more complicated mathematics.

For the formal exposition of the approach, I return to the model developed earlier, but with a modified rule for the determination of private sector expectations.[70] This rule now takes the form

$$\epsilon^e = \begin{cases} 0 & \text{as long as } \epsilon_{t-1} = 0, \\ \dfrac{1}{\alpha_c}(\tau + \tilde{y}) & \text{otherwise.} \end{cases} \tag{3.20}$$

It stipulates that agents believe in the stability of the fixed exchange rate as long as the central bank sticks to its commitment. By contrast, once expectations are frustrated, the private sector anticipates the optimal depreciation rate derived in Equation 3.5 for all future periods. To make this a plausible strategy, we assume that regime switches are irreversible. In other words, the authorities would have no chance of recommitting to a fixed exchange rate after having abandoned it at any point in time.

Based on this expectations mechanism, we can derive the loss associated with cheating through comparing the future losses associated with maintaining the fixed exchange rate and with discretionary policy making, respectively.

Noting that the shock variable has a mathematical expectation of $E[\mu] = 0$ and thus disappears from the calculation, the expected period loss in the case of cheating can be determined as

$$E[L_c^d] = \frac{1}{2}\frac{1+\alpha_c}{\alpha_c}(\tau + \tilde{y})^2, \tag{3.21}$$

with an expected period depreciation rate of

$$E[\epsilon] = \frac{1}{\alpha_c}(\tau + \tilde{y}) \tag{3.22}$$

and an output level of

$$E[y] = -\tau. \tag{3.23}$$

By contrast, the expected future period loss in the case of a fixed exchange rate would amount to

$$E[L_c^f] = \frac{1}{2}(\tau + \tilde{y})^2, \tag{3.24}$$

consistent with Expression 3.16.

Taking the difference between Equations 3.21 and 3.24 yields the future period punishment P that a decision to break the exchange rate commitment in the current period would engender. It amounts to

$$E[P] = E[L_c^d] - E[L_c^f] = \frac{1}{2}\frac{1}{\alpha_c}(\tau + \tilde{y})^2. \tag{3.25}$$

Finally, the present value of all future period punishments—from the perspective of a decision maker acting in period $T-1$—amounts to

$$E_{T-1}[P_T] = \beta \sum_{s=t}^{\infty} \beta^{s-t} \left[\frac{1}{2}\frac{1}{\alpha_c}(\tau + \tilde{y})^2\right] \tag{3.26}$$

or

$$E_{T-1}[P_T] = \frac{\beta}{1-\beta}\left[\frac{1}{2}\frac{1}{\alpha_c}(\tau + \tilde{y})^2\right]. \tag{3.27}$$

In these expressions, β is a factor indicating the inter-temporal preference of the monetary authority. The larger its size, the more the authorities value future losses compared to present losses in their decision making and, hence, the more effective is the punishment as a commitment device.

A rational monetary policy maker will weigh this expected punishment against the one-time incentive associated with reneging on the exchange rate commitment familiar from Equation 3.13. Formally, this comparison would lead the central bank to renege on its exchange rate promise if

$$\frac{1}{2}\frac{1}{1+\alpha_c}(\tau + \mu + \tilde{y})^2 - \frac{\beta}{1-\beta}\left[\frac{1}{2}\frac{1}{\alpha_c}(\tau + \tilde{y})^2\right] > 0, \tag{3.28}$$

or, after rearranging, if

$$\frac{\alpha_c}{1+\alpha_c}\Phi > \frac{\beta}{1-\beta}, \tag{3.29}$$

with $\Phi = (\tau + \mu + \tilde{y})^2/(\tau + \tilde{y})^2$.

In a situation where this condition holds, the incentives associated with a surprise depreciation are stronger than the associated pains in the form of higher future policy losses. Thus, the central bank should be expected to exit the peg. It is easy to see from Expression 3.29 that this condition is more likely to be met if the central bank has a low preference for price stability compared to output stabilization (embodied in a low α_c), the output target is ambitious, a strong supply shock hits the economy, and/or structural distortions, including those created by taxes on output, are significant. By contrast, the more the central bank cares about future welfare, the less likely a devaluation will become.

This short exposition of the sources of the credibility problem plaguing currency pegs and of the two basic strategies to partially fix it provides the background for the main discussion in the following sections: the analysis of how the inclusion of political factors alter the chances of a peg's survival in difficult times.

3.3 Uncertainty and the role of elections

The first extension of the basic model aimed at better understanding the political dimension of currency crises emphasizes the role of uncertainty with respect to the policy preferences of future policy makers. In particular, I will examine to what extent the prospect of a handover in government may impact on the central bank's decision of whether or not to exit from a currency peg. While this analysis is concerned chiefly with the effect of elections as the typical way of organizing leadership transitions in democracies, the results are applicable to a broader range of events, including situations characterized by a heightened threat of coups or other political actions that would lead to the ousting of the incumbents.

The theme that elections could be harmful to the stability of a fixed exchange rate has been highlighted by many narrative accounts. For example, Frankel (2005) notes that many of the recent emerging market crises occurred around election times, with pressure building in the run-up to the ballot and a full crisis typically erupting soon thereafter. This pattern is attributed to a typical policy maker's attempt to delay a politically costly devaluation until after the election, in the meantime hoping to improve its chance of remaining in power. Moreover, after the election, a renewed mandate from the electorate may help limit the loss in political capital associated with a devaluation or, in cases of a government transition, the blame for macroeconomic incompetence could be shifted to the successors. Such political calculations would match with the evidence in the crisis cases of Mexico in 1994, Korea in 1997, and Brazil in 1998–99.

Several models offer an analytical treatment of the channels through which up-coming elections change the incentives for an incumbent government deciding on the optimal path for the exchange rate. In particular, they show how imminent elections could create an incentive to delay a devaluation and may lead to sharper corrections once the new administration took over.

For example, Meon (2004) attributes the incentive of delaying devaluations in pre-election periods to the signaling effect that the incumbent's exchange rate policy has on the electorate. Using a loss function augmented with terms to reflect both the cost of losing office and the government's quality in defending the peg, the author shows in a framework similar to the one presented in Section 3.2 that even an incompetent policy maker (meaning an administration that incurs higher costs in defending the peg than a more knowledgeable one) could have an incentive to avoid exchange rate realignments before elections to maintain office. Other theoretical work based on the political business cycle literature comes to qualitatively similar results.[71]

By contrast, other models take election probabilities as exogenously given. They focus mainly on the question of how election-induced uncertainty over the policy preferences of a future holder of office would affect exchange rate decisions in the pre-election period.

In a single-period framework, this uncertainty could enter the government's exchange rate decision indirectly through its effect on depreciation expectations. Meon (2001) highlights this mechanism by developing a model in which expectations depend on the anticipated reaction of the government to a stochastic supply shock. The shock is, however, only realized after the election. Election politics come into play as the two parties competing for office differ in their set of preferences (expressed, in the context of our basic model, in diverging choices of α_c). In this setting, private sector expectations should be expected to reflect each party's optimal policy response to the anticipated supply shock weighted with the parties' respective probability of winning the ballot. The resulting dynamics could force even a strongly committed incumbent off the peg, should it have a low probability of surviving in power.

Analyzing the impact of elections on the repeated game between the central bank and the private sector offers another, and perhaps more realistic, way of formally showing the destabilizing impact that anticipated government transitions could have on fixed exchange rate regimes. Using a technique borrowed from Meon and Rizzo (2002), the following exposition shows how the multi-period approach introduced in Section 3.2.2 can be extended to capture the effect of uncertainty about future election outcomes on the authorities' decision, on top of the economic considerations already familiar from the earlier discussion.

Specifically, I assume that elections are scheduled for period T, following the period in which the incumbent policy maker needs to decide on the optimal course of exchange rate policy. The opposition party will win the ballot with an exogenously given probability p, so that the incumbent's re-election probability in our two-party model is equal to $(1-p)$. To facilitate the discussion, it is assumed that all actors know that the opponent, if elected, would always choose to devalue rather than defend the peg. As the public would direct its anger about the devaluation to the opposition party, the current incumbent would be left out of the blame and face no punishment.

With this slight modification to the multi-period model, one can easily determine the impact of the upcoming election on the central bank's optimization problem. While the one-off incentive to devalue in $T-1$ remains unchanged from Equation 3.13, the expected future punishment associated with this strategy now needs to be weighted by the probability of being re-elected, which is $(1-p)$. Therefore, the expected positive punishment described in Equation 3.27 would change to

$$E_{T-1}[P_T] = (1-p)P_T = (1-p)\frac{\beta}{1-\beta}\left[\frac{1}{2}\frac{1}{\alpha_c}(\tau+\tilde{y})^2\right]. \tag{3.30}$$

Subtracting the loss expressed in Equation 3.30 from the benefit associated with cheating then yields[72]

$$\frac{\alpha_c}{1+\alpha_c}\Phi > (1-p)\frac{\beta}{1-\beta} \tag{3.31}$$

as a necessary condition for the collapse of the fixed exchange rate. Comparing this expression to Inequality 3.29 reveals that the introduction of uncertainty over the election outcome, and thus a certain chance for the incumbent of not being held accountable for future pains associated with a floating exchange rate, tilts the balance of incentives in favor of a devaluation.

Of course, restricting the analysis to the case of one single election in the future is unrealistic. At least in democratic societies, governments face the verdict of the electorate with some periodicity, typically at the beginning of every multi-year term for the executive. To adapt the model to this more complex but also more interesting case, and again following Meon and Rizzo (2002), the length of each executive's term in office as provided in the constitution is depicted by a new variable M, and I assume that there is no option to recommit to an exchange rate peg once the initial promise has been broken. Other assumptions remain unchanged from before: the central bank decides whether to devalue in $T-1$, the next elections are held in period T, and the incumbent would not incur losses from any future term in which the current opposition holds office.

The adoption of a multi-election framework complicates the calculation of expected losses, as there is now a certain probability for an exit from the peg at the beginning of each future term—if the opposition wins. This problem occurs independently of whether or not the incumbent sticks to its exchange rate commitment in period $T-1$. To pin down the optimal strategy for the central bank at this juncture, we need to determine the expected present value of all future losses for both the case of exercising the devaluation option (Λ_T^{flex}) and the case of maintaining the currency peg (Λ_T^{fix}) for at least another period.

If the central bank devalues at $T-1$, the expected punishment for each future period would be given by the difference in policy losses between the scenarios with a floating and a fixed exchange rate, respectively. These losses have already been determined in Equation 3.25. Aggregating period losses to term losses,[73] adjusting for infinite future terms, and weighting the punishment by the probability of remaining in office for each future term yields

$$E_T[\Lambda_T^{\text{flex}}] = \sum_{s=T}^{\infty} \beta^{(s-T)M} \left[(1-p)\ell_{\text{inc}}^{d}\right]$$

or

$$E_T[\Lambda_T^{\text{flex}}] = (1-p)\frac{1}{1-\beta^M}\frac{1-\beta^M}{1-\beta}\left[\frac{1}{2}\frac{1+\alpha_c}{\alpha_c}(\tau+\tilde{y})^2\right] \tag{3.32}$$

as the expected policy loss associated with this scenario.

The calculation of future payoffs is more difficult when the central bank maintains the currency peg in period $T-1$. This stems from the fact that three potential policy outcomes for each future term need to be factored into the equation: the current incumbent could continue maintaining the peg, the current incumbent could abandon the peg, and the current opposition party could abandon the peg.

In any future term in which the opposition were in charge, the current incumbent would by assumption not face any loss. By contrast, if the incumbent were in office and the currency peg survived until the particular term under consideration, the term loss associated with maintaining the peg would amount to

$$\ell_{inc}^{fix} = \frac{1-\beta^M}{1-\beta}\frac{1}{2}(\tau+\tilde{y})^2.$$

The further we look into the future, the more unlikely this scenario becomes, as it requires an election victory for the incumbent in all of the intervening terms since the one starting with year T. In case the incumbent kept office but would opt for a floating exchange rate regime, the term loss would amount to

$$\ell_{inc}^{flex} = \frac{1-\beta^M}{1-\beta}\frac{1}{2}\frac{1+\alpha_c}{\alpha_c}(\tau+\tilde{y})^2.$$

Putting all these pieces together and weighting prospective term losses with election probabilities (assuming as a best guess that these probabilities would not change in future periods) yields the discounted future policy loss associated with defending the fixed exchange rate at $T-1$ as

$$\begin{aligned} E_T[\Lambda_T^{\text{fix}}] &= (1-p)\ell_{\text{inc}}^{\text{fix}} + p\ell_{\text{flex}}^{\text{opp}} \\ &\quad + a^M\left[(1-p)^2\ell_{\text{inc}}^{\text{fix}} + p(1-p)\ell_{\text{inc}}^{\text{flex}} + p\ell_{\text{opp}}^{\text{flex}}\right] \\ &\quad + a^{2M}\left[(1-p)^3\ell_{\text{inc}}^{\text{fix}} + (1-p)[1-(1-p)^2]\ell_{\text{flex}}^{\text{inc}} + p\ell_{\text{opp}}^{\text{flex}}\right] + \cdots \end{aligned} \tag{3.33}$$

or, after rearranging,

$$E_T[\Lambda_T^{\text{fix}}] = \sum_{s=T}^{\infty} \beta^{(s-T)M}\Big[(1-p)(1-p)^{s-T}\ell_{\text{inc}}^{\text{fix}} + (1-p)[1-(1-p)^{s-T}]\ell_{\text{inc}}^{\text{flex}} + p\ell_{\text{opp}}^{\text{flex}}\Big]$$
$$= \frac{1-p}{1-(1-p)\beta^M}\ell_{\text{inc}}^{\text{fix}} + (1-p)\left(\frac{1}{1-\beta^M} - \frac{1}{1-(1-p)\beta^M}\right)\ell_{\text{inc}}^{\text{flex}} + p\frac{1}{1-\beta^M}\ell_{\text{opp}}^{\text{flex}}. \tag{3.34}$$

Using Equations 3.32 and 3.35, the central bank's expected punishment in case of an exit from the peg in $T-1$ can then be determined as

$$E_{T-1}[P_T] = \beta\left(E_T[\Lambda_T^{\text{flex}}] - E_T[\Lambda_T^{\text{fix}}]\right) = \beta(1-p)\frac{1}{1-(1-p)\beta^M}\frac{1-\beta^M}{1-\beta}\frac{1}{2}\frac{1}{\alpha_c}(\tau+\tilde{y})^2. \tag{3.35}$$

Finally, as before, this punishment needs to be compared to the immediate benefit associated with giving up the peg (see Equation 3.13). This comparison shows that devaluation becomes optimal if the following inequality holds:[74]

$$\frac{\alpha_c}{1+\alpha_c}\Phi > \beta(1-p)\frac{1}{1-(1-p)\beta^M}\frac{1-\beta^M}{1-\beta}. \tag{3.36}$$

The sensitivity of this condition to changes in the political conditions affecting the incumbent's time horizon is simulated in Figure 3.1. Specifically, the three graphs in the panel simulate how the policy maker's optimal exchange rate decision depends on changes in its time preference, in the probability of winning the upcoming election, and in the length of the executive's electoral term. Whenever the net gains emerging from a devaluation at $T-1$ exceed the costs associated with the future punishment (or as long as $I_{T-1} - E_{T-1}[P_T] > 0$ holds), a rationally acting central bank would opt out of the peg. Otherwise, the peg would be maintained in the current period. Moreover, the graphs in the panel distinguish between two cases: one in which the realization of the exogenous supply shock is equal to its mathematical expectation of zero (full line), and one in which an exogenous shock of size $\mu = 0.2$ hits the economy (dotted line).

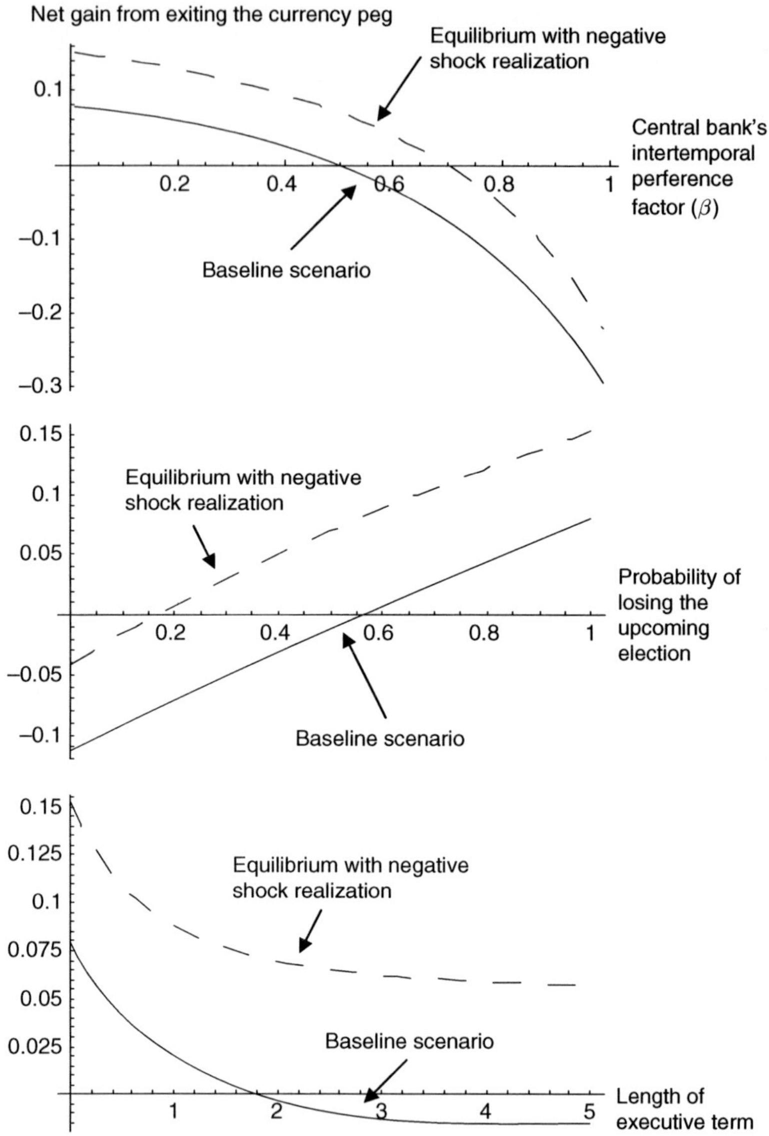

Figure 3.1 Elections and the Stability of Fixed Exchange Rates
Notes: $\alpha_c = 0.7$, $\tau = 0.5$, $\tilde{y} = 0.02$.

All the reported results make intuitive sense. First, the more the central bank is concerned about its welfare in future periods, the lower is the probability of reneging on its commitment to the fixed exchange rate regime (upper panel). For example, with a 50 percent chance of winning next period's election and a term length of four years, a government weighing future losses with a factor of at least 0.5 in its decision function would leave the currency peg intact as long as the shock realization is not much worse than its mathematical expectation. By contrast, the factor would need to increase to about 0.7 to 'insure' the economy against a devaluation when hit by the negative supply shock.

Re-election prospects can also greatly influence the incumbent's exchange rate decision (middle panel). The higher the chance of losing the next election, the less the current government will take into account the negative impact of its decision to abandon the peg on its future welfare, even if it is re-elected at a later point in time. Using the same parameterization as before and considering the shadow of the future with a factor of 0.5 in current decision making, the authorities would give up the peg in the baseline scenario whenever their re-election prospects shrink to below 50 percent. A substantial increase in re-election prospects would be required to induce the incumbent to defend the peg in case the economy is hit by the shock.

Finally, the length of an executive term clearly matters for the survival of the peg (lower panel). In particular, a very short-term length implying frequent elections can have a dramatic negative effect on the stability of a fixed exchange rate. This result is driven by the fact that each future election may represent an additional test of the peg, given the underlying assumption that an opposition victory would always cause the peg to collapse. While constitutionally anchored terms should not be less than four years under normal conditions, a shorter *de facto* term length could reflect the situation of a country with very weak political institutions suffering from frequent turnovers in government, including irregular ones.

3.4 A fiscal veto player

A political actor with the clout to override the central bank's decision of whether or not to defend a fixed exchange rate when times get tough is a veto player. In this section, I will show how a fiscal policy maker could indirectly play such a role through using its power to set the level of taxation on firms' output. In particular, the analysis will reveal that currency crises could become much more probable (or even inevitable) in cases where the fiscal authority and the monetary policy maker differ significantly in the weight they attach to exchange rate stability relative to other policy objectives.

Veto player analysis has become fashionable in recent years as a tool to study decision making in many policy areas, including macroeconomic policy. Originating in comparative political science, the approach departs from the premise that political outcomes in a wide array of situations can be understood better by examining the configuration and interests of veto players. This group of privileged political actors can include not only individual politicians and political parties, but also institutional actors such as a central bank or a supreme court that act as checks on the executive and whose agreement is necessary for any change of policy from the prevailing status quo.[75]

Typically, veto players derive the power to shape policy outcomes from provisions in a country's constitution, their exposed position in the political system, or their role in government bureaucracy. Moreover, their influence over policy results depends often on their slot in the sequence of decisions leading to the final outcome. In particular, agenda-setting actors can use their first-mover advantage to shape policy proposals in such a way as to maximize the chances that others accept what they want.

Whether the presence of veto players is a good or a bad thing depends on the circumstances. As more consensus building becomes necessary before a decision is taken, veto players should increase the stability of a political system. But at the same time, this very fact may impair the ability of the political process to respond quickly to a changing environment. Hence, the presence of veto players may represent a burden, particularly in crisis situations when speed is of the essence to implement an adjustment program aimed at restoring investor confidence.[76]

Existing veto player studies in the area of monetary and exchange rate policy typically depart from challenging a fundamental assumption of the economic literature on monetary policy credibility—the feasibility and, even more important, the irrevocability of the transfer of monetary policy to an independent central bank.[77] In fact, the argument goes, political actors can always (threaten to) affect central bank decisions and, in an extreme scenario, reverse them. As private agents are aware of these dynamics, their inflation expectations should reflect this residual risk to the central bank's independence, particularly in countries where the inflation preferences of key veto players differ significantly from those of the central bank.[78]

On a theoretical level, these issues are explored in Keefer and Stasavage (2000) and Keefer and Stasavage (2003). Specifically, these studies examine how the number and preferences of veto players can help determine to what extent the delegation of authority to an independent central bank would mitigate the inflation bias inherent in monetary policy making. To this aim, they develop a closed-economy model with no constraints on the inflation rate that features one or more political actors with veto power over monetary policy decisions. These veto players, which could include the executive and the legislature, strive to minimize their respective loss functions that differ with regard to the actors' inflation-aversion. It is further assumed that in a baseline scenario without an independent central bank, an (inefficiently high) default inflation outcome would prevail when the two veto players cannot agree on a shared target rate. By contrast, with an independent and inflation-averse central bank enjoying agenda-setting power, the default inflation rate would be the target proposed by the monetary authority.

In such a setting, delegation of authority to an independent central bank can help improve inflation outcomes for the society if at least two veto players exist. Specifically, the central bank would propose a rate of inflation that leaves the most inflation-averse veto player no worse off than in the case where all veto players override the central bank and subsequently agree on a new and higher rate of inflation. Of course, this strategy would not be feasible in the presence of only one veto player. In this alternative scenario, the inflation outcome would merely reflect this individual player's preference, and an independent central bank could not improve society's welfare.

In Keefer and Stasavage (2002), the same authors use a similar methodology to analyze whether the presence of veto players would have an impact on the stability of a currency peg. Contrary to the result for the closed economy, they conclude that the presence of a high number of such actors should not be expected to strengthen the credibility of a peg. This pessimistic view is grounded in the fact that the inflation rate consistent with the maintenance of a fixed exchange rate vis-à-vis a low-inflation anchor country would typically be much lower than even the one preferred by the most inflation-averse domestic player (after all, the peg should import anti-inflation credibility). This would leave no room for the continuation of a fixed exchange rate regime as a negotiated solution. Moreover, the authors argue that exchange rate policy, more clearly than domestic monetary policy, would be the prerogative of a single veto player, the executive, with the result that the default depreciation outcome should closely reflect this actor's individual preferences.

From a theoretical perspective, these results pertaining to fixed exchange rate regimes are troubling. In particular, the *a priori* denial of a role for veto players with respect to the currency peg's credibility precludes any analysis of how changes in the preferences or composition of key actors in macroeconomic policy making would impact a fixed exchange rate's likelihood of survival over time.

Against this backdrop, I suggest a different modeling strategy that highlights the potential for intra-governmental conflict, that is, conflict among segments of the executive. Specifically, I show how a fiscal policy maker could undermine the efforts of an independent central bank to maintain a currency peg when faced with a sufficiently adverse economic environment, even if the monetary authority itself remains strongly committed to defending the prevailing regime.

3.4.1 Currency crises and fiscal policy decisions

The recent experience with currency crises in countries such as Argentina, Ecuador, and Turkey suggests that a fiscal policy stance perceived by investors to be unsustainable is often closely associated with the collapse of a fixed exchange rate regime. The Argentinean experience might be particularly instructive in this regard, given that the central bank remained strongly in favor of defending the currency board regime, which in itself was perceived as a very strong institutional backup for the Peso's peg to the U.S. dollar amidst growing pressure in 2001 (see Sections 2.3 and 2.4).

But whereas the empirical evidence relating fiscal policy outcomes to exchange rate crises appears to be strong in some cases, second-generation crisis models typically do not capture this link well.[79] Most existing models are based on a policy trade-off between exchange rate stability and output stabilization; the approaches that do incorporate aspects of fiscal policy in the central bank's decision function ignore the real side of the economy (see, in particular, Cole and Kehoe, 1996; Obstfeld, 1994; Velasco, 1996).

From our perspective, however, the neglect of a fiscal dimension in a crisis model based on the Phillips-curve trade-off is primarily a lost opportunity in a second respect: an explicit modeling of fiscal policy making could provide a useful channel to apply veto player analysis to the context of currency crises. In particular, a model with an autonomous fiscal authority enables us to better account for conflicts of interest over exchange rate policy within the executive branch of government, caused through diverging preferences over macroeconomic outcomes among the monetary and the fiscal policy maker. Such conflicts of interest appear to be highly plausible given the different incentives that the players are facing. Most importantly, while a, more or less, independent central bank should typically enjoy some degree of isolation from the political process, a fiscal policy maker faces a periodic challenge of re-election. As a result, the latter can be expected to be more concerned about the effects of macroeconomic policy on the electorate, which in turn should translate into more opportunistic behavior informed by short-term considerations.[80]

In the following technical exposition, we extend a standard second-generation crisis model to incorporate explicitly these considerations and discuss their implications for the stability of a fixed exchange rate regime. As will be shown, the fiscal player enjoys *de facto* veto power over the central bank's decision of whether or not to abandon a prevailing currency peg through its authority over tax policy. This result will be developed in stages. The discussion will first focus on the optimal decision-making strategies for the central bank and the fiscal policy maker, before turning to an analysis of intra-governmental conflict that could, in some cases, undermine the stability of a currency peg. Then, introducing a stochastic element into the fiscal authority's spending target, I will show how endogenous expectations can lead to multiple equilibria—in much the same way as in Obstfeld's classic second-generation crisis model (see Obstfeld, 1994, 1996).

For the integration of a fiscal perspective into the basic framework, I draw on research pioneered by Alesina and Tabellini (1987). These authors have been among the first scholars to discuss the welfare implications arising from the integration of an autonomous fiscal authority as a second optimizing policy maker into the familiar Phillips-curve framework. This type of analysis has re-emerged recently in the context of the debate on how varying degrees of cooperation between the national fiscal authorities and the European Central Bank impact the welfare level of union members.[81] But the methodology has not yet been applied to analyzing the stability of currency pegs.

The model is specified by five equations relating output, exchange rate depreciation, and the level of taxation to the decision functions of three types of actors, which are the private sector, the central bank, and the fiscal authority. As in the basic model discussed earlier, the economy's log output y is determined from the supply side. Assuming purchasing power parity to hold, period production follows[82]

$$y = \epsilon - \epsilon^e - \tau. \tag{3.37}$$

The central bank decides on the period's depreciation rate based on the loss function already established in Equation 3.14, which includes a cost term $C = \bar{c}$ in case the institution reneges on its pre-announced commitment to maintain a fixed exchange rate throughout the period. Hence, we can write

$$L_c = \frac{1}{2}\alpha_c \epsilon^2 + \frac{1}{2}(y - \tilde{y})^2 + C(\epsilon), \tag{3.38}$$

with

$$C(\epsilon) = \begin{cases} 0 & \text{if } \epsilon = 0, \\ \bar{c} & \text{if } \epsilon > 0. \end{cases}$$

The fiscal authority faces a loss function similar to the one of the central bank. In choosing the optimal level of taxation, however, the fiscal player has to strike a balance between three conflicting policy objectives, namely, a stable exchange rate, an output level close to $\tilde{y}$, and a realization of government spending consistent with the target level $\tilde{g} > 0$. This expenditure target could reflect the political preferences of society about the extent of the welfare state and the degree of state interventionism in the economy, but also the impact of corruptive practices embedded in the political system.[83] Specifically, the loss function takes the form

$$L_f = \frac{1}{2}\alpha_f \epsilon^2 + \frac{1}{2}(y - \tilde{y})^2 + \frac{1}{2}\alpha_g (g - \tilde{g})^2, \tag{3.39}$$

with α_f and α_g expressing the relative weights of the inflation and spending objectives in the fiscal authority's decision rule.

The fiscal authority needs to implement a balanced budget in every period, implying that expenditure g matches the period's tax revenue τ, so that[84]

$$g = \tau. \tag{3.40}$$

Finally, as in the basic model, private agents hold rational expectations and have perfect knowledge of the decision functions of the other players. Therefore, agents make no systematic errors in their forecast of the period's exchange rate depreciation, which allows us to write

$$\epsilon^e = E[\epsilon]. \tag{3.41}$$

Decisions are taken in the following sequence. First, the central bank announces its commitment to defend the fixed exchange rate for another period, and society decides on the size of the punishment term $\bar{c}$ associated with the implementation of a surprise devaluation. Moreover, this stage involves the disclosure of targets for output and public spending as well as of the various actors' preference parameters. Subsequently, the private sector forms its depreciation expectations. Then, the fiscal authority chooses the taxation level before the central bank decides on its exchange rate policy, and output is produced. As before, the sequential model can be solved by starting with the decision problem of the central bank and then working backwards toward the beginning of the game.

Similar to the analysis in Section 3.2.2, the depreciation rate of the exchange rate that minimizes the central bank's policy loss can be found by differentiating Equation 3.38 with respect to ϵ as

$$\epsilon^d = \frac{1}{1+\alpha_c}(\epsilon^e + \tau + \tilde{y}), \tag{3.42}$$

which implies a policy loss of

$$L_c^d = \frac{1}{2}\frac{\alpha_c}{(1+\alpha_c)}(\epsilon^e + \tau + \tilde{y})^2 + \bar{c}. \tag{3.43}$$

By contrast, the loss associated with maintaining the fixed peg would amount to

$$L_c^f = \frac{1}{2}(\epsilon^e + \tau + \tilde{y})^2. \tag{3.44}$$

Based on this information, the central bank has an incentive to devalue as long as the associated benefits exceed the costs involved, or as long as the inequality

$$I_c = L_c^f - L_c^d = \frac{1}{2}\frac{1}{(1+\alpha_c)}(\epsilon^e + \tau + \tilde{y})^2 - \bar{c} > 0 \tag{3.45}$$

holds. Put differently, unless the punishment $\bar{c}$ incurred in the case of exercising the devaluation option is high enough, the central bank always has an incentive to renege on its exchange rate commitment and devalue *after* the private sector and the fiscal authority have revealed their behavior for the period.

As can be seen by solving Inequality 3.45 for τ, a sufficiently high level of taxation implemented through the fiscal authority would lead the central bank to reconsider its promise to defend the currency peg. Specifically, once the tax take increases beyond the threshold level τ^*, which can be determined as

$$\tau^* = \sqrt{2(1+\alpha_c)\bar{c}} - \epsilon^e - \tilde{y}, \tag{3.46}$$

a rationally acting central bank would respond to the fiscal player's tax decision by exiting from the fixed exchange rate. Therefore, the fiscal authority enjoys a strategic advantage vis-à-vis the central bank, as it can force its counterpart off the peg through a sufficiently high level of taxes. In other words, the fiscal authority effectively enjoys veto power over exchange rate policy by virtue of its position in the sequence of decision making.

Acknowledging that the fiscal authority has the power to make the maintenance of a fixed peg too costly for the central bank is a first step to grasp its crucial role in exchange rate matters. But it is even more important to understand under what conditions a collapse of the peg would be in the fiscal authority's best interest. An answer to this question can be found by examining the fiscal policy maker's decision rule.

Specifically, to find the level of its policy instrument that minimizes the authority's period losses, I take the partial derivative of Equation 3.39 with respect to τ, which can be written as

$$\frac{\partial L_f}{\partial \tau} = \alpha_f \epsilon \frac{\partial \epsilon}{\partial \tau} + (y - \tilde{y}) \frac{\partial y}{\partial \tau} + \alpha_g (g - \tilde{g}) \frac{\partial g}{\partial \tau}. \tag{3.47}$$

This expression shows that the optimal tax choice depends on the partial derivatives of output and depreciation with respect to taxes. As these derivatives are not independent of the exchange rate regime in place, one needs to calculate them for both the scenario in which the central bank maintains the currency peg and the scenario in which the bank chooses to devalue.

In the presence of a fixed exchange rate, ϵ cannot be used for the stabilization of output. Hence, the exchange rate does not respond to changes in taxation, implying $\partial \epsilon / \partial \tau = 0$.

By contrast, in the case of a devaluation, the partial derivative of the devaluation rate ϵ^d becomes $\partial \epsilon / \partial \tau = 1/(1 + \alpha_c)$. The central bank would thus see value in mitigating output distortions caused by the income tax through a higher dose of depreciation. As a result, output is affected less from increased taxation than under a fixed exchange rate regime: the derivative of output to taxes becomes $\partial y / \partial \tau = -\alpha_c/(1 + \alpha_c)$, which is clearly smaller than under a currency peg ($\partial y / \partial \tau = -1$). Finally, given the simple budget constraint from Equation 3.40, public spending responds in equal proportion to a change in taxation ($\partial g / \partial \tau = 1$), regardless of the exchange rate regime in place.

Using these partial derivatives and substituting Equations 3.37, 3.40, and 3.42 into 3.47, one obtains

$$\tau^d = \frac{\alpha_g (1 + \alpha_c)^2}{\alpha_c^2 + \alpha_f + \alpha_g (1 + \alpha_c)^2} \tilde{g} - \frac{\alpha_c^2 + \alpha_f}{\alpha_c^2 + \alpha_f + \alpha_g (1 + \alpha_c)^2} (\epsilon^e + \tilde{y}) \tag{3.48}$$

as the optimal taxation level under the devaluation scenario.

Table 3.1 Three Macroeconomic Policy Scenarios

	Fiscal Authority	Central Bank
Scenario A	τ^d	$\epsilon^d = \frac{1}{1+\alpha_c}(\epsilon^e + \tau^d + \mu + \tilde{y})$
Scenario B	τ^c	$\epsilon = 0$
Scenario C	τ^*	$\epsilon^* = \frac{1}{1+\alpha_c}(\epsilon^e + \tau^* + \mu + \tilde{y})$

Together with the optimal depreciation rate for the exchange rate from Equation 3.42, this choice of tax revenue defines Scenario A in Table 3.1.

Alternatively, optimal taxes in the case of a continuation of the currency peg can be found to be

$$\tau^c = \frac{1}{1+\alpha_g}(\alpha_g \tilde{g} - \epsilon^e - \tilde{y}), \tag{3.49}$$

defining Scenario B in combination with a stable exchange rate.[85]

The derivation of optimal taxes conditional on the exchange rate regime in place is, however, only the first step in deriving the optimal tax decision. As the fiscal authority is in a position to force its 'will' upon the central bank through acting prior to the monetary policy maker, it is important to know which of the two scenarios the institution would prefer. Hence, the next step involves comparing the policy losses accruing to the fiscal policy maker in the two scenarios.

Using Equations 3.39, 3.42, 3.48, and 3.49, I calculate a policy loss of

$$L_f^d = \frac{1}{2}\left(\frac{\alpha_g(\alpha_c^2 + \alpha_f)}{\alpha_c^2 + \alpha_f + \alpha_g(1+\alpha_c)^2}\right)(\epsilon^e + \tilde{g} + \tilde{y})^2 \tag{3.50}$$

for Scenario A and of

$$L_f^c = \frac{1}{2}\frac{\alpha_g}{(1+\alpha_g)}(\epsilon^e + \tilde{g} + \tilde{y})^2 \tag{3.51}$$

for Scenario B.

Subtracting the loss associated with the flexible exchange regime (L_f^d) from that incurred in the presence of a currency peg (L_f^c) yields the loss difference

$$L_f^c - L_f^d = \frac{\alpha_g^2(1+2\alpha_c-\alpha_f)}{2(1+\alpha_g)(\alpha_c^2+\alpha_f+\alpha_g(1+\alpha_c)^2)}(\epsilon^e+\tilde{g}+\tilde{y})^2, \tag{3.52}$$

which, under the plausible assumption that the inflation-aversion of the central bank is at least as strong as that of the fiscal authority,[86] shows that the fiscal branch is always better off under a flexible exchange rate. Given this result, we should not be surprised if the fiscal authority always has a preference for choosing taxes in such a way as to force the fixed exchange rate's collapse.

But the fiscal player is not always in a position to impose its preferred macroeconomic regime upon the central bank. As we know from Equation 3.46, the central bank will only devalue when taxation exceeds the threshold level τ^*. This condition, in turn, creates a floor for the public spending target $\tilde{g}$ that indirectly induces the monetary authority to abandon the fixed exchange rate. Hence, the public expenditure target set by society becomes a crucial fundamental of the fixed exchange rate's credibility.

Formally, we can find the minimum level of the spending target that enables the fiscal authority to induce a devaluation by combining Equations 3.46 and 3.48 and solving for $\tilde{g}$ as

$$\tilde{g}^d = \frac{\alpha_c^2+\alpha_f+\alpha_g(1+\alpha_c)^2}{\alpha_g(1+\alpha_c)^2}\sqrt{2(1+\alpha_c)\bar{c}} - \epsilon^e - \tilde{y}. \tag{3.53}$$

This threshold increases in α_c and α_f, which represent the preferences of the monetary and fiscal policy makers for exchange rate stability relative to their other policy objectives. By contrast, it decreases in the fiscal player's spending preference α_g, as a higher emphasis on public spending heightens the pressure on the central bank to offset the output effect of increased taxation by a dose of surprise depreciation.[87]

With the identification of the critical spending target $\tilde{g}$, we have reached a first important result regarding the impact of fiscal policy decisions on the stability of a currency peg: whenever $\tilde{g} > \tilde{g}^d$, the fiscal authority will rationally choose τ^d over τ^c and thereby provoke a collapse of the fixed peg.

Figure 3.2 illustrates this result graphically. In its upper panel, the tax rates τ^c and τ^d are plotted as functions of the spending target $\tilde{g}$.

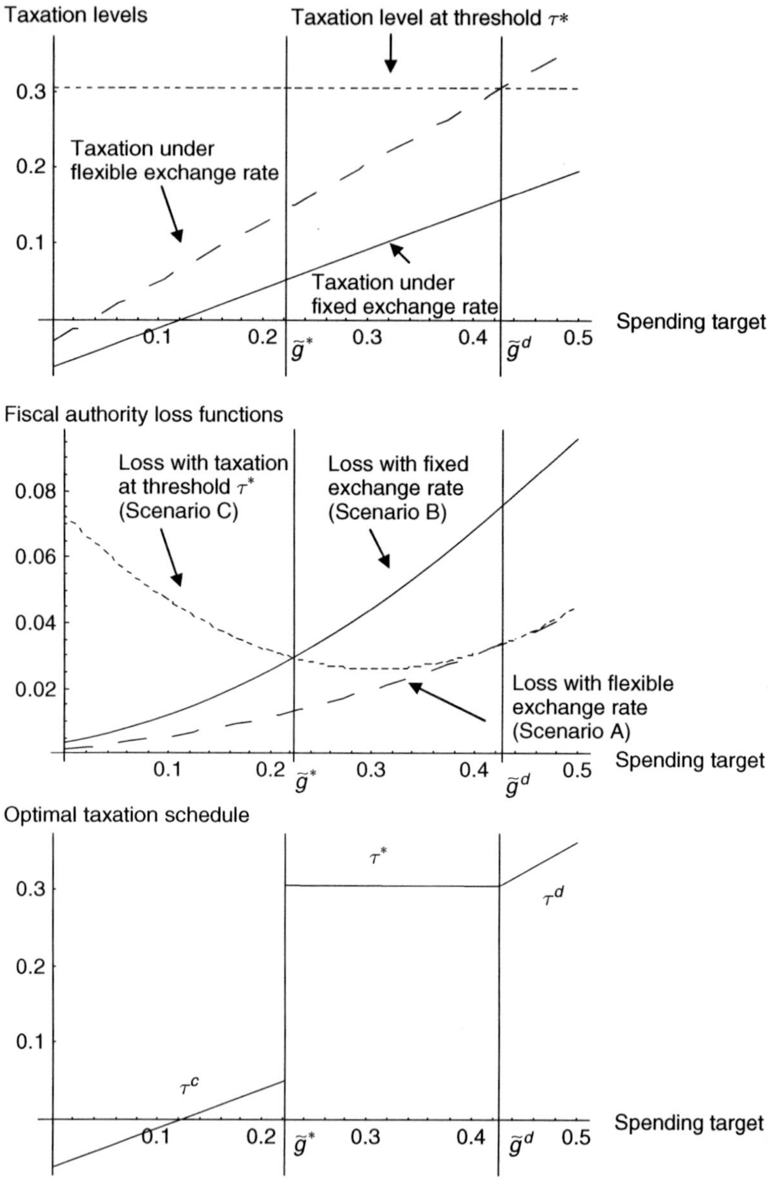

Figure 3.2 The Fiscal Authority's Optimal Tax Choice
Notes: $\alpha_c = 0.7$, $\alpha_f = 0.3$, $\alpha_g = 1$, $\epsilon^e = 0.1$, $\tilde{y} = 0.02$, $\bar{c} = 0.05$.

Furthermore, the horizontal line indicates the level of taxation (τ^*) that is associated with the threshold condition in Equation 3.46—the minimum tax rate necessary for triggering a collapse of the currency peg.

The middle panel shows the policy losses accruing to the fiscal authority in the various scenarios as a function of the spending target $\tilde{g}$. Consistent with the analytical discussion, the graph reveals that the combination of a taxation level τ^d and a depreciation rate ϵ^d in Scenario A always yields a smaller policy loss than Scenario B. But the fiscal authority is not in a position to force this scenario upon the central bank in every state of nature. As signaled in the upper panel, a necessary condition for such an initiative to succeed is that the tax rate τ^d exceeds the threshold level τ^*. This, in turn, requires that the spending target $\tilde{g}$ takes at least a value of 0.42. Otherwise, the loss-minimizing Scenario A would be out of reach for the fiscal authority.

That said, the first two panels of Figure 3.2 convey yet another important message: a failure to enforce Scenario A does not necessarily mean that the fiscal authority would prefer Scenario B compared to other feasible options.

To prove this point analytically, I introduce a Scenario C that combines the minimum tax rate τ^* consistent with an exit from the peg with the associated devaluation rate ϵ^* (see Table 3.1).[88] Combining Equations 3.39 and 3.46, the corresponding loss level can be obtained as

$$L_f^{\tau^*} = \left(\frac{\alpha_c^2 + \alpha_f}{1+\alpha_c}\right)\bar{c} + \frac{1}{2}\alpha_g(\epsilon^e + \tilde{g} + \tilde{y} - \sqrt{2(1+\alpha_c)\bar{c}})^2. \qquad (3.54)$$

We already know from Equation 3.46 that the fiscal player, acting prior to the central bank, could bring about this scenario. The middle panel, which contains both Scenarios B and C, shows that it is also in the fiscal policy maker's interest to choose τ^* rather than τ^c for a range of spending targets to the left of $\tilde{g}^d$.[89] This region, where the policy loss under Scenario C is lower than that associated with Scenario B, is limited on its left-hand side by the spending target $\tilde{g}^*$.

Analytically, this second critical spending target can be derived by setting Equation 3.51 equal to Equation 3.54 and solving for $\tilde{g}$ to obtain[90]

$$\tilde{g}^* = \frac{1+\alpha_g}{\alpha_g}\sqrt{(2(1+\alpha_c)\bar{c}} - \frac{1}{\alpha_g}\sqrt{\frac{2(1+\alpha_g)(1+2\alpha_c-\alpha_f)\bar{c}}{1+\alpha_c}} - \epsilon^e - \tilde{y}. \quad (3.55)$$

If the spending target remains below this threshold, τ^c is implemented and the currency peg survives. But if the spending target is set at or above that level, a rationally acting fiscal authority would choose τ^* and in the process push the central bank toward an exit from the fixed exchange rate regime.

The lower panel of Figure 3.2 summarizes graphically the results of this discussion by plotting the optimal tax choice for the fiscal authority as a function of the public expenditure target $\tilde{g}$. As long as the spending target remains below $\tilde{g}^*$, the fiscal policy maker would choose τ^c and the currency peg would survive. However, as soon as $\tilde{g}$ exceeds $\tilde{g}^*$, the institution would seek to bring about an exit from the peg: it would do so by implementing τ^* in an intermediate range of $\tilde{g}$, and by choosing τ^d whenever it faces a spending target of at least $\tilde{g}^d$.

3.4.2 The scope for intra-governmental conflict

The preceding analysis already suggests that a currency peg may be consistent with only a relatively small range of targets for public spending. It also establishes that the fiscal policy maker holds *de facto* veto power over whether the central bank can deliver on its commitment to defend a fixed exchange rate regime. The following pages will be dedicated to examining more closely to what extent intra-governmental conflict could arise over exchange rate issues between the fiscal policy maker and a monetary authority enjoying varying degrees of operational independence.

Before proceeding, however, it is important to understand better the role of the private sector in influencing the policy decisions of the two branches of the executive.[91] Given the simple structure of our model that, so far, does not include any stochastic element, the private sector's expectations should always settle on one of two possible states: either agents anticipate the survival of the fixed exchange rate for another period and set their expectations accordingly at $\epsilon^e = 0$, or expectations converge toward a devaluation equilibrium, in which case the expected depreciation rate should become $\epsilon^e = E[\epsilon]$.

Using this information, one can determine several regions of a currency peg's credibility that are conditioned on the state of the fiscal

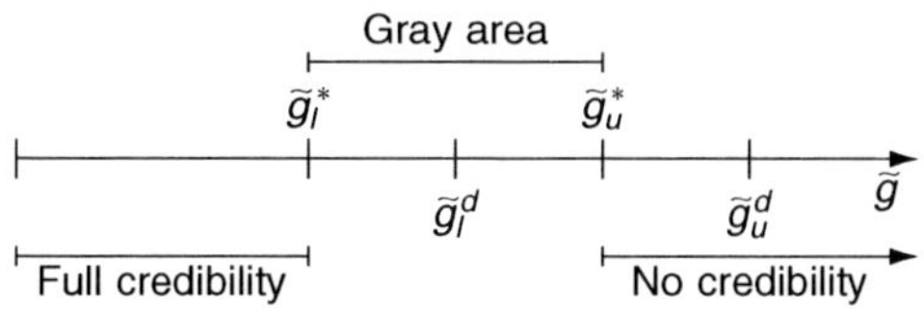

Figure 3.3 Regions of Exchange Rate Credibility

authority's spending target[92]: a region in which the peg is fully crisis-proof, an intermediate or gray region in which the fate of the fixed exchange rate is at the mercy of investor sentiment, and a region where the state of fundamentals is so bad that the fixed parity cannot survive, regardless of what the private sector thinks. In Figure 3.3, the first two regions are separated by the threshold $\tilde{g}_l^*$ and the second pair by $\tilde{g}_u^*$.

The first step in the formal derivation of these thresholds involves finding the rational depreciation expectations that are consistent with a scenario in which the central bank breaks its commitment to the currency peg.[93] Recalling from Section 3.2 that the level of τ^* is instrumental for the stability of the fixed exchange rate, these equilibrium expectations can be found by solving Equation 3.42 for $\epsilon^e = \epsilon$ and substituting this expression into 3.46 as

$$\epsilon^e = \frac{1}{\sqrt{1+\alpha_c}}\sqrt{2\bar{c}}. \tag{3.56}$$

The left threshold $\tilde{g}_l^*$ that separates the fully credible region of the peg from the gray zone of partial credibility can then be determined by substitution of Equation 3.56 in 3.55 as

$$\tilde{g}_l^* = \left(\frac{(1+\alpha_c)(1+\alpha_g) - \sqrt{(1+\alpha_g)(1+2\alpha_c - \alpha_f)} - \alpha_g}{\alpha_g\sqrt{1+\alpha_c}} \right)\sqrt{2\bar{c}} - \tilde{y}. \tag{3.57}$$

To the right of this spending target, the credibility of the peg depends on expectations. If they converge toward the pessimistic equilibrium described in Equation 3.56, the fixed exchange rate collapses. But if agents remain optimistic and believe in a continuation of the peg (implying $\epsilon^e = 0$), then the peg could survive for a range of $\tilde{g}$ realizations to the right of $\tilde{g}_l^*$.

This gray area of partial credibility is delimited on its right-hand side by $\tilde{g}_u^*$. At this point, the spending target becomes so ambitious that the prevailing currency regime is abandoned even in the presence of favorable expectations. By using $\epsilon^e = 0$ in Equation 3.55, this second threshold can be identified as

$$\tilde{g}_u^* = \left(\frac{(1+\alpha_c)(1+\alpha_g) - \sqrt{(1+\alpha_g)(1+2\alpha_c-\alpha_f)}}{\alpha_g\sqrt{1+\alpha_c}} \right) \sqrt{2\bar{c}} - \tilde{y}. \qquad (3.58)$$

From the perspective of a policy maker, the gray area spanning the region between $\tilde{g}_l^*$ and $\tilde{g}_u^*$ in Figure 3.3 is particularly worrisome, as the survival of the fixed exchange rate is at the mercy of the private sector's animal spirits. However, it is also clear that this gray zone only arises because underlying fundamentals are dangerously weak, in this case illustrated through a discomfortingly high-spending target for the fiscal policy maker.[94]

After having derived the optimal strategies for all groups of actors in the veto player model, we can now turn to one of the key issues that this framework seeks to shed light upon: the impact of intra-governmental conflict on the stability of a currency peg. Conceptually, such conflict between the fiscal authority and the central bank can be modeled through two channels.

First, and most directly, policy preferences over the optimal course of exchange rate policy could differ among the two branches of government. For example, whereas identical (or very similar) anti-inflation preferences α_c and α_f would signal an absence of conflict along this dimension, increasing the central bank's inflation-aversion while leaving the fiscal authority's preference unchanged on a relatively low level would increase the potential for conflict.

Secondly, the fiscal authority's temptation to spend should affect the stability of a fixed exchange rate. In particular, the more ambitious the expenditure plans of the fiscal policy maker (expressed by a high α_g) are, the lesser the administration's concern about the importance of exchange rate stability would be. It would be particularly interesting to see to what extent the actions of a spending-prone government could be mitigated in its impact on the currency peg through a high degree of operational independence for the monetary authority.

Table 3.2 Intra-Governmental Conflict Over Exchange Rate Policy

		α_c				
		0.3	0.7	1	1.3	1.7
α_g	0.3	*(0.03/0.00)* *(0.06/0.28)*	*(0.03/0.00)* *(0.15/0.24)*	(0.03/0.00)	(0.03/0.00)	(0.03/0.00)
	0.7	**(0.07/0.00)** **(0.07/0.30)**	*(0.07/0.00)* *(0.15/0.24)*	*(0.07/0.00)* *(0.20/0.22)*	(0.07/0.00)	(0.07/0.00)
	1.0	**(0.09/0.00)** **(0.09/0.37)**	*(0.09/0.00)* *(0.15/0.24)*	*(0.09/0.00)* *(0.20/0.22)*	*(0.09/0.00)* *(0.25/0.21)*	(0.09/0.00)
	1.3	**(0.10/0.00)** **(0.10/0.41)**	*(0.10/0.00)* *(0.15/0.24)*	*(0.10/0.00)* *(0.20/0.22)*	*(0.10/0.00)* *(0.25/0.21)*	(0.10/0.00)
	1.7	**(0.12/0.00)** **(0.12/0.46)**	*(0.12/0.00)* *(0.15/0.24)*	*(0.12/0.00)* *(0.20/0.22)*	*(0.12/0.00)* *(0.25/0.21)*	(0.12/0.00)
	2.0	**(0.13/0.00)** **(0.13/0.49)**	**(0.13/0.00)** **(0.15/0.24)**	*(0.13/0.00)* *(0.20/0.22)*	*(0.13/0.00)* *(0.25/0.21)*	(0.13/0.00)

Note: The numbers in parentheses describe the choices of (τ/ϵ) consistent with every pair of preferences. Outcomes set in italics denote the part of the gray region in which the tax choice is either τ^c or τ^*. Outcomes set in bold describe the region in which the tax choice is either τ^c or τ^d. $\alpha_f = 0.3$, $\tilde{g} = 0.2$, $\tilde{y} = 0.02$, $\tilde{c} = 0.05$; all values in the table are rounded.

To get a sense of how the interests of the fiscal and monetary policy makers interact with exchange rate stability, I conduct a series of numerical simulations (Table 3.2). Specifically, I calculate the equilibrium outcomes for various preference configurations as expressed in parameters α_c and α_g for both optimistic and pessimistic expectations. In these simulations, the emergence of intra-governmental conflict over exchange rate policy is facilitated through the presence of a fiscal policy maker with a very low degree of inflation-aversion ($\alpha_f = 0.3$). This assumption is made to reflect that the fiscal policy maker faces stronger short-term incentives than the central bank to please its political constituency, and hence would typically attach a higher weight to the output and spending objectives compared with his concern for a stable exchange rate (and thus low inflation).[95]

In the first case with optimistic expectations ($\epsilon^e = 0$), the currency peg is not put at risk for any of the preference configurations considered. In other words, independent of the specific values we assign to the central bank's inflation-aversion α_c and the fiscal authority's appetite for spending α_g, the fiscal authority would always implement a taxation level of τ^c that is compatible with continuing the currency peg. Taxation levels would increase in proportion to the fiscal authority's appetite for spending, but would not be affected by the central bank's inflation-aversion.

But Table 3.2 clearly shows that such a benign outcome would only be guaranteed in a setting that combines a highly inflation-averse central bank with a spending-averse fiscal policy maker. In all other cases, there exists a second possible equilibrium in which a shift from optimistic to pessimistic expectations would lead to the peg's collapse. Specifically, for a relatively low spending target and intermediate inflation-aversion, pessimistic expectations would induce a transition from Table 3.1's Scenario B to Scenario C, in which the fiscal policy maker implements τ^* rather than τ^c. For a higher spending target combined with a lesser degree of inflation-aversion on the part of the central bank, the fiscal authority could even achieve its preferred outcome of Scenario A with a taxation level of τ^d.

These simulations help clarify how the self-interested behavior of a fiscal policy maker in conjunction with fragile private sector expectations could heighten the vulnerability of a currency peg for a broad range of plausible preference configurations. In other words, the veto player model suggests that a fixed exchange rate would always remain fragile unless an extremely tough central bank is supported in its efforts to maintain the currency peg by a prudent fiscal policy that strictly limits public spending.

3.4.3 A stochastic fiscal target

In the basic veto player model developed above, I abstracted from uncertainty emerging from exogenous shocks that could impact the economy. This simplifies the analysis but ignores the fact that fixed exchange rates are vulnerable to events like a sizable negative supply shock or the sudden realization of large contingent liabilities on the government's balance sheet. Moreover, it offers no account of how private sector expectations would be formed.

To account for such disturbances, I will refine the analysis in the following by introducing a stochastic element into the model framework. This enables us to show how expectations interact with the anticipated magnitude of a shock to affect the cost-benefit calculation of the central bank. For some parameter values, the stochastic model gives rise to multiple equilibria and thus to the potential for self-fulfilling currency crises.[96]

Whereas most second-generation crisis models feature a stochastic element in the determination of the economy's output (as in Equation 3.1), our model incorporates a stochastic shock in the fiscal policy maker's spending target $\tilde{g}$. This shock captures the potential for contingent expenditures that the fiscal policy maker may face with some positive probability if things turn bad. I prefer this approach to the traditional one because my main focus lies in examining the impact of fiscal policy choices on a fixed exchange rate's credibility. Moreover, it enables me to incorporate a key dimension of many third-generation crisis models in the framework: the notion that in open economies, currency crises are often closely linked to financial distress in the domestic banking or non banking corporate sectors, which, in turn, could give rise to contingent liabilities for the fiscal authority.[97]

Specifically, in the following analysis, the spending target $\tilde{g}$ will be interpreted as being the sum of two components:

$$\tilde{g} = \tilde{g}_0 + z. \tag{3.59}$$

The term $\tilde{g}_0$ depicts expenditure items that society expects the policy maker to meet in each period regardless of the state of nature. By contrast, z represents a stochastic component of the target. Its level for the period under review becomes public knowledge *after* private agents formed their depreciation expectations, but before the fiscal and monetary policy makers choose their policy instruments. The other steps in the sequence of decision making remain unchanged from Section 3.4.1. That said, private agents are assumed to know that the shock follows a uniform probability distribution over the interval $[-Z, Z]$, implying a mathematical expectation of $E[z] = 0$. To ensure that the overall spending target is always positive, I introduce the restriction $Z < \tilde{g}_0$.

As private agents are aware of the shock distribution in setting their depreciation expectations for the upcoming period, their assessment should reflect both the likelihood of a shock exceeding the critical value triggering the peg's collapse and the shock's anticipated size in case such an event actually materializes. Specifically, as agents would be potentially confronted with all three of the policy scenarios described in Table 3.1, the best guess of ϵ at the moment of negotiating wage contracts is a probability-weighted average of the depreciation rates associated with Scenarios A to C. Formally, this expectations term can be written as

$$E[\epsilon] = \text{Prob}(\nu < \nu^*) * 0 + \text{Prob}(\nu^* < \nu < \nu^d) * E\left[\epsilon | \nu^* < \nu < \nu^d\right] + \text{Prob}(\nu > \nu^d) * E[\epsilon | \nu > \nu^d]. \tag{3.60}$$

In this expression, and analogous to the thresholds $\tilde{g}^*$ and $\tilde{g}^d$ from Section 3.4.1, ν^* describes the minimum realization of the shock that would cause the fiscal authority to choose τ^* rather than τ^c. A shock exceeding ν^d would even allow for the implementation of the fiscal authority's most preferred tax rate τ^d. Consistent with the uniform distribution of ν, the probabilities for the shock to fall within each of the three areas delineated by the two thresholds ν^* and ν^d are $\text{Prob}(\nu < \nu^*) = (\nu^* + Z)/2Z$, $\text{Prob}(\nu^* < \nu < \nu^d) = (\nu^d - \nu^*)/2Z$, and $\text{Prob}(\nu > \nu^d) = (Z - \nu^d)/2Z$.

Furthermore, the private sector can perfectly anticipate the monetary authority's policy response conditional on the observance of the shock (see Table 3.1). First, as long as ν remains below ν^*, the central bank would stick to the currency peg. In this case, expectations should converge toward $E[\epsilon | \nu < \nu^*] = 0$. By contrast, Equations 3.42 and 3.46 suggest that the central bank would react to a shock occurring in the interval $[\nu^*, \nu^d]$ through a depreciation rate of

$$E[\epsilon^*] = \frac{1}{\sqrt{1+\alpha_c}} \sqrt{2\bar{c}}. \tag{3.61}$$

As ν is uniformly distributed, the expected shock realization in this parameter range is $E[\nu | \nu^* \leq \nu < \nu^d] = (\nu^* + \nu^d)/2$.

Finally, if the shock exceeds ν^d, the monetary policy maker would likely respond by implementing

$$E[\epsilon^d] = \frac{\alpha_g(1+\alpha_c)}{\alpha_c^2 + \alpha_f + \alpha_g(1+\alpha_c)^2} (\tilde{g}_0 + \epsilon^e + E[\nu | \nu > \nu^d] + \tilde{y}), \tag{3.62}$$

with $E[\nu | \nu \geq \nu^d] = (\nu^d + Z)/2$.

Having collected all the necessary information and substituting Equations 3.61 and 3.62 into 3.60, it becomes possible to write the private sector's depreciation expectations as a function of the shock's threshold levels as

$$\epsilon^e = f(\nu^*, \nu^d) = \left(\left(\frac{\nu^d - \nu^*}{2Z}\right)\left(\frac{\sqrt{2\bar{c}}}{\sqrt{1+\alpha_c}}\right)\right.$$
$$+\left(\frac{Z-\nu^d}{2Z}\right)\left(\frac{\alpha_g(1+\alpha_c)}{\alpha_c^2+\alpha_f+\alpha_g(1+\alpha_c)^2}\right)\left.\left(\tilde{g}_0 + \frac{\nu^d+Z}{2} + \tilde{y}\right)\right)\Big/$$
$$\left(1 - \left(\frac{Z-\nu^d}{2Z}\right)\left(\frac{\alpha_g(1+\alpha_c)}{\alpha_c^2+\alpha_f+\alpha_g(1+\alpha_c)^2}\right)\right). \quad (3.63)$$

This expectations expression can then be used as an input in Equations 3.55 and 3.53 to determine the shock thresholds ν^* and ν^d. Given that the shock level ν^* determines the fate of the currency peg by separating the case in which the fiscal authority would prefer its continuation from that in which it would favor its collapse, we can infer that the peg would be abandoned whenever

$$\sqrt{2\bar{c}} \leq \frac{\alpha_g\sqrt{1+\alpha_c}}{(1+\alpha_c)(1+\alpha_g) - \sqrt{(1+\alpha_g)(1+2\alpha_c-\alpha_f)}}(\nu^* + \tilde{g}_0 + f(\nu^*, \nu^d) + \tilde{y}). \quad (3.64)$$

By the same reasoning, the minimum shock size ν^d compatible with the fiscal policy maker's preferred taxation level τ^d rather than τ^c must be a solution to

$$\sqrt{2\bar{c}} \leq \frac{\alpha_g(1+\alpha_c)^2}{(\sqrt{1+\alpha_c})(\alpha_c^2+\alpha_f+\alpha_g(1+\alpha_c)^2)}\left(\nu^d + \tilde{g}_0 + f(\nu^*, \nu^d) + \tilde{y}\right). \quad (3.65)$$

Presenting a solution to the system established by Equations 3.63–3.65 in graphical terms, Figures 3.4 and 3.5 show how the central bank's decision of whether or not to give up the peg depends on the interaction between private sector expectations and the shock realization ν. Specifically, the figures plot the transformed punishment term $\sqrt{2\bar{c}}$ associated with an exit from the peg together with $\alpha_g\sqrt{1+\alpha_c}/(1+\alpha_c)(1+\alpha_g) - \sqrt{(1+\alpha_g)(1+2\alpha_c-\alpha_f)}\ (\nu + \tilde{g}_0 + f(\nu, \nu^d) + \tilde{y})$—the central bank's modified policy loss in case of a devaluation that is conditioned on the realization of ν.[98]

For the set of parameter values used in the earlier parts of this chapter, the system delivers only one economically plausible equilibrium for ν^*: taking into account all available information, private agents

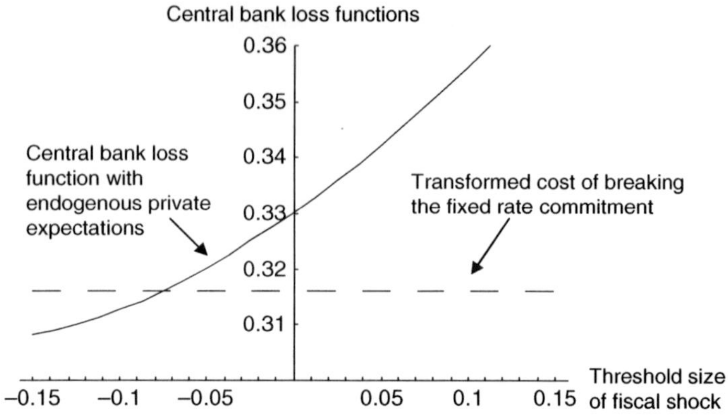

Figure 3.4 A Stochastic Economy: One Equilibrium
Notes: $\alpha_c = 0.7$, $\alpha_f = 0.3$, $\alpha_g = 1$, $\tilde{g}_0 = 0.2$, $\tilde{y} = 0.02$, $\bar{c} = 0.05$.

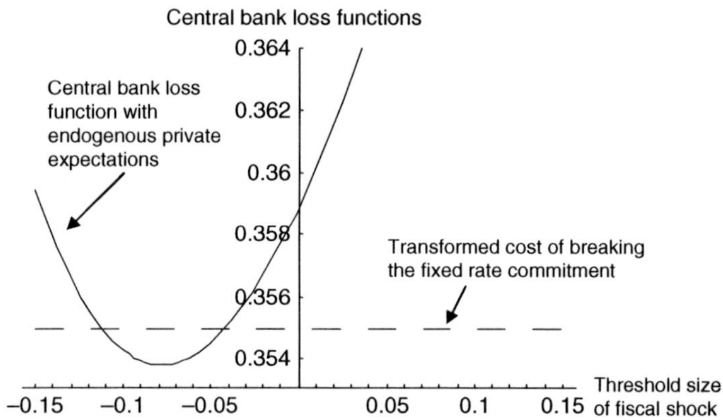

Figure 3.5 A Stochastic Economy: Two Equilibria
Notes: $\alpha_c = 0.7$, $\alpha_f = 0.3$, $\alpha_g = 2$, $\tilde{g}_0 = 0.2$, $\tilde{y} = 0.02$, $\bar{c} = 0.063$.

would settle on depreciation expectations of 18 percent, implying that the shock necessary to trigger a collapse of the fixed exchange rate would need to exceed -0.07.[99] Moreover, the fiscal authority would be able to implement its preferred tax rate τ^d rather than τ^* in case the shock exceeds the threshold $\nu^d = 0.12$ (not shown in the figure).

As the realization of ν is confined to the interval between $-Z=-0.15$ and $Z=0.15$, the fixed peg would survive in only 27 percent of the possible outcomes. In other words, unless the shock would lead to a sizeable decline in the fiscal authority's spending target, we should not expect the central bank to defend the fixed exchange rate.

By contrast, Figure 3.5 presents the graphical solution to a system for modified parameter values that were chosen to produce multiple equilibria within the defined shock range. With a doubled spending preference of the fiscal policy maker ($\alpha_g = 2$) and a punishment slightly higher than before ($\bar{c}=0.063$ instead of 0.05), the two possible solutions for ν^* fall inside the interval $[-Z, Z]$. In this case, the threshold value for the shock necessary to induce the collapse of the fixed exchange rate can no longer be easily inferred. Rather, it depends in a circular way on the state of expectations.

In a relatively benign equilibrium, private agents would settle on depreciation expectations of 17 percent. In this case, the currency peg would fall only if the period shock realization exceeded -0.04. As a result, the peg would enjoy a 37 percent change of survival. However, once expectations turned pessimistic for some exogenous reason, private agents would anticipate a 25 percent devaluation, implying that only a strong contraction of the fiscal policy maker's spending target (a minimum shock of -0.11) could save the fixed exchange rate. This would be highly unlikely: in 87 percent of the potential outcomes, the fixed exchange rate would be abandoned.

The results show that the potential for self-fulfilling crises identified in Section 3.4.2 does not disappear when augmenting the model with a stochastic element as a way to endogenize the mechanism for expectations formation, a finding that is consistent with the results of other second-generation models. This leaves the analyst in an uncomfortable position: while it is possible to determine whether the economy operates in a gray area that exposes the currency peg to a heightened danger of collapse, nothing within the model structure tells him why expectations would shift from a good to a bad equilibrium. However, we have also seen that the multiplicity of equilibria may be endogenous, that is, whether there exists a unique equilibrium or more depends on the underlying structure of the economy, institutional factors, and the preferences of the policy makers.[100]

We can retain from this section that a fiscal policy maker can threaten the continuation of a currency peg with its taxation choices in case it attaches sufficient importance to a high level of public spending compared with other policy objectives. The fiscal branch thus enjoys indirect veto power over the central bank's exchange rate decisions, and the resulting potential for intra-governmental conflict can greatly endanger the stability of a fixed exchange rate regime—particularly in an environment in which private agents lose faith in the willingness of the policy makers to continue with the peg.

3.5 Lobbying and exchange rate stability

Governments depend on the support of voters and other societal groups for their survival in power. It is thus reasonable to expect that the preferences of interest groups and the electoral base of the ruling coalition are reflected in macroeconomic policy outcomes, particularly in democracies. In this section, I will develop an extension of the basic model that accounts for such dynamics. Specifically, it will be shown how the optimizing behavior of a labor union could affect the exchange rate decisions of the central bank through a fiscal policy channel and, in extreme cases, give rise to a currency crisis.

The attractiveness of focusing on interest groups rather than political parties to understand macroeconomic outcomes derives from the observation that the economic preferences of actors are relatively difficult to aggregate into one party line.[101] In particular, a party that competes for an electoral majority needs to be an instrument of political integration and thus risks blurring its economic preference profile in the process of forging compromises between many contrasting interests (see, in particular, Lipset and Rokkan, 1967).

For the analysis of the link between interest groups and exchange rate outcomes, the extension of a sociological model of inflation to an open economy context has become the most widely used approach.[102] It starts from the premise that exchange rate outcomes reflect a political balance of power between various interest groups that are concerned about the distributional consequences of policy making. For example, export and import competing industries would prefer a low external value of the currency, while consumers and the nontradable goods sector would prefer a high one. In addition, the banking sector may be hostile to any large volatility in exchange rates, given that its balance sheet exposure to currency risk may render it vulnerable to liquidity or solvency crises.[103]

Empirically, this approach has been tested in a variety of contexts. For example, in a case study of the Mexican crisis in 1994–95, Frieden (1997) emphasizes that the continuation of a strong Peso policy was a key element in the ruling party's strategy to maintain and broaden the support of the politically powerful urban middle classes in the run-up to the presidential elections. Hence, devaluation was delayed until after the ballot, when it was forced upon the government through a sudden reversal of capital flows. The same author argues in a different paper that the Southern member states of the European Communities could only redirect their policies toward endorsing the objective of European Monetary Union through a gradual shift in political power toward pro-European interest groups. In particular, internationally operating firms that depended on stable exchange rates and continued access to the markets of their European neighbors became strong supporters of the case for further monetary integration (see Frieden, 2002).[104]

Notwithstanding its apparent appeal, the framework described above suffers from two problems. First, it does not offer any insights as to the incentives of an interest group to take lobbying action: it simply assumes that political influence is proportional to the size of a particular interest group in a country's population (see also Eichengreen, 1998).

Secondly, the fact that distributional costs and benefits of exchange rate policies are widely dispersed suggests that under normal circumstances, interest groups should have trouble acting collectively on the issue. The maintenance of a fixed exchange rate regime, for example, could benefit all consumers when a devaluation would reduce their purchasing power, thus reducing individual incentives to lobby. Indeed, the fiscal policy maker may be a much more obvious lobbying target, given its ability to target the benefits of tax exemptions or subsidies with great precision to particular sectors.

The model developed below offers an alternative approach that addresses these weaknesses while preserving a potentially significant effect of lobbying on exchange rate outcomes. Building on the framework developed in Section 3.4 as well as on recent work by Neugart (2003), it seeks to capture the influence of interest groups on the central bank's exchange rate decision via a fiscal policy channel.[105]

Specifically, I assume that a labor union is concerned both with the protection of real wages against wage erosion and the level of employment. Having these objectives, the union could benefit from offering side payments to the fiscal policy maker in exchange for the implementation of a level of taxation that is lower than in the absence of lobbying. In turn, this would lead to a less depreciated exchange rate than would otherwise be the case. In this model, as will be seen, adjustments in exchange rate policy could thus reflect a shift in the labor union's policy preferences or changes in the government's susceptibility to lobbying.

Deviating from the discussion in the preceding sections, the lobbying model will be built around a discretionary framework for the implementation of exchange rate policy. Hence, the central bank does not commit to the defense of any particular exchange rate with a view to influence the decisions of the private sector and the fiscal authority. Moreover, we normalize the level of the log exchange rate in period $t-1$ to $e_{t-1}=0$. This allows us to use the current period's exchange rate level e_t interchangeably with the period's depreciation rate $\epsilon = e_t - e_{t-1}$. A high e hence indicates a highly depreciated home currency relative to the foreign money. Both simplifications help facilitate the technical analysis.

Written in logs, output is supply-determined and follows

$$y = e - w - \tau. \tag{3.66}$$

Output depends positively on the level of the exchange rate e,[106] and negatively on nominal wages w and the level of taxation on firms' output τ.

The central bank decides on exchange rate policy based on its loss function

$$L_c = \frac{1}{2}\alpha_c e^2 + \frac{1}{2}(y - \tilde{y})^2, \tag{3.67}$$

which, except for including the level of the exchange rate rather than its period rate of depreciation, is identical to the expression used in the earlier sections of this chapter.

The fiscal policy maker's decision function, however, does now reflect the possibility of lobbying. Specifically, its aggregate welfare level Ξ_f is determined by both the state of the economy and the level of financial contributions received from the interest group. This is captured in a policy loss function of the form

$$\Xi_f = \lambda L_f - (1-\lambda)M, \tag{3.68}$$

with

$$L_f = \frac{1}{2}\alpha_f e^2 + \frac{1}{2}(y-\tilde{y})^2 + \frac{1}{2}\alpha_g(g-\tilde{g})^2. \tag{3.69}$$

In this composite function, L_f characterizes the loss element stemming from the economic optimization problem of the policy maker, while M represents the level of financial contributions. λ, with $0 \leq \lambda < 1$, is a parameter measuring the government's aversion to lobbying. The higher its value, the stronger is the policy maker's resistance to changing his economically optimal policy program in exchange for bribes.[107]

As the fiscal authority is forced to implement a balance budget, the period's tax revenue τ has to match expenditure g, or

$$g = \tau. \tag{3.70}$$

The labor union strives to minimize a loss function L_u, which accommodates both a real wage target and an employment objective.[108] In particular, it seeks to protect real wages by minimizing the deviation of nominal wages w from the expected price level e^e, while at the same time achieving an output level as close as possible to the target $\tilde{y}$. Furthermore, the union needs to consider the disutility arising from any payment of financial contributions $M(\tau)$ aimed at influencing the fiscal policy maker. Hence, its decision function can be written as

$$L_u = \frac{1}{2}(w-e^e)^2 + \frac{1}{2}\alpha_u(y-\tilde{y})^2 + M(\tau), \tag{3.71}$$

with α_u expressing the weight attached to the real wage objective relative to the employment target: the higher this parameter value, the more the union is inclined to trade off the goal of real wage protection for an improved output performance of the economy to reduce prevailing unemployment levels.

As before, private agents are endowed with rational expectations, so that $e^e = E[e]$. Given that the model economy is not exposed to any stochastic shock, this assumption implies that expectations regarding fiscal and monetary policy choices do not include any forecasting error.

Decisions are made sequentially. After having observed the policy targets and the preference parameters of all agents, the labor union decides on the level of financial contributions offered to the fiscal policy maker. Then, the fiscal authority chooses the period's taxation level to fund its operations. Having observed the tax schedule, the union announces its nominal wage target, which, assuming that employers accept, enters the economy's production function as market wage. In the last step of the process, the central bank chooses the period's depreciation rate and output is produced.

The labor union enters the game at two different stages to avoid a time inconsistency problem. To influence the tax schedule, the union needs to offer side payments prior to the fiscal authority's policy decision. But if the interest group had decided on its nominal wage target at the same time, the fiscal policy maker would have no incentive *ex post* to honor its promise to keep tax rates at a lower-than-optimal level: only a credible threat by the union of using its power to counteract any deviating tax decision by choosing a higher wage target can keep the fiscal player locked in the bargain.

To show the impact of lobbying on the central bank's exchange rate decision and the whole economy, it is first necessary to derive the equilibrium that would prevail in the absence of any financial contributions extended from the interest group to the fiscal policy maker. This pure economic equilibrium can then be taken as a benchmark for determining the political equilibrium. As will be seen, the political equilibrium becomes an attractive solution for the labor union and the fiscal policy maker because it enables the former to improve its welfare even if it fully compensates the fiscal policy maker for the disutility caused by deviating from the economically optimal tax choice. To distinguish among the two cases, a $*$ superscript will be assigned to all outcomes associated with the economic equilibrium, while a p superscript will identify those emerging in the presence of lobbying.

Given the sequential nature of the decision-making process, the model is solved by backward induction. Differentiating Equation 3.67 with respect to e yields the period's exchange rate level as

$$e^* = \frac{1}{1+\alpha_c}(w^* + \tau^* + \tilde{y}). \tag{3.72}$$

In addition to the factors familiar from the preceding discussion, the central bank pays attention to the wage level set by the union: higher nominal wages lead to a more depreciated exchange rate as the central bank seeks to partially offset the associated negative effect on firms' output.

The labor union's nominal wage offer is determined next. Using Equations 3.66 and 3.72 in 3.71, the partial derivative of the union's loss function with respect to the wage level w can be found to be

$$\frac{\partial L_u}{\partial w^*} = \frac{1}{(1+\alpha_c)^2}(\alpha_c w^* - \tau^* - \tilde{y})\left(\frac{\alpha_c}{(1+\alpha_c)^2}\right) + \frac{\alpha_c^2\alpha_u}{(1+\alpha_c)^2}(w^* + \tau^* + \tilde{y})\left(\frac{\alpha_c^2\alpha_u}{(1+\alpha_c)^2}\right).$$

Solving for w then yields

$$w^* = \frac{1}{\alpha_c}\left(\frac{1-\alpha_c^3\alpha_u^2}{1+\alpha_c^2\alpha_u^2}\right)(\tau^* + \tilde{y}) \tag{3.73}$$

as the optimal wage choice for the union.

Finally, if its decision were based exclusively on economic considerations, the fiscal policy maker would choose the level of taxation with a view to minimize its loss function as specified in Equation 3.69. This optimal tax take can be found by substituting Equations 3.72 and 3.73 in 3.69 as

$$\tau^* = \frac{1}{\alpha_c^2 + \alpha_f + \alpha_c^2\alpha_g(1+\alpha_c^2\alpha_u^2)^2}\left(\alpha_c^2\alpha_g(1+\alpha_c^2\alpha_u^2)^2\tilde{g} - (\alpha_c^2 + \alpha_f)\tilde{y}\right). \tag{3.74}$$

While Equations 3.72–3.74 describe the model's equilibrium outcome in the absence of lobbying, the optimization problem for the fiscal policy maker and the labor union changes if there is scope for financial contributions. The former needs to consider in its decision function the value it derives from accepting bribes (see Equation 3.68), while the latter needs to determine how much it is prepared to invest in its lobbying activities.

To derive the policy outcome consistent with this scenario, I assume that the fiscal authority would not accept any welfare level inferior to that obtained in the absence of lobbying. This requires that the labor union needs to choose its contributions offer M to meet the condition[109]

$$\lambda L_f^* = \lambda L_f^p - (1-\lambda)M, \tag{3.75}$$

which in turn implies a minimum contribution level of

$$M = \frac{\lambda}{1-\lambda}(L_f^p - L_f^*). \tag{3.76}$$

This reasoning on the part of the fiscal authority determines what the union would have to pay in order to induce the government to deviate from the taxation level prevailing in the absence of lobbying.

The next step involves finding a solution to the labor union's own optimization problem with respect to the tax rate τ^p, taking into account the costliness of the financial contributions it may offer to the fiscal authority. Substituting Equations 3.76 and 3.70 into 3.71 and taking the partial derivative of the resulting expression with respect to the tax rate yields

$$\frac{\partial L_u}{\partial \tau^p} = (w^p - e^p)\frac{\partial (w^p - e^p)}{\partial \tau^p} + \alpha_u(y^p - \tilde{y})\frac{\partial y^p}{\partial \tau^p}$$
$$+ \frac{\lambda}{1-\lambda}\left(\alpha_f e^p \frac{\partial e^p}{\partial \tau^p} + (y^p - \tilde{y})\frac{\partial y^p}{\partial \tau^p} + \alpha_g(\tau^p - \tilde{g})\right).$$

Based on this derivative, we can determine the tax rate τ^p that enables the labor union to minimize its welfare loss as

$$\tau^p = \frac{1}{\Phi}\left(\lambda\alpha_c^2\alpha_g\left(1+\alpha_c^2\alpha_\mu^2\right)^2\tilde{g} - (\alpha_c^2 + \lambda\alpha f - (\lambda-1)(\alpha_c^3\alpha_\mu^2)^2)\tilde{y}\right), \tag{3.77}$$

with $\Phi = \alpha_c^2 + \lambda\alpha_f + \lambda\alpha_c^2\alpha_g(1+\alpha_c^2\alpha_\mu^2)^2 - (\lambda-1)(\alpha_c^3\alpha_\mu^2)^2$.

When comparing this taxation level with τ^*, one can see that the two tax rates typically differ, with the difference being a function of the government's susceptibility to lobbying embodied in λ. Moreover, Equation 3.77 shows that the more the government is concerned with economic welfare relative to financial contributions (approximated by λ converging toward 1), the more the tax rate τ^p would become similar to τ^*.

The sensitivity of the fiscal authority's decision to the availability of financial contributions can be visualized in a simple simulation exercise (Figure 3.6). As expected, the level of taxation on firms' output

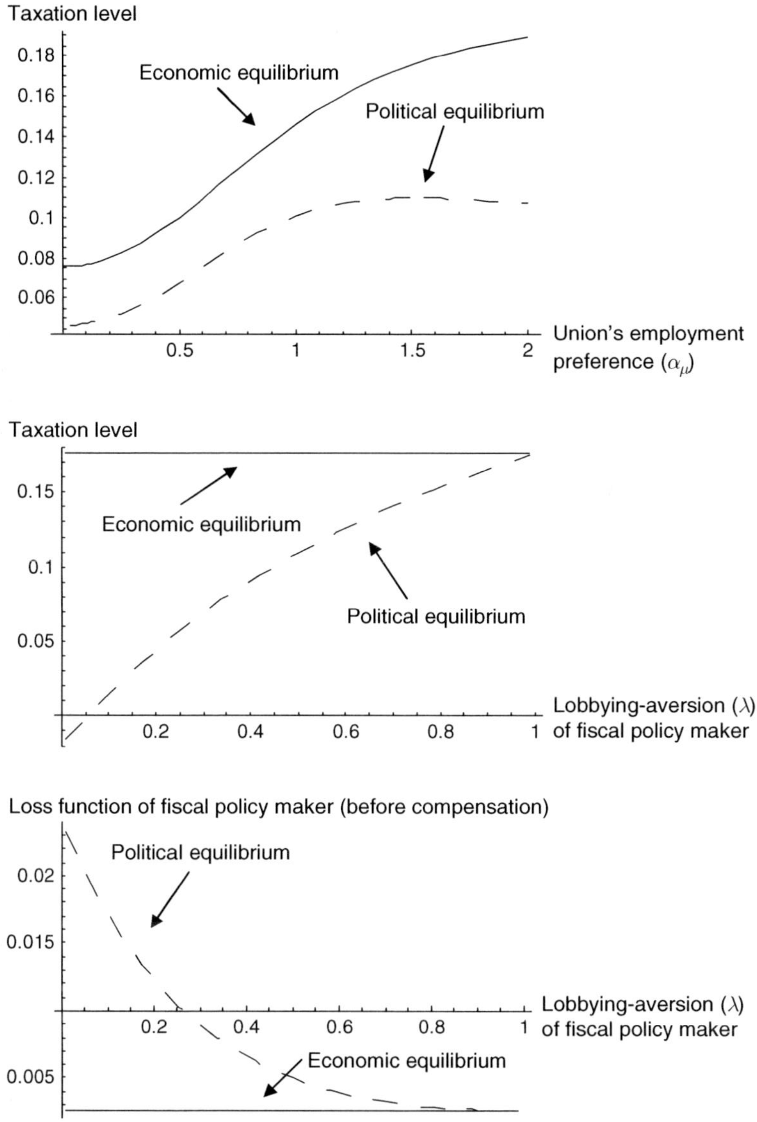

Figure 3.6 Lobbying and Fiscal Policy Decisions
Notes: $\alpha_c = 1$, $\alpha_f = 0.3$, $\alpha_g = 1$, $\alpha_u = 1.5$, $\tilde{g} = 0.2$, $\tilde{y} = 0.02$.

is lower in the political equilibrium than in the absence of lobbying. Hence, the interest group succeeds in its attempt to bring about a tax regime that is favorable to employment growth.

But there are two caveats to this general observation. First, the higher the union's employment preference, the less successful the pressure group would be in securing a low level of taxes (upper panel). Underlying this outcome is the fact that, to some extent, the fiscal policy maker can exploit the growing goodwill of the union to exercise wage restraint by being more selfish about its own chief concern, which is financing a high level of public expenditure through taxation.

Secondly, the scope for lobbying is clearly affected by the nature of the fiscal policy maker. If the authority is very receptive to bribes, it can be expected to tolerate a tax level that is considerably lower than in the absence of lobbying (middle panel). But the less receptive the policy maker becomes, the more the tax rate in the political equilibrium approaches that are associated with a decision based solely on economic considerations.

A look at the fiscal authority's loss function can help explain this last observation. As the lower panel reveals, a high degree of openness to lobbying leads the government to tolerate a large deviation from the economic welfare level that would be optimal in its judgment. This tolerance decreases with a growing lobbying-aversion. This is partly due to the fact that economic considerations would become more important in the authority's decision function, but also reflects the fact that the union would find it less attractive to spend significant amounts of money on seeking to influence a counterpart that is difficult to access—the associated costs would no longer be worth the effort.

Broadening our perspective to the entire economy, we can see that the lower taxes induced through the lobbying activities lead to higher output, higher real wages, and less exchange rate depreciation than in the economic equilibrium (Table 3.3). By 'buying' lower taxes, the interest group thus offers a helping hand to the central bank in the latter's effort to limit the optimal period depreciation of the exchange rate. This said, the simulations show that the differences in outcome between the political and the economic equilibria tend to disappear with an increase in the fiscal policy maker's resistance to interest group influence.

Table 3.3 The Impact of Lobbying on the Economy

	λ		
	0.3	0.5	0.7
L_f^*	0.00265	0.00265	0.00265
L_f^p	0.00903	0.00512	0.00335
L_u^*	0.01101	0.01101	0.01101
L_u^p	0.00502	0.00729	0.00903
M	0.00273	0.00247	0.00162
τ^*	0.17589	0.17589	0.17589
τ^p	0.06935	0.10964	0.14069
e^*	0.06027	0.06027	0.06027
e^p	0.02749	0.03989	0.04944
w^*	–0.07534	–0.07534	–0.07534
w^p	–0.0343	–0.04986	–0.06181
y^*	–0.04027	–0.04027	–0.04027
y^p	0.00749	–0.01987	–0.02944

Note: $\alpha_c = 1$, $\alpha_f = 0.3$, $\alpha_g = 1$, $\alpha_u = 1.5$, $\tilde{g} = 0.2$, $\tilde{y} = 0.02$; all values in the table are rounded.

In general, the various results of the theoretical discussion should make us rather sceptical of the likelihood of a currency peg's survival in crisis episodes if such an arrangement were not embedded into a broadly favorable political environment. They also suggest clearly that a narrow look at central bank independence, or at the institutional back up of a fixed exchange rate regime in the form of a fixed cost associated with reneging on an exchange rate commitment, may not be sufficient to fully capture the potential vulnerabilities underlying a currency peg. But the proof lies in the eating: the case for accepting political-economy models as an alternative to purely economic models for explaining and predicting currency crises ultimately needs to rely on enhanced explanatory power, not only in theory but also in practice. It is the task of the next chapter to examine whether the data actually show any robust evidence suggesting a role for political factors in the occurrence of currency crises.

4
The Role of Politics in Crisis Prediction

4.1 Introduction

Predicting currency crises is difficult. Doing so successfully would imply outperforming well-informed market participants at forecasting sudden shifts in investor confidence, a task in which even professionals, including the big commercial rating agencies and the IMF, often fail.[110] The difficulties encountered in explaining such events may be partially linked to the changing nature of the channels through which vulnerabilities build; in the words of Kindleberger (1989), 'one knows a financial crisis when it happens,' but it is difficult to generalize about such events given the idiosyncracies involved in each case. Moreover, predictability may be impaired by the endogeneity of the policy responses that are taken in light of mounting crisis risk, and by the potential for sentiment-driven speculative attacks, which may not be associated with any clear pattern in the evolution of a limited set of fundamentals underlying the exchange rate.[111]

But the widespread disregard for the political-economy dimension of currency crises in the mainstream literature may also play a role in explaining the relatively poor prediction performance of many statistical models. As argued forcefully in the previous chapters, one should expect that the political environment matters for a country's vulnerability to currency crises. In particular, governments would consider the political costs and benefits in their decision of whether to exit from a currency peg, which in turn should reflect factors such as the incumbent's ideological preferences, the administration's time horizon, and the institutional constraints it faces in reaching policy decisions.

Against this background, this chapter sets out to investigate the empirical relationship between political factors and the probability of currency crises in some detail. Using a large set of political indicators for a diverse sample of 69 countries over the 1975–97 period, the chapter will first describe the data and then estimate a variety of logit models to determine the extent to which the inclusion of political indicators could make a difference in crisis prediction. This will show that several political indicators are indeed associated with a heightened probability of crisis, but also that these findings are not very robust across model specifications.

The study distinguishes itself from other work that has recently been done in the field through its conservative design, aimed at a thorough testing of the results. In particular, the methodology used for the multi-variate analysis controls for temporal dependence and autocorrelation in the data as well as for the influence of a country's per capita income level; each political variable needs to demonstrate its explanatory power in model specifications that encompass a broad range of other political measures; and extensive robustness tests are performed with regard to the country and time coverage of the data. Finally, the analysis reveals that the specific choice of crisis indicator can play an important role in biasing the results of large scale cross-country studies on the political economy of currency crises.

Before proceeding with the statistical analysis, a short survey of the existing empirical studies on the political economy of currency crises will help to assess their achievements as well as their weaknesses more clearly. Then, the data set and the empirical strategy will be described, which involves both the estimation of pooled logit regressions and fixed-effects panels. A discussion of the key findings from both the descriptive analysis and the various logit models will follow, including the robustness of results and the models' in-sample forecasting performance. Finally, I will look more closely at the behavior of currency markets around election episodes, and at the impact of the composition of the legislature for whether left-leaning governments are more prone to currency crises than others.

4.2 Literature survey

The econometric literature on currency crises has grown rapidly since the mid-1990s but has not yet reached maturity. In fact, a strong consensus on the fundamentals of currency crises is still outstanding, and many early-warning-systems (EWS) models—which typically rely on a set of macroeconomic and financial indicators to detect crisis vulnerabilities—fail to robustly predict the occurrence of currency crises.[112]

Against this background, a growing sense of frustration has led a number of researchers to include political factors in the list of regressors.[113] In this section, I will quickly review the key characteristics of this relatively new literature and present its main findings on the linkage between political conditions and currency crises, before discussing some of its methodological weaknesses. The interested reader can consult Appendix B for a more detailed description of the various studies underlying this survey.

In general, the econometric work on the political economy of currency crises has relied on the methodology established in some of the more prominent economic studies, with authors broadening the range of independent variables to better account for political conditions. This practice is reflected in the dominant use of cross-country panel regressions rather than time-series approaches,[114] the widespread reliance on an index of exchange market pressure to identify crisis periods, which due to its binary nature lends itself best to logit or probit analysis (see Section 4.3.1), and an increasing focus on forecasting through the use of leading rather than contemporaneous independent variables.

In terms of country coverage, the analysis has focused on both advanced economies and the developing world, with the latter drawing increasing interest in recent years. This closely reflects the changing patterns in the regional distribution of currency events: whereas the early 1990s were dominated by the 1992–93 crises within the European Exchange Rate Mechanism and its periphery, the dramatic increase in short-term private capital flows to emerging market economies, and hence the potential for sudden reversals in investor sentiment, prepared the ground for a variety of large capital account crises in this country category since the mid-1990s. Major improvements in data availability have facilitated this expansion in country coverage. In particular, many of the political-economy studies make use of indicators from the World Bank's Database of Political Institutions (DPI) or the University of Maryland's Polity IV database, both of which provide detailed political and institutional information virtually on every country in the world.[115]

The shared hypothesis underlying all political-economy models is that the credibility of a government's commitment to a fixed exchange rate regime should depend on its ability and willingness to defend the arrangement when faced with market pressure. In turn, the ability and willingness to do so successfully should be at least as much a function of the administration's interests and political strength as being conditioned upon a healthy macroeconomic environment. Thus, the political-economy literature sets out to test the statistical effect on crisis probabilities of a variety of political and institutional variables that are thought to be systematically related to a government's economic policy preferences and its capacity to implement the policy agenda in a given institutional environment.

Arguably, the literature has directed most of the attention to the link between political uncertainty and currency crises. The underlying hypothesis is that the probability of an exit from the currency peg should increase with a short-term perspective on the part of the incumbent policy maker, as the costs and benefits of defending a peg under adverse conditions are asymmetrically distributed over time (see Section 3.3). The findings of several studies support such a view, showing a close association between currency crises and election periods for both advanced and emerging economies. In particular, evidence on Latin American countries reveals that currency crises tend to occur in the first several months after a vote takes place.[116] Further empirical support pointing to a close relation between political uncertainty and currency crises is produced by Bernhard and Leblang (2000) and Leblang (2003a), which do not stop at the election link but employ a broader concept of political uncertainty from which to infer the probability of leadership change.[117]

That said, even in this most researched subfield, it is not possible to draw strong conclusions from the available evidence. For example, in a study that carefully distinguishes between pre-election, post-election, and other periods, Leblang (2003b) finds that developing-country governments are more likely to defend the currency after the elections compared to tranquil times (albeit the probability of a successful defense is lower than in the pre-election period). Moreover, several studies incorporating an election indicator as part of a broader set of political variables fail to establish statistically significant effects.[118]

A similarly mixed pattern of findings emerges with regard to the explanatory power of other political factors, including interest group pressure, the role of veto players, the extent of democratic government, and the policy maker's ideological preferences.

To some extent, this outcome may reflect the difficulties associated with finding suitable empirical instruments for measuring the impact of a particular political factor on crisis probabilities. One area in which this problem may be prominent is the analysis of lobbying, where the influence of a sectoral interest group is typically approximated through the share of the interest group's economic sector in a country's GDP (see, for example, Frieden, Ghezzi, and Stein, 2001; Leblang, 2003b). This very crude measure may not capture well the incentives to lobby or the actual power of the interest group, especially if the relevant economic sector consists of individual agents with heterogenous policy preferences.[119]

But inconclusive results may also reflect that the direction of effect is not always clear from a theoretical perspective. For example, in the field of veto player analysis, one could argue that the odds of a successful exchange rate defense should be substantially reduced through less flexible decision making in the presence of intra-governmental conflict or a large number of veto players (see Section 3.4). On the other hand, veto players may sometimes play a positive role in preventing excessive volatility in the political process (see, for example, MacIntyre, 2001). Given these theoretical ambiguities, it should not come as a surprise that the empirical evidence remains weak and even produces contradictory results. For example, while Leblang (2003b) fails to find evidence on the link between divided government and the likelihood of a successful defense of a currency peg, Leblang and Satyanath (2006) and Chiu and Willett (2006) show that the presence of veto players typically increases the likelihood of a currency crisis.[120]

A similar issue may plague the studies that investigate the impact of a country's regime type on crisis vulnerability. On the one hand, one could expect that the credibility of macroeconomic policy makers should be enhanced through the provision of transparent and timely information on policies and a system of checks and balances that would hold the government accountable, conditions that are more common in democracies than in authoritarian regimes (Bremmer, 2006). In addition, Leblang (2005) argues that democratically elected governments may have a stronger incentive to defend a fixed exchange rate as a failure to do so could lead to a loss of office. On the other hand, authoritarian governments may find it easier to impose the adjustment measures required in a crisis situation to sustain a currency peg (see Edwards and Santaella, 1993; Frieden, Ghezzi, and Stein, 2001). Indeed, while Leblang and Satyanath (2006) find weak evidence of a positive link between the degree of a country's democratic development and currency crises for varying samples of developing and emerging market economics, Block (2003) establishes the opposite result based on his sample of 23 emerging market countries.[121]

Finally, failure to establish clear stylized facts could be caused by the presence of signalling behavior on the part of a government that risks blurring its true preferences. For example, while some studies confirm the theoretical priors that partisan shifts to the left should be positively correlated with speculative attacks (see Bernhard and Leblang, 2000; Block, 2003; Leblang, 2002), Leblang (2003b) finds that right-wing governments in developing countries are less likely to defend a currency peg than others. Potentially, this latter finding may reflect that left-leaning administrations depend more on a commitment to a currency peg to signal their competence, and hence have a stronger incentive to defend it when faced with a speculative attack, in spite of their alleged closeness to labor interests.[122]

Turning to the economic as opposed to the statistical relevance of the literature's findings, the results also appear to be rather sobering. First, the marginal effects of political variables on crisis probabilities—to the extent that they are reported in the studies—are often found to be very small. For example, Leblang (2003b) reports that for the two key political variables included in his study, left-wing governments are 1.18 percent more likely during a campaign and electoral period to defend the exchange rate than during non-electoral periods, while right-wing governments are 0.27 percent less likely than others to defend their exchange rate when facing market pressure. In terms of quantitative impact, these effects are consistent with what is found in Leblang (2003a), reporting that a one standard deviation increase in the probability of a constitutional change in government raises the probability of a speculative attack by a mere 1.16 percent.[123]

The basic picture does not change when looking at the overall prediction performance of the models. For example, Leblang and Satyanath (2006) find that even in the best-performing specification, the inclusion of government turnover and divided government in standard EWS models can typically improve only marginally the latters' forecasting accuracy.[124] Specifically, in an out-of-sample forecasting exercise for three different EWS models, the inclusion of both variables would increase the share of correct predictions in one case by 7 percent relative to the baseline specification, but by less than 2 percent in the case of the other two models.[125] Clearly, such results are not compelling enough to make a strong case for including political conditions in forecasting models as a means to better predict currency crises.

To some extent, a more careful approach to selecting the country sample and to formulating the hypotheses that are subjected to empirical testing may help to improve the robustness of findings on the linkage between political factors and currency crises, even if this would imply some loss of generality.[126] In particular, researchers could pay increased attention in the choice of country sample to its regional composition, the time period under review, and the countries' economic development stage, in the hope that a more homogenous country composition would lead to stronger results on the link between political conditions and the probability of currency crisis. Moreover, researchers could seek to construct indicators that better capture the particular political and institutional context of the countries under review, including through the use of interaction variables that condition the impact of political factors on the state of a country's institutional environment.[127]

But research designs should also address better the potential for omitted variables bias. In particular, authors tend to single out a limited number of political factors and test for their statistical significance without sufficiently considering their potential links to other political and institutional conditions. Perhaps unintentionally, this problem is well illustrated in Leblang and Satyanath (2006): when including all five political variables in the regressions at the same time, none of them retains its significance across all three types of forecasting models.[128] This unsatisfactory outcome shows how multicollinearity among explanatory variables can lead to large standard errors for individual variables. More fundamentally, it warns that restricting the study design to a small set of fundamentals may give rise to the risk of confusing correlation with causality; developments may actually be driven by other, latent variables with the observed indicators merely moving in the same direction as the underlying ones.

A more thorough application of model selection strategies could help guarding against this risk of finding spurious relationships. For example, exploratory econometric work could begin with a general model and then use a testing-down approach to reduce the number of explanatory variables in a step-wise procedure. In addition, econometric models focusing on the association between political factors and currency crises could seek to better control for a country's level of economic development as approximated by its per capita income. This would help ensure that the coefficients pick up the part of the political variables' effect on currency crises that is not already captured through a country's stage of development.[129]

Finally, many studies have not satisfactorily addressed issues relating to endogeneity and serial correlation in the data. To some extent, the former problem could be resolved by lagging the independent variables with a view to avoiding the potential for currency crises causing a deterioration in political conditions rather than vice versa. The latter issue could be addressed through the inclusion of a survival variable in the study design, which captures for each observational unit the time elapsed since the last crisis event (see Beck, Katz, and Tucker, 1998).[130]

4.3 Data set and empirical strategy

In this section, I describe the data sample used in our empirical study, introduce a variety of political factors whose impact on the probability of experiencing a currency crisis will be examined, and present the empirical strategy for estimating a range of logit models based on a large panel of countries.

4.3.1 Country sample and crisis measure

This analysis follows most other political-economy studies in using a cross-section approach spanning a broad sample of countries. Such a design caters best to the fact that within-country variance in political data tends to be very low, as many indicators measuring structural characteristics of a polity change little over time. Specifically, the data set contains annual observations for a total of 69 countries over the period 1975–97. Given our interest in testing the robustness of the association between political factors and currency crises across countries with respect to their income levels and location, the sample includes advanced economies, emerging market countries, and other developing countries from all geographical regions.[131]

For the identification of currency crises, I follow standard practice in relying on a pressure index.[132] Based on monthly changes in nominal exchange rates and foreign reserve holdings of the central bank, the index signals periods of extreme pressure in currency markets whenever its level for a particular country month exceeds a certain threshold.

Specifically, with e defining the price of the foreign reference currency in terms of the local money and r_t representing the level of central bank reserves, the index p for month t can be determined as

$$p_t = \Delta e_t - \alpha \Delta r_t \tag{4.1}$$

with

$$\alpha = \frac{\sigma_e}{\sigma_r}. \tag{4.2}$$

α is a parameter that ensures that the conditional volatilities of the two index components are equal. Without this adjustment, the conditional volatility of reserves would typically be much higher than that of the exchange rate, causing index movements to be driven mainly by the evolution of the former component.

Complementing this standard measure is a second indicator, p_t^s, which takes into account the evolution of the index over a three-month period ending with period t (see Schnatz, 1998). This additional measure, which seeks to smooth the indicator's behavior over time, is calculated as

$$p_t^s = p_t + \frac{1}{2} p_{t-1} + \frac{1}{4} * p_{t-2}. \tag{4.3}$$

In both cases, a depreciation of the home currency and a loss in central bank reserves cause the index to increase.

Crisis periods are called for a given country *i* in month *t* whenever the index exceeds its mean μ by a certain distance, which is measured as a multiple Ω of the standard deviation σ of the index.[133] To avoid calling the same episode of exchange market pressure twice, we impose a 24-month window of exclusion after each initial crisis call.[134]

In a formal form, the decision rule to identify currency crises can thus be written as

$$\mathrm{CRS}_{i,t} = \begin{cases} 1 & \text{if } p_{i,t} \geq \mu_i^p + \Omega * \sigma_i^p \text{ and } p_i < \mu_i^p + \Omega * \sigma_i^p \text{ for } t_{-23} - t_{-1} \\ 0 & \text{otherwise} \end{cases} \tag{4.4}$$

Compared to qualitative crisis measures, the pressure index has the advantage of objectivity. Moreover, compared to simpler crisis measures such as those relying exclusively on a steep nominal exchange rate depreciation, it has the advantage of also identifying as a crisis successful defenses against a speculative attack, as long as the central bank has lost a sufficient amount of reserves in the process. [135]

Even if the index follows a transparent identification rule, it is still sensitive to several choices related to its implementation. First, index volatility can be measured separately for each country or across countries. In the first case, the index picks up times of extreme pressure in the foreign exchange market relative to the mean period change for each individual country; in the second, the index identifies crises relative to the cross-country mean. Secondly, the choice of threshold can affect the number of episodes called.

To address this specification uncertainty, I rely on a variety of crisis indicators based on country-specific volatility measures (CRS, CRSSM), on the smoothing formula (CRSSM) from Equation 4.3, and on the cross-country volatility calculation (CRCRS). For each of these options, the analysis further differentiates between weak crises (CRS2, CRSSM2, CRCRS2) that are called whenever the index exceeds its mean by two standard deviations, and strong crises that are based on a three-standard-deviation threshold (CRS3, CRSSM3, CRCRS3).[136] Finally, as additional checks for the results, I calculate an index calling a crisis in cases where the monthly nominal exchange rate depreciation exceeds 15 percent (see Frankel and Rose, 1996), and run the regressions based on the crisis calls contained in Glick and Hutchison (1999).

The overlap in crisis calls among the various measures is rather low. It ranges between 36 percent and 66 percent for any pair of indicators.[137] For example, most small crises (CRS2, CRSSM2) are concentrated in Europe, while most strong crises (CRS3, CRSSM3) originate in Latin America (see Table 4.1). Moreover, the bias in the distribution of crises toward the Latin American region becomes even more pronounced when looking at the cross-country standard deviation measure, in which case two-thirds of all crisis occurrences are confined to this region.

Table 4.1 Sensitivity of the Crisis Indicator to Specification Issues

Measure	**Crisis Frequencies**					
	Africa	**Asia**	**Europe**	**Latin**	**RoW**	**Total**
CRS2	19	39	73	48	15	194
CRSSM2	19	35	72	47	11	184
CRCRS2	12	9	6	62	4	93
CRS3	13	22	21	37	6	99
CRSSM3	12	20	28	35	5	100
CRCRS3	8	4	4	38	2	56
Country-years	175	286	442	477	88	1,468
Measure	**Crisis Probabilities**					
	Africa	**Asia**	**Europe**	**Latin**	**RoW**	**Total**
CRS2	0.11	0.14	0.17	0.10	0.17	0.13
CRSSM2	0.11	0.12	0.16	0.10	0.13	0.13
CRCRS2	0.07	0.03	0.01	0.13	0.05	0.06
CRS3	0.07	0.08	0.05	0.08	0.07	0.07
CRSSM3	0.07	0.07	0.06	0.07	0.06	0.07
CRCRS3	0.05	0.01	0.01	0.08	0.02	0.04

Crisis probabilities are calculated as the ratio of crises occurrences over total country-years.

4.3.2 The choice of regressors

The discussion in the previous chapter and the survey of the existing econometric literature provide many testable hypotheses about the linkage between political factors and the probability of currency crises. Specifically, we should expect that the regime type of a country, the time horizon of the incumbent administration, its partisan orientation, interest group pressure, and institutional constraints in the form of veto players should all matter for the stability of a currency peg. The following discussion will introduce the empirical proxies for each of these factors before providing an overview of the economic control variables used in the study. For an overview of the variables together with their data sources and the assumed direction of correlation with currency crises, see Tables 4.2 and 4.3.

4.3.2.1 Regime type

As discussed earlier, the direction of the effect running from regime type to crisis probabilities is not clear. On the one hand, democracy

Table 4.2 Political Variables: Overview

	Description	Source	Direction
POLITY	Index of democractic government	Polity IV	±
LEFTGOV	Dummy for left-leaning government	WB	+
AGRI	Share of agricultural sector in GDP	WDI	±
INDUSTRY	Share of industrial sector in GDP	WDI	+
SERVICES	Share of service sector in GDP	WDI	±
ELECTION	Legislative/executive election	WB	+
TURNOVER	Annual turnover of veto players	WB	+
YEARS	Years-in-office of chief executive's party	WB	±
GOVMAJ	Parliamentary majority of government	WB	−
GOVCOH	Party concentration index of gov. coalition	WB	−
OPPCOH	Party concentration index of opposition	WB	±
VETO	Number of veto players	WB	+
POLARIZ	Polarization of political system	WB	+
CBI	Central bank independence	CU92	−

Note: WB refers to the World Bank's Database of Political Institutions (version 3.0); Polity IV to the Polity IV database of the University of Maryland; WDI to the World Bank's World Development Indicators; and CU to Cukierman (1992).

could lead to more transparent and accountable policy making, and hence to more credibility. But this advantage could be offset in crisis situations by the fact that democratic governments may encounter greater difficulties in organizing the necessary political consensus for the policy adjustment needed to defend the peg compared with their more authoritarian counterparts.

To examine the impact of regime type on currency crises, we rely on the POLITY variable from the Polity IV database. This indicator, which increases with the degree of democracy, takes into account such criteria as the competitiveness of political participation, the openness and competitiveness of executive recruitment, and constraints on the chief executive.[138]

4.3.2.2 Partisanship and interest group pressure

LEFTGOV is a dummy variable that is intended to test whether currency crises are more probable in the presence of left-leaning governments. In the case of presidential systems, it takes a value of 1 whenever the party of the chief executive has a left-leaning orientation. For parliamentary democracies, it tracks coalition governments that include a left-wing party.

Lobbying on economic policy issues is assumed to be organized along sectoral interests. The political weight of these interests is approximated by the share of the respective sector—agriculture, manufacturing, and services—in a country's GDP. The direction of effect is difficult to predict: firms operating mainly in the domestic market may benefit from an exit from the peg when the monetary tightening associated with its defense stifles economic activity through high interest rates. Support for such a strategy should also be expected from tradable-goods producers that are concerned about the effects of an overvalued real exchange rate on their competitiveness. By contrast, firms that would be hard hit by the effects of a sharp exchange rate depreciation on their balance sheets should be in favor of maintaining the peg. This would most likely be the case for financial institutions that often hold substantial unhedged foreign currency exposure on their balance sheets. On balance, these considerations lead to the assumption that the manufacturing sector would most likely be in favor of an exit from the peg. However, the preferences of the (often very heterogenous) agriculture and services sectors are far less predictable.

To account for the fact that the preferences over exchange rate policies should be particularly relevant for policy making in open economies, the models interact the sectoral shares in a country's GDP with an openness measure of the economy.[139]

4.3.2.3 Uncertainty about future policy choices

The willingness to defend a fixed exchange rate regime should be expected to suffer in cases where policy making is guided by a short time horizon. In such cases, an incumbent would likely put a premium on the immediate gains associated with abandoning the peg in a crisis episode (see Section 3.3). To capture the uncertainty over the current administration's time horizon, the models include a series of variables taken from DPI.

The ELECTION dummy signals whether the current period is an election year. Being sensitive to the type of political system, the variable records executive elections in presidential systems and legislative elections in parliamentary democracies. As upcoming elections should increase uncertainty over the incumbent's continued stay in power, one would expect the indicator to be positively correlated with currency crises.

Heightened political instability could also follow from a high turnover in the country's key decision makers. This is captured through the TURNOVER indicator based on the DPI's Stabs measure, linking the incidences of changes in a country's key decision makers within a given calendar year to the total number of such political actors.[140]

Besides these two rather straightforward measures affecting an incumbent's time horizon, the models will test the significance of a variety of additional factors that could be associated with political instability, albeit in a more indirect way.

First, the potential for political instability could be affected through the time elapsed since the last change in the ruling party. This is measured by the YEARS variable, which counts the number of years that the chief executive's party (as opposed to the chief executive himself) has already spent in power. The direction of its link with currency crises is, however, unclear. As argued in Bernhard and Leblang (2000) and Leblang (2003a), governments tend to be most vulnerable to challenges when they begin their time in power. As cabinets survive over time, the risk of exit declines because they acquire political capital, consolidate power, and hone leadership skills. But if parties remain in power for long periods of time, risks about their time horizon could resurface due to such factors as leadership fatigue or the electorate's growing desire for change.[141]

Secondly, administrations with a stronger hold on power should have a higher chance of political survival than those associated with fragmented coalitions and fragile parliamentary majorities. These dimensions are captured through GOVMAJ, recording the fraction of parliamentary seats held by the government; GOVCOH, a measure of government cohesion; and OPPCOH, which describes the fragmentation of the incumbent's parliamentary opposition.[142]

4.3.2.4 Institutional constraints on policy making

The scope for an administration to implement the adjustment measures necessary to fend off a looming currency crisis may be limited through the institutional constraints it faces in its decision making. In particular, the existence of a large number of veto players could render it difficult to organize the political support required for a peg's successful defense.

The VETO variable captures this aspect through counting the number of decision makers in the political system whose consent is needed to implement a change in policies from the prevailing status quo.[143] Rather than counting the veto players in a system, POLARIZ (based on the DPI's Polariz2 indicator) measures the ideological distance between the governing coalition and the opposition based on the partisan orientation of each veto player. The higher the polarization measure, the more ideological factors should burden the political process, and the more difficult it should become to forge a consensus over policies.[144]

Finally, given its prominent role in exchange rate policies, the analysis looks closely at the central bank's place in the polity. Specifically, it is expected that a more independent, inflation-averse central bank would be more inclined to defend a currency peg. To account for this eventuality in the models, the analysis uses the index of legal independence (CBI) that was developed by Cukierman (1992). Based on criteria including appointment, dismissal and terms of office of the governor, central bank objectives, and the limitations on the bank's ability to lend to the public sector, the index increases with the independence of the bank.[145]

4.3.2.5 Economic control variables

As the objective is to examine whether political factors could yield additional insights regarding the emergence of currency crises, it is necessary to control for a set of macroeconomic and financial variables. For guidance, I rely on the results of the vast literature on EWS models that suggests a range of indications to capture a country's crisis vulnerability. While the preference would be for a parsimonious set of indicators, I seek to minimize the risk of omitting a relevant indicator through testing a variety of economic variables in the model's baseline specification (see Table 4.3).[146]

A strong consensus in the empirical literature on currency crises has developed regarding the role of indictors that signal vulnerabilities of the external capital account.[147] In particular, measures of reserve cover have been found to be closely related with the break of a crisis. I thus include the M2-to-reserves ratio (M2/RES) as a very broad measure of the potential for capital flight out of the domestic currency; and RESERVES to report the growth in central bank reserves relative to a long-term trend.[148]

Measures of current account performance also tend to be important crisis predictors. In particular, a marked appreciation of the real exchange rate relative to trend is typically found to be a key determinant of crisis vulnerability.[149] I construct the real exchange rate variable (RER) for each country year as the real exchange rate's

Table 4.3 Economic Variables: Overview

	Description	Source	Direction
M2/RES	Ratio of broad money to reserves	IFS	+
RESERVES	Growth in central bank reserves	IFS	−
RER	Real exchange rate level	IFS	−
EXPORTS	Export growth	IFS	−
IMPORTS	Import growth	IFS	−
GDP	Real output growth	WDI	−
INT	Advanced country interest rate	IFS	+
OPENNESS	Exports plus imports over GDP	IFS, WDI	±
BANKING	Occurrence of a banking crisis	GH 1999	+

Note: IFS refers to the IMF's International Financial Statistics; WDI to the World Bank's World Development Indicators; and GH1999 to Glick and Hutchison (1999).

deviation from its long-term linear trend against the U.S. dollar or, in the case of European countries, the Deutsche Mark. As a higher value of this indicator signals a more depreciated real exchange rate, one would expect a negative association of this measure with currency crises.

Two closely related variables are exports growth (EXPORTS) and imports growth (IMPORTS). A slowdown in export growth would be expected to signal competitiveness issues; a slowdown in import growth may be a sign of a weakening domestic economy, particularly after an initial post-stabilization consumption boom (see Calvo and Végh, 1999). By contrast, given that most studies fail to find a statistically significant effect of the external current account balance itself on crisis probabilities, I abstain from using this indicator.

Finally, I include the nominal GDP growth rate as an indicator that could signal the need for a devaluation from the side of the real economy; the level of advanced country interest rates (INT) as a proxy for global liquidity conditions,[150] a proxy measure for an economy's openness (OPENNESS), as well as a dummy variable (BANKING) to capture the potential effect of a front-running banking crisis on the likelihood of a currency event.[151]

To ensure that the continuous variables are comparable across countries, the annual observations for each variable are normalized by transforming them into deviations from the country-specific mean over 1975–97.

4.3.3 Empirical strategy

Following the mainstream in the econometric literature on currency crises, I use a cross-section approach to maximize the number of observations available for estimation and a logit model to accommodate the binary nature of the dependent variable based on the pressure index.[152] However, as straightforward logit analysis is highly problematic in binary time-series cross-section studies, I seek to control for cross-section and temporal dependence (see Beck, Katz, and Tucker, 1998).

To deal with panel heteroskedasticity (the problem that the regression residuals may vary systematically across countries), I always estimate a fixed effects (fe) panel, in addition to a model based on pooled data and including regional dummies, as the former allows for better control of unobservable and time-invariant country-specific effects. I do not rely exclusively on the fe specification, as the fixed effects estimator eliminates the cross-sectional variation in the panel which could contribute to identification, wipes out the country cases that show no variance in the data over time, and may aggravate the problem of multi-collinearity among the regressors.[153]

Controlling for time dependence in the data is advisable because currency crises tend to cluster in episodes characterized by a particularly bad international economic environment. I deal with this issue by including a set of annual dummies in the regressions, which should help in controlling for financial contagion across countries and thus in separating related crisis causes from country-specific vulnerabilities.

Furthermore, each of the specifications includes a variable labeled SURVIVAL that counts the years elapsed since the time of the last crisis event to control for serially correlated errors—the fact that current crisis probabilities may be affected by the time elapsed since the last crisis event (see Beck, Katz, and Tucker, 1998).[154]

Finally, the predictive power of political variables should ideally be assessed independently of a country's level of economic development. This may represent a significant challenge, given that a comparison of variable means along per capita income categories often reveals a high degree of correlation with a country's level of economic development (Table 4.4). Unfortunately, most existing studies

Table 4.4 Political Variables: Comparison of Means by Country Type

	Advanced	Emerging	Other Developing
POLITY	9.851	2.514	1.743
LEFTGOV	.600	.362	.397
AGRI	2.967	6.742	12.357
INDUSTRY	16.870	20.218	17.014
SERVICES	30.750	27.979	31.520
ELECTION	.286	.200	.189
TURNOVER	.157	.133	.162
YEARS	3.451	6.280	6.995
GOVMAJ	.568	.713	.710
GOVCOH	.719	.842	.848
OPPCOH	.522	.531	.677
VETO	4.787	2.909	2.402
POLARIZ	1.104	.312	.238
CBI	.342	.327	.321

that make use of a large country sample do not control for this pattern. In this study, a series of per capita terms (per capita, per capita,^{2} per capita^3) will seek to address this risk, and should help separating the effect on crisis probabilities stemming from a country' stage of development from that associated with the state of political indicators.

Reflecting all of these considerations, the baseline logit equation can be written as

$$L = \ln\left(\frac{P(\mathrm{CRS}_{i,t}=1)}{1-P(\mathrm{CRS}_{i,t}=1)}\right) = \alpha + X_{i,t\_1}\beta + P_{i,t\_1}\delta + D\gamma + s\rho + \epsilon_{i,t}, \quad (4.5)$$

where α is a constant, X is a matrix of economic indicators for country i, P is a matrix of political variables for country i, D is a matrix of dummy variables that control for regional and temporal dependence as well as a country's per capita income level, and s is the survival variable. β, δ, γ, and ρ are coefficients to be estimated, and ϵ is an error term assumed to be i.i.d. and normal. To minimize endogeneity issues, all economic and political indicators are lagged one year.

Moreover, in the fixed effects specifications, the error term of Equation 4.5 is assumed to allow for a decomposition into

$$\epsilon_{it} = \mu_i + \upsilon_{it}, \quad (4.6)$$

with μ_i being an unobservable country-specific fixed effect. The remaining stochastic disturbance υ_{it} is assumed to be independent and identically distributed.

4.4 Key findings

After having described the basic setup of the study, we are ready to proceed with the empirical testing of the hypotheses. In a first step, the study will focus on the findings from a descriptive analysis that relates the mean values of individual independent variables to the probability of experiencing currency crises. Based on these preliminary results, I will then estimate a variety of logit models that can control for co-variance among the regressors.

4.4.1 Descriptive statistics

A descriptive analysis to gauge whether the behavior of an indicator in the run-up to a currency crisis differs systematically from its behavior in tranquil periods can be based on *t*-tests on the equality of means. To this aim, the sample observations are grouped into two categories depending on whether the CRS indicator calls a crisis. The variable means in the two subgroups are then compared to each other, with a view to find statistically significant differences among the two subgroups. To show the sensitivity of results to the choice of independent variable, the tests are performed both for the weak crisis measure (CRS2) and for the strong crisis indicator (CRS3).

As there is reason to assume that many of the political factors introduced above should only be relevant when the degree of political competition in a country exceeds a certain minimum threshold, I perform the equality of means tests based on two samples. In the first case, the tests make use of all available observations for any given variable, and thus maximize the information contained in the underlying data. By contrast, in the second case, the sample is restricted to those observations for which a country's democratic institutions are developed beyond a certain threshold level. Specifically, to identify cases of full democracies, I use the World Bank's legislative index of electoral competition (LIEC): country-year observations are only retained in this subsample when the index signals a high degree of electoral competition (LIEC = 7). Below this threshold, the administration would typically not be subjected to meaningful legislative scrutiny.[155]

Unavoidably, restricting the sample to cases with full democracy comes at a cost in terms of sample size; almost one-third of all country-years need to be dropped from the analysis. Moreover, some countries disappear completely from the sample, including Ivory Coast, Singapore, and Zimbabwe, and permissible observations for others tend to be clustered in the more recent past.[156]

4.4.1.1 *Political variables*

For strong currency crises (CRS3), the *t*-tests on the equality of means between crisis and noncrisis periods reveal statistically significant differences for POLITY, YEARS, and ELECTION. While the tests indicate statistically significant differences for the entire sample, additional explanatory power is gained by restricting the tests to the cases of full democracies (see Table 4.5). For two other variables—the two lobbying indicators INDUSTRY and SERVICES—the tests show statistically significant differences only for full democracies.

Table 4.5 Equality of Means Test for Political Variables

	Full Sample			Full Democracies		
	CRS = 1	**CRS = 0**	**#**	**CRS = 1**	**CRS = 0**	**#**
			Strong Crises (CRS3)			
POLITY	3.84*	4.97*	1403	5.94***	7.44***	1011
LEFTGOV	0.40	0.43	1468	0.41	0.50	1050
AGRI	6.42	7.16	1459	5.55	5.80	1045
INDUSTRY	16.65	18.27	1459	14.52*	16.95*	1045
SERVICES	26.28	30.18	1459	23.16***	28.58***	1045
ELECTION	0.29*	0.22*	1468	0.39***	0.23***	1050
TURNOVER	0.12	0.15	1354	0.10	0.16	986
YEARS	6.72**	5.27**	1461	5.94***	4.27***	1049
GOVMAJ	0.67	0.66	1329	0.59	0.59	1040
GOVCOH	0.81	0.80	1325	0.79	0.77	1037
OPPCOH	0.59	0.56	1203	0.59	0.56	1020
VETO	3.28	3.39	1433	3.93	4.05	1038
POLARIZ	0.42	0.55	1346	0.60	0.77	951
CBI	0.34	0.34	1051	0.34	0.34	788
			Weak Crises (CRS2)			
POLITY	5.36	4.82	1403	7.52	7.31	1009
LEFTGOV	0.50**	0.42**	1468	0.56*	0.48*	1048
AGRI	5.87**	7.30**	1459	4.99*	5.91*	1045
INDUSTRY	18.80	18.06	1459	17.48	16.68	1045
SERVICES	30.73	29.79	1459	28.90	28.11	1045
ELECTION	0.24	0.22	1468	0.28	0.23	1048
YEARS	6.02*	5.27*	1461	5.13**	4.26**	1049
TURNOVER	0.12	0.15	1354	0.13	0.16	984
GOVMAJ	0.66	0.66	1329	0.60	0.59	1038
GOVCOH	0.77	0.80	1325	0.75	0.77	1035
OPPCOH	0.58	0.56	1203	0.56	0.54	1018
VETO	3.55	3.35	1433	4.12	4.02	1036
POLARIZ	0.59	0.53	1346	0.77	0.76	949
CBI	0.33	0.34	1051	0.34	0.34	786

Note: Results of *t* tests on the equality of means between crisis and non crisis episodes. Probability of erroneous rejection of null-hypothesis (no difference between means) at the *0.1 percent-level, the **0.05 percent-level, and the ***0.01 percent-level.

Regarding the direction of association, the results suggest that the likelihood of experiencing a crisis increases strongly after election years, and is positively correlated with the number of years an incumbent administration has already spent in office. By contrast, the probability of currency crises decreases with the degree of democracy in a country and the weights of the agricultural and services sector in the overall economy. Once we proceed to the logit analysis, it will be interesting to examine whether these results survive when controlling for the stage of a country's economic development; as strong crises tend to be concentrated in middle-income countries that typically score lower on democracy and have less developed manufacturing and services sectors than advanced economies, the correlations between political variables and currency crises may lose their significance.

The association of currency crises with YEARS is confirmed for the case of weak crises (CRS2). In addition, crises are more likely in the presence of left-leaning governments, and in countries with relatively small agricultural sectors. That said, the means of ELECTION and POLITY are no longer statistically different among crisis and noncrisis periods when relying on conventional significance levels.

Episodes of crises do not seem to be systematically different with regard to the other political indicators included in the data set, including the measures of the executive's parliamentary support and of the institutional constraints placed on the executive through the presence of veto players. The latter result is surprising, particularly with regard to central bank independence (CBI), which should have been expected to make a difference for the probability of a currency crisis.

4.4.1.2 Economic variables

The *t*-tests on the economic variables broadly confirm the priors formed on the basis of the theoretical literature and previous empirical studies (see Table 4.6). Moreover, the tests tend to report statistically stronger results than in the case of the political variables, and tend not to be sensitive to whether the sample includes all available observations or merely country-years with well-developed democracies.

The measures of foreign exchange cover (M2/RES and RESERVES) signal that crisis episodes typically are dramatically different from

Table 4.6 Equality of Means Test for Economic Variables

	Full Sample			**Full Democracies**		
	CRS = 1	CRS = 0	#	CRS = 1	CRS = 0	#
			Strong Crises (CRS3)			
M2/RES	40.32***	−2.86***	1468	25.65***	−5.86***	1050
RESERVES	−63.17***	8.86***	1466	−60.01**	11.40**	1050
RER	−11.73***	1.24***	1439	−9.88***	1.03***	1043
EXPORTS	−59.60*	8.51*	1468	−62.97**	6.81**	1050
IMPORTS	−72.55***	7.21***	1468	−65.09	8.06	1050
GDP	−8.70	−4.50	1455	6.64	1.38	1042
INT	7.91*	1.06*	1468	8.89**	−2.42**	1050
OPENNESS	0.49	0.56	1459	0.43**	0.51**	1045
BANKING	0.05	0.05	1437	0.06	0.04	1043
			Weak Crises (CRS2)			
M2/RES	15.68***	−2.33***	1468	9.20***	−5.92***	1050
RESERVES	−33.17**	9.67**	1466	−23.35*	11.63*	1050
RER	−6.37***	1.40***	1439	−5.20***	1.22***	1043
EXPORTS	−62.87**	14.09**	1468	−33.16*	8.04*	1050
IMPORTS	−37.33***	7.80***	1468	−25.46**	7.96**	1050
GDP	−19.93	−2.48	1455	−4.54	2.78	1042
INT	5.70	0.89	1468	5.11**	−2.79**	1050
OPENNESS	0.55	0.55	1459	0.51	0.51	1043
BANKING	0.03	0.05	1437	0.03	0.05	1043

Note: Results of *t* tests on the equality of means between crisis and non crisis episodes. Probability of erroneous rejection of null-hypothesis (no difference between means) at the *0.1 percent-level, the **0.05 percent-level, and the ***0.01 percent-level.

calm periods: in the run-up to a crisis, broad money tends to considerably exceed central bank reserves, while the latter tend to grow much below trend. Moreover, strong evidence suggests that the competitiveness of the export sector suffers prior to the outbreak of a crisis, with the RER measure indicating a more appreciated real exchange rate and mean exports growth (EXPORTS) slowing dramatically.

There is also some evidence that crisis periods are associated with a weaker domestic economic environment, as suggested by the strongly negative deviation in mean imports growth (IMPORTS) from trend. However, while the GDP variable shows the expected negative sign in three out of four test specifications, the difference in means fails to reach statistically significant levels. No evidence is found with regard to the role of a banking crisis as a trigger for currency events.

Finally, global economic conditions seem to matter for crisis probabilities. Specifically, interest rates in the systemically important countries—the United States and Germany—tend to be higher prior to crisis episodes, decreasing the incentive to invest in local currency assets and thus potentially contributing to a reversal in investor sentiment.

4.4.2 Political-economy logit models

The equality of means tests do not control for linkages among the explanatory variables and thus risk overstating the explanatory power of individual regressors.[157] By contrast, logit models that can accommodate more than one independent variable offer a framework for taking into account potential interactions among the predictors. In particular, they allow us to assess whether the individual political variables found to be statistically related to currency crises in the preceding analysis retain their significance when entered jointly into an estimation framework that controls for economic conditions. Moreover, the logit approach offers a convenient way of comparing the in-sample forecasting performance of political-economy models with that of more parsimonious specifications.

As above, the logit estimations are performed both for the weak and the strong crisis indicators to gauge the sensitivity of results to the intensity of currency crises. Moreover, the various models differ in how they control for panel heteroskedasticity (the fact that error terms may systematically differ among sample countries), and in the number of regressors included. Specifically, in the results tables presented below, columns A and C summarize the findings based on a fixed effects estimator, whereas the models underlying columns B and D are estimated with pooled data. To control for cross-section variance in the data, the latter models include dummy variables for emerging and advanced economies. Moreover, while columns A and B always show the estimation results of the most general model specification based on the regressors identified in Tables 4.2 and 4.3, columns C and D report the results of reduced models. These emerge from implementing a step-wise testing down procedure in which, at each step, the variable with the lowest *t*-statistic is eliminated from the specification until all of the remaining indicators are significant at conventional levels.[158]

4.4.2.1 Identifying the set of macroeconomic controls

Before proceeding with the estimation of the political-economy models, however, we need to identify those macroeconomic indicators from the comparison of means exercise in Section 4.3.2 that retain their statistical significance in a logit framework. These measures will provide a basis for adding the various political factors to the model specification, and will be used in the estimation of a benchmark model that serves as a basis for assessing the additional predictive power, if any, of the political-economy specifications.

For the strong crisis indicator, the various model specifications are consistent in finding M2/RES, RER, and IMPORTS to be highly significant predictors of currency crises (Table 4.7). Specifically, a high ratio of M2-to-reserves, an overvalued real exchange rate relative to its long-term trend, and slow growth in imports all contribute to a heightened probability of crisis. However, the statistical significance of RESERVES disappears, probably due to the fact that this variable is highly correlated with the M2/RES indicator.

Moreover, the estimations based on pooled data reveal that crises are more probable in emerging market economies compared with other developing countries (the baseline specification) or advanced economies, while the fixed effects estimations reveal the importance of crisis history captured by SURVIVAL: a long episode of calm on the exchange markets tends to increase the probability of seeing a crisis in the future. The other economic controls do not seem to be related to currency crises at conventional significance levels.

The key findings carry over to the estimations based on the weak crisis indicator CRS2 (Table 4.8). The notable exception to this general rule is IMPORTS, which ceases to be associated with currency crises in a statistically meaningful way. While the pooled regressions confirm the high crisis vulnerability of emerging market countries, they also find advanced economies to be more susceptible to weak currency crises than developing countries that do not yet enjoy emerging market status. Finally, SURVIVAL is now highly significant in any model specification, regardless of whether or not fixed effects are included.

Based on these findings, we can narrow down the choice of economic controls to be retained in the political-economy models to the

Table 4.7 Economic Benchmark Model: Results for Strong Crises

	A (fe)	B	C (fe)	D
M2/RES	.005***	.005***	.005***	.005***
	(.002)	(.001)	(.001)	(.001)
RESERVES	−.000	−.000		
	(.001)	(.001)		
RER	−.033***	−.039***	−.034***	−.039***
	(.009)	(.007)	(.009)	(.007)
EXPORTS	−.000	−.000		
	(.000)	(.000)		
IMPORTS	−.002**	−0.002***	−.001**	−.001***
	(.001)	(.001)	(.001)	(.001)
GDP	.001	.001		
	(.001)	(.001)		
INT	.003	.006		
	(.006)	(.006)		
OPENNESS	−.118	−.123		
	(1.328)	(.305)		
BANKING	.054	.015		
	(.530)	(.525)		
EMC		.634**		.689**
		(.296)		(.291)
OECD		.110		.165
		(.344)		(.338)
SURVIVAL	.215***	.019	.215***	.023
	(.047)	(.029)	(.047)	(.028)
#	1170	1328	1214	1365
Pseudo − R^2	.244	.145	.243	.145
Log Likelihood	−192.99	−292.60	−198.06	−299.37

Note: Probability of erroneous rejection of null-hypothesis (no difference) at the *0.1 percent-level, the **0.05 percent-level, and the ***0.01 percent-level.

level of broad money-to-reserves (M2/RES), the deviation of the real exchange rate from trend (RER), and, in the case of the strong crisis indicator, the growth rate of imports (IMPORTS). In addition, the findings suggest including the SURVIVAL variable in all specifications to capture serial correlation in the data.

4.4.2.2 Adding political indicators

Having determined the set of economic controls that are suitably retained in a baseline logit specification, the next step consists of

Table 4.8 Economic Benchmark Model: Results for Weak Crises

	A (fe)	B	C (fe)	D
M2/RES	.004***	.002*	.004***	.003***
	(.001)	(.001)	(.001)	(.001)
RESERVES	−.000	−.000		
	(.000)	(.000)		
RER	−.019***	−.024***	−.018***	−.022***
	(.006)	(.005)	(.006)	(.005)
EXPORTS	−.001	−.000		
	(.000)	(.000)		
IMPORTS	−.001	−.001		
	(.001)	(.001)		
GDP	.000	.000		
	(.001)	(.001)		
INT	.004	.005		
	(.004)	(.004)		
OPENNESS	.317	.262		
	(.907)	(.189)		
BANKING	−.609	−.608		
	(.466)	(.461)		
EMC		.539**		.521**
		(.233)		(.227)
OECD		.911***		.914***
		(.246)		(.239)
SURVIVAL	.237***	.062**	.243***	.058**
	(.037)	(.025)	(.036)	(.024)
#	1336	1395	1367	1434
$Pseudo-R^2$	.182	.112	.176	.104
Log Likelihood	−356.28	−486.50	−363.66	−499.29

Note: Probability of erroneous rejection of null-hypothesis (no difference) at the *0.1 percent-level, the **0.05 percent-level, and the ***0.01 percent-level.

adding the political indicators described in Table 4.2 to the list of regressors.[159] As discussed above, the political-economy models control for temporal independence (notably cross-country contagion of crises) and a country's stage of development by including year dummies and a series of per capita terms.

Even in the presence of these extensive controls, up to four political variables are found to be good predictors of strong currency crises (Table 4.9). As a comparison of results across the various specifications shows, these findings survive the step-wise elimination process that narrows down the number of indicators in the estimations, and are not sensitive to the inclusion of country dummies.

Table 4.9 Political-Economy Model: Results for Strong Crises

	A (fe)	B	C (fe)	D
POLITY	−.027	.016		
	(.076)	(.036)		
LEFTGOV	.100	.003		
	(.478)	(.317)		
AGRI	−.066	−.020		
	(.102)	(.038)		
INDUSTRY	−.037	.013		
	(.061)	(.025)		
SERVICES	−.015	−.017		
	(.054)	(.017)		
ELECTION	.566*	.530*	.565**	.597**
	(.329)	(.307)	(.282)	(.263)
TURNOVER	−.210	.027		
	(.663)	(.603)		
YEARS	.053	.062**	.053	.049**
	(.048)	(.027)	(.033)	(.019)
GOVMAJ	−.740	−.788		
	(2.067)	(1.168)		
GOVCOH	−.008	−.407		
	(1.33)	(.780)		
OPPCOH	−.475	.190		
	(.941)	(.582)		
VETO	.702**	.017	.513***	.146*
	(.273)	(.128)	(.160)	(.087)
POLARIZ	−1.025**	−.128	−.827**	−.135
	(.459)	(.263)	(.365)	(.209)
M2/RES	.006**	.007***	.005***	.005***
	(.003)	(.002)	(.002)	(.002)
RER	−.033***	−.041***	−.037***	−.041***
	(.011)	(.009)	(.009)	(.007)
IMPORTS	−.002*	−.002*	−.001*	−.001*
	(.001)	(.001)	(.001)	(.001)
EMC		.570		.676**
		(.440)		(.318)
OECD		−.823		.273
		(.949)		(.669)
SURVIVAL	.269***	.007	.272***	.011
	(.062)	(.034)	(.055)	(.031)
#	752	945	1082	1256
Pseudo − R^2	.336	.186	.302	.163
Log Likelihood	−114.81	−203.05	−164.08	−266.99

Note: Probability of erroneous rejection of null-hypothesis (no difference) at the *0.1 percent-level, the **0.05 percent-level, and the ***0.01 percent-level.

From the subset of variables that are related to the incumbent's time horizon, ELECTION and YEARS are found to be positively correlated with crisis episodes. This confirms our hypothesis that elections should be a leading indicator of exchange market pressure. Consistent with the univariate analysis, the results for the YEARS indicator also suggest that factors such as leadership or voter fatigue and increased rigidity in the bureaucracy are likely to outweigh any positive effects that a long stay in power may have on an administration's ability to maintain a successful currency peg.

The positive coefficient for VETO, which is, however, only significant in the pooled estimations, suggests that a high number of veto players gives rise to increased vulnerability—potentially due to the fact that policy adjustment to emerging imbalances becomes more difficult when it requires the consent of a large number of political actors. The second variable measuring institutional constraints on the executive, POLARIZ, appears to be negatively associated with crises in the models that control for country-specific effects. This finding is difficult to explain on theoretical grounds, as one would expect that difficulties in reaching agreement on policy reforms should increase with the ideological distance between the key decision makers.[160]

Re-estimating the model based on the weak crisis indicator (CRS2) changes considerably the results pertaining to the various measures of political conditions (Table 4.10). The only variable that retains its statistical significance is YEARS, while the other political factors associated with the occurrence of strong crises lose their explanatory power. By contrast, the LEFTGOV variable that measures the ideological orientation of the administration in power now becomes significant in three out of four specifications. This result points to a heightened vulnerability of left-leaning governments to weak currency crises, in line with what could be expected by the theoretical literature.

In both the strong and the weak crisis specifications, the explanatory power of the economic controls and the SURVIVAL variable is not affected by the inclusion of political indicators. They always show the expected signs and remain typically highly significant.[161]

On balance, the estimations find that a variety of political conditions systematically affect the probability of currency crises. These results are reflected in the test statistics assessing the overall

Table 4.10 Political-Economy Model: Results for Weak Crises

	A (fe)	B	C (fe)	D
POLITY	.016	.026		
	(.056)	(.030)		
LEFTGOV	.449	.366*	.525**	.448**
	(.305)	(.221)	(.243)	(.176)
AGRI	−.136	−.023		
	(.084)	(.027)		
INDUSTRY	−.027	.001		
	(.041)	(.019)		
SERVICES	.045	−.000		
	(.032)	(.012)		
ELECTION	.108	.138		
	(.238)	(.228)		
TURNOVER	.003	.251		
	(.422)	(.394)		
YEARS	.012	.056**	.047*	.042***
	(.033)	(.022)	(.024)	(.014)
GOVMAJ	.799	.520		
	(1.291)	(.859)		
GOVCOH	−.825	−.202		
	(.943)	(.563)		
OPPCOH	.265	.164		
	(.647)	(.442)		
VETO	−.052	−.014		
	(.144)	(.094)		
POLARIZ	−.070	.028		
	(.249)	(.182)		
M2/RES	.005***	.006***	.005***	.003***
	(.002)	(.002)	(.001)	(.001)
RER	−.012	−.022***	−.019***	−.022***
	(.007)	(.007)	(.006)	(.005)
EMC		.640*		.605**
		(.352)		(.238)
OECD		.593		.507
		(.631)		(.435)
SURVIVAL	.299***	.073***	.257***	.066***
	(.049)	(.028)	(.038)	(.024)
#	943	1001	1366	1431
Pseudo − R^2	.200	.121	.193	.120
Log Likelihood	−247.01	−352.98	−356.14	−490.11

Note: Probability of erroneous rejection of null-hypothesis (no difference) at the *0.1 percent-level, the **0.05 percent-level, and the ***0.01 percent-level.

Table 4.11 Standard Measures of Model Performance

	Strong Crises		**Weak Crises**	
	C (fe)	**D**	**C (fe)**	**D**
		Political-Economy Models		
Pseudo – R^2	0.302	0.163	0.193	0.120
AIC	7.399	0.479	12.035	0.730
Likelihood ratio (%)	99	95	99	99
		Economic Models		
Pseudo – R^2	0.243	0.145	0.176	0.104
AIC	7.827	0.478	12.114	0.734

Note: Probability of erroneous rejection of null-hypothesis (no difference) at the *0.1 percent-level, the **0.05 percent-level, and the ***0.01 percent-level.

performance of the reduced political-economy models relative to the baseline specification relying exclusively on economic fundamentals (Table 4.11).

While it can be expected that the *Pseudo* – R^2 increases with the number of parameters used in a model, log likelihood ratio tests typically reject the null hypothesis that the additional variables in the political-economy models are jointly insignificant at the 99 percent-level (Table 4.11).[162] Moreover, a comparison of the Akaike Information Criterion (AIC) among the various specifications suggests that the political-economy models are slightly more efficient than the baseline logits—the gains in terms of improved statistical performance are not fully offset by the models' increased complexity.[163]

4.4.2.3 *Marginal effects*

To get a sense of the magnitude of the parameter estimates, I calculate marginal effects to show how the predicted probability of a currency crisis changes with a variation in individual independent variables.[164] Specifically, I calculate the change in the likelihood of a crisis associated with a one-standard deviation increase or one-unit increase for dichotomous variables in each independent variable, while holding all other measures constant at their sample means.

In general, changes in political conditions do not significantly alter the probability of experiencing a strong currency crisis. For example, the advent of a presidential or parliamentary election increases the probability of a currency crisis in the year following the ballot by 1.14 percent, whereas a one-standard deviation increase in the number of veto players and in the years that the incumbent's party has already spent in office increase the likelihood of seeing a crisis by 0.44 percent and 0.50 percent, respectively. These effects are not very large in size, but are comparable to those associated with changes in the macroeconomic fundamentals.[165]

By contrast, political factors significantly affect the probability of a crisis when the weak crisis indicator is used. A particularly strong effect is associated with the presence of a left-leaning government, heightening the chance of seeing a crisis by 5.3 percent, and thus by more than a long tenure of the ruling party in office (2.9 percent) or adverse changes in macroeconomic conditions.[166]

While these magnitudes themselves may not be sufficient to cause the break of a currency crisis, the effects associated with an adverse change in political conditions may just be strong enough to push a country into crisis when the economic environment is already fragile. I visualize these vulnerabilities by plotting the changes in the probability of a currency crisis that are associated with election years and left-wing governments, conditional on the state of key macroeconomic fundamentals (Figures 4.1 and 4.2): in situations where the reserve cover of the central bank is already low or the real exchange rate shows signs of dangerous overvaluation, the likelihood of seeing a crisis is significantly increased when political risks are on the rise, too.

4.4.2.4 *Predicting currency crises*

So far, I have focused on the question of whether the inclusion of political factors can improve the understanding of currency crises *relative* to a baseline model that relies exclusively on economic factors. Unfortunately, these comparisons do not provide a good measure of how well the various models actually fit the underlying data or, in other words, how well they perform in the actual prediction of the currency crises that are included in our data set.[167]

Thus, to obtain an idea of their goodness-of-fit, I submit the various models to an (in-sample) forecasting exercise. This provides an intuitive yardstick of whether or not the inclusion of political indicators in crisis models would be worth the extra effort. Specifically, I define

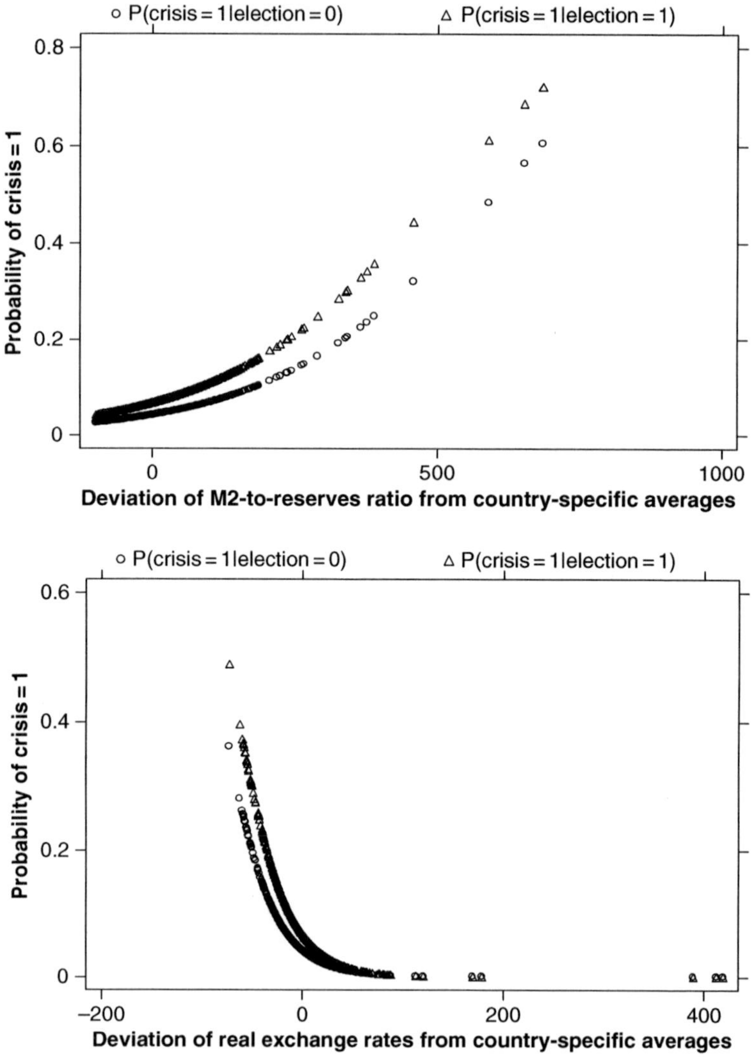

Figure 4.1 Strong Crises: Marginal Effect of Elections

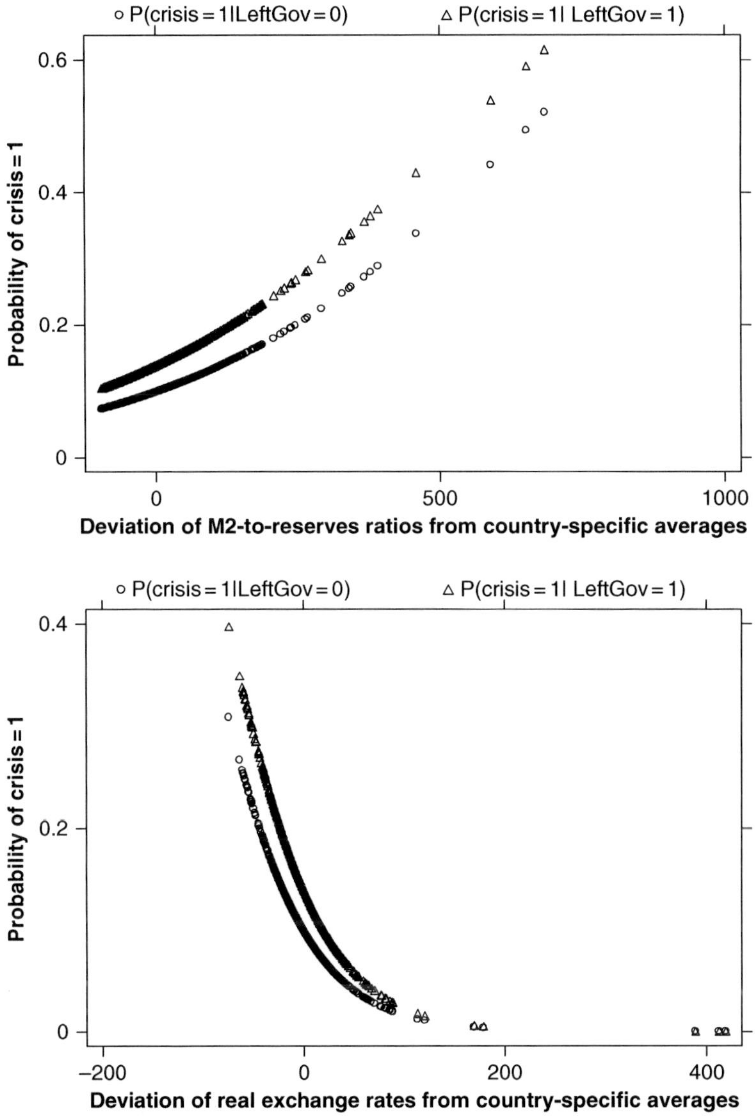

Figure 4.2 Weak Crises: Marginal Effect of Left-leaning Governments

a forecast as being a crisis call whenever the predicted probability for a given country year exceeds the probability of crisis in the underlying sample as indicated by the number of crises in the total sample of country years. Based on this criterion, the probability threshold is 7.1 percent for calling a strong crisis and 13.1 percent for identifying a weak crisis. Setting such a relatively low threshold should improve the model's accuracy in correctly predicting crisis events (often referred to as the sensitivity of the model), but at the same time typically causes the number of false alarms (crisis calls for observations where none happened, referred to as a model's specificity) to rise relative to a more ambitious cutoff point.[168]

In this exercise, the political-economy models outperform the baseline specifications (Table 4.12), albeit only by a small margin. For the strong crisis indicator (CRS3), adding political factors to the specification increases the number of crisis events correctly called from 61 to 65 out of a total of 88 cases, while at the same time reducing the number of false alarms from 335 to 322. In the case of the weak crisis indicator (CRS2), the number of crisis calls does not change compared to the baseline specification, but the addition of political variables still leads to a fall in false alarms from 416 to 406 cases.

Notwithstanding the better performance of the models that contain political variables relative to those that do not, the high number of false alarms in *any* of the specifications is disturbing.[169] Hence,

Table 4.12 Forecasting Crises: In-sample Prediction Performance

	Economic Model			Political-Economy Model		
	Strong Crises, Crisis Threshold $c = 0.071$					
	CRS = 1	CRS = 0	total	CRS = 1	CRS = 0	total
$P(CRS = 1) > c$	61	335	396	65	322	387
$P(CRS = 0) < c$	27	833	860	23	846	869
Total	88	1168	1256	88	1168	1256
r^2_{count}	0.712			0.725		
	Weak Crises, Crisis Threshold $c = 0.131$					
	CRS = 1	CRS = 0	total	CRS = 1	CRS = 0	total
$P(CRS = 1) > c$	131	416	547	131	406	537
$P(CRS = 0) < c$	57	827	884	57	837	894
Total	188	1243	1431	188	1243	1431
r^2_{count}	0.670			0.676		

when the objective is to maximize the number of correct predictions as a share of the total sample (measured as r^2_{count}) rather than only the number of correct crisis calls, the models do not perform well. Conceptually, raising the probability threshold for calling crises should help to address this issue. However, it would imply a greatly reduced ability of the models to identify crisis vulnerabilities correctly, as a reduction in false alarms would be accompanied by a significantly weakened performance in identifying true crises.[170]

4.5 Robustness checks

The evidence generated by the various models is consistent with the view that currency crises are more likely to occur when the political outlook is fragile. But the regression results also show that the findings on political variables, contrary to those related to macroeconomic indicators, are quite sensitive to model specification issues. This situation is clearly not very encouraging, as it leaves little room for robust conclusions on the empirical link between politics and currency crises.

In general, the source of the problem may lay in the fact that the impact of political conditions on the probability of a crisis is greatly influenced by a country's development stage and geographical location, which cannot be fully controlled for by the per capita terms and income dummies included in the specifications.[171] The results of a variety of robustness tests appear to broadly confirm such an impression.

First, re-estimating the political-economy models for the full set of alternative dependent variables established in Section 4.3.1 shows that these indicators are much more sensitive to the model specification than the macroeconomic measures (Table 4.13).[172] While the ratio of broad money-to-reserves as well as the real exchange rate deviation from trend remain highly significant predictors in almost all model variants, the results for the political variables are more mixed.

For the alternative strong crisis measures, YEARS and VETO show the most robust association with currency crises. By contrast, the results for ELECTION and POLARIZ are much less stable, with the coefficients even changing their sign in some specifications. The alternative models based on the weak crisis indicators tend to be

Table 4.13 Robustness to Variation in the Dependent Variable

	CRS	CRSSN	CRCRS	CRSFR	CRSGH
			Strong Crisis Indicators		
ELECTION	.565**	.338	.556	−.156	−.342
	(.282)	(.277)	(.437)	(.420)	(.375)
YEARS	.053	.037	.179**	.094**	.085*
	(.033)	(.032)	(.070)	(.047)	(.046)
VETO	.513***	.285**	.011	.426**	.175
	(.160)	(.118)	(.215)	(.202)	(.140)
POLARIZ	−.827**	−.494	.369	−.123	−1.133***
	(.365)	(.320)	(.526)	(.481)	(.425)
M2/RES	.005***	.007***	.004*	.008***	.008***
	(.002)	(.002)	(.002)	(.002)	(.003)
RER	−.037***	−.030***	−.031***	−.032***	.003
	(.009)	(.008)	(.010)	(.009)	(.004)
IMPORTS	−.001*	−.001**	−.001*	−.000	.000
	(.001)	(.007)	(.001)	(.001)	(.001)
SURVIVAL	.272***	.175***	.198**	.193	.219***
	(.009)	(.048)	(.079)	(.073)	(.061)
#	1082	1123	522	627	476
Pseudo − R^2	.302	.241	.386	.376	.218
Log Likelihood	−164.08	−184.01	−77.03	−91.75	−123.68
			Weak Crisis Indicators		
YEARS	.047*	.039*	.048	.079*	.084**
	(.024)	(.024)	(.034)	(.044)	(.042)
LEFTGOV	.525**	.485**	.060	.217	−.043
	(.243)	(.245)	(.390)	(.477)	(.379)
M2/RES	.005***	.004***	.004**	.006***	.005**
	(.001)	(.001)	(.002)	(.002)	(.002)
RER	−.019***	−.030***	−.017***	−.035***	.000
	(.006)	(.007)	(.006)	(.009)	(.004)
SURVIVAL	.257***	.116***	.087	.016	.120**
	(.038)	(.034)	(.053)	(.063)	(.059)
#	1366	1366	710	660	520
Pseudo − R^2	.193	.138	.220	.304	.140
Log Likelihood	−356.14	−368.18	−156.81	−109.7	−148.78

Note: Probability of erroneous rejection of null-hypothesis (no difference) at the *0.1 percent-level, **0.05 percent-level, and the ***0.01 percent-level.

consistent in finding a statistical link between currency crises and YEARS, but LEFTGOV loses its statistical power in those specifications that include a larger number of emerging market crises (CRCRS2, CRSFR, and CRSGH).

A second series of robustness tests, therefore, directly examines to what extent a country's income level and geographical location influence the link between political factors and currency crises. A strong crisis specification that controls for a country's income type by interacting the political variables with the emerging market dummy suggests that most of the statistical power vested in political variables seems to emanate from advanced economies, with ELECTION, VETO, and POLARIZ losing significance in a middle-income country context (Table 4.14).[173] That said, YEARS does not follow a similar pattern but retains its significance when interacted with the emerging economy dummy, reducing the overall positive effect of the length of an administration's tenure on the probability of crisis. A similar exercise for weak crises suggests that the LEFTGOV variable is a relevant predictor only for advanced economies.

Estimations that distinguish between geographical regions show that ELECTION is a significant predictor of strong crises in European and Latin American countries, but not in Asia. None of the other political variables retain their statistical power at conventional significance levels. Variation across regions produces more robust results for weak crises, with YEARS retaining its significance in all specifications and LEFTGOV in the regressions for Europe and Latin America (see Tables C.2 and C.3).

Finally, variation of the time window underlying the regressions suggests that several political factors are more relevant for the explanation of currency crises in the 1970s and 1980s compared with the more recent past (see Table C.4). This is particularly true for the link between LEFTGOV and weak crises, which is significant at the 99 percent-level prior to 1990 but loses its explanatory power thereafter. This result could reflect that left-leaning governments prior to 1990 were more inclined to implement Keynesian-style demand management policies aimed at boosting employment, before policy preferences changed in response to an increased openness of the domestic economy.

It is more difficult, however, to explain the pattern of results for VETO, ELECTION, and POLARIZ. In fact, the loss of explanatory

Table 4.14 Robustness to a Country's Stage of Development

	Strong Crises	Weak Crises
LEFTGOV		.696**
		(.347)
LEFTGOV*EMC		−.426
		(.557)
ELECTION	1.273**	
	(.584)	
ELECTION*EMC	−1.073	
	(.736)	
YEARS	.275**	.040
	(.134)	(.060)
YEARS*EMC	−.252*	−.017
	(.140)	(.069)
VETO	.862**	
	(.428)	
VETO*EMC	−.390	
	(.486)	
POLARIZ	−1.645**	
	(.742)	
POLARIZ*EMC	1.451	
	(.905)	
M2/RES	.008***	.006***
	(.003)	(.002)
IMPORTS	−.002**	
	(.001)	
RER	−.044***	−.022***
	(.011)	(.007)
SURVIVAL	.301***	.274***
	(.067)	(.045)
#	793	1015
Pseudo − R^2	.358	.190
Log Likelihood	−111.10	−282.69

Note: Probability of erroneous rejection of null-hypothesis (no difference) at the *0.1 percent-level, the **0.05 percent-level, and the ***0.01 percent-level.

power for the veto player indicator after 1990 and the parallel emergence of ELECTION and POLARIZ as significant predictors could be driven by a shift in the distribution of crisis occurrences toward emerging market countries: while advanced economies accounted for 26 percent of strong crises prior to 1990s, their share declines to a mere 10 percent thereafter.

4.6 Extensions

To end this empirical chapter, I shall take a closer look at two issues in the political economy of currency crises: the extent to which currency markets behave differently in election periods, and the influence of the composition of the legislature on the link between left-leaning governments and crises.

4.6.1 The link between elections and crises

A number of the logit models discussed above find a positive statistical association between elections and currency crises for the countries included in the sample, albeit only for the case of strong crises. The robustness tests further suggest that this pattern of elections front-running currency crises is observable mainly for European and Latin American countries, but not for the group of emerging market economies as a whole.

In this section, the logit analysis is complemented by an approach based on monthly rather than annual data. Specifically, I examine the monthly evolution of the nominal exchange rate and of the pressure index within a 19-month window centered on the election month *T* for the 320 election episodes that the 69 sample countries experienced over 1975–97. This descriptive analysis reveals a more refined pattern of market behavior than would be observable from annual data. Moreover, it can serve as a robustness check to test whether the findings generated by Frieden, Ghezzi, and Stein (2001) on 26 Latin American countries would also hold for a more diverse group of countries.[174]

Aggregating the results over all regions clearly shows that election periods tend to be correlated with a high degree of month-to-month volatility in currency markets (Figure 4.3). Consistent with what one would expect, the most pronounced changes in both the pressure index and the exchange rates are concentrated in the period shortly after the ballot takes place, with both indicators peaking in the second post-election month.

Breaking down the data along geographical lines provides some additional insights. In particular, Latin American countries experience the highest level of currency market volatility among all regions, with the average monthly deprecation of the nominal exchange rate reaching 19 percent in the second post-election month (Figure 4.4).

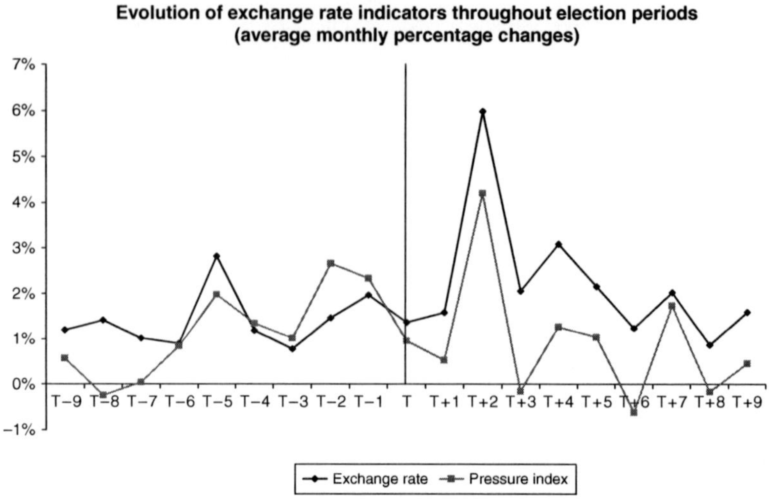

Figure 4.3 Full Country Sample: The Impact of Elections

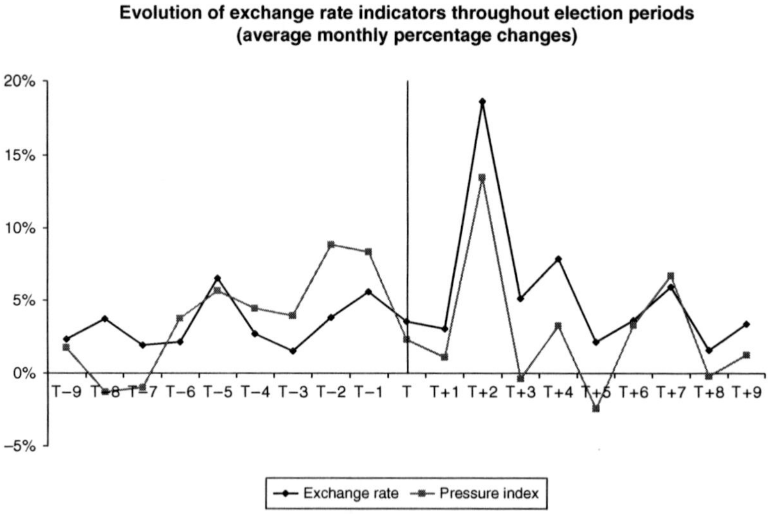

Figure 4.4 Latin American Countries: The Impact of Elections

But an interesting pattern also emerges in the run-up to elections: the pressure index records substantial movement in the two months prior to the ballot, while the actual exchange rate depreciation is much less pronounced. This pattern suggests that country authorities typically respond to mounting investor concerns in the pre-election period through using central bank reserves to stabilize their currencies. If they did not, the electorate would probably interpret the downward pressure on the exchange rate as policy incompetence.

The pattern for European countries is very different from the one observed in Latin America (Figure 4.5). First, the monthly changes in the market indicators are much weaker and remain typically within a band of plus/minus one percent. Secondly, the post-election peak in the indicators only emerges in the fourth post-election month, and then only for the pressure index that on average increases to about 3.3 percent. Thus, impulses from elections to the foreign exchange market tend to be quite muted and quite delayed in the case of European countries, and, perhaps as a result of most countries maintaining a more or less rigid peg to the Deutsche Mark over much of the period under review, are confined to movements in the pressure index.

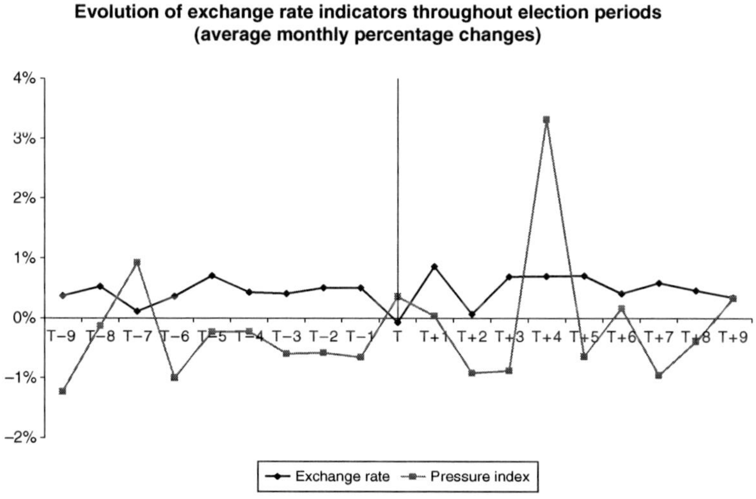

Figure 4.5 European Countries: The Impact of Elections

The results from this analysis based on higher frequency data supports strongly the finding that the probability of a currency crisis increases after an election took place, with a particularly strong effect being observable for Latin American countries. It also suggests a reason why many logit estimations based on annual data fail to report a statistically significant linkage: given that the strongest movements in the indicators take place within a window of just two-to-four months after the ballot, the annual data frequency may be too low to identify the correlation in all cases.

4.6.2 The link between left Governments and crises

Both the theoretical discussion and the preceding empirical analysis suggest the existence of a link, albeit limited to the case of weak crises, between left-leaning administrations and the occurrence of currency crises. However, the strength of the link between ideological orientation and exchange rate policy should depend on the political environment in which the policy maker operates. In particular, it would be plausible to assume that the scope for advancing the ideological agenda may be constrained by the composition of the legislature; an executive faced with a comfortable majority in parliament or with a fragmented opposition should clearly be in a better position to push through its agenda than an administration working under less favorable conditions.[175]

I follow up on this idea by linking the LEFTGOV indicator in the weak crisis model with two of the measures describing the composition of the legislature. LEFTGOV*MAJ takes the value of the MAJ variable in case the incumbent government is left-leaning, and takes a value of zero otherwise. Thus, this variable measures the parliamentary strength that a left-leaning incumbent has relative to the conservative opposition: the higher the measure, the larger is the share of total seats in parliament supporting government. Similarly, LEFTGOV*OPPCOH takes the value of OPPCOH in the case of a left-leaning incumbent and zero otherwise. This variable increases in the political concentration of the parliamentary opposition, and reaches its maximum value of one when the opposition seats are all taken by members of a single party.

The regressions reveal that the positive link between left-leaning governments and currency crises is only retained in the case of strong opposition parties: LEFTGOV* OPPCOH is statistically significant and

Table 4.15 Weak Crises: The Impact of Left-leaning Governments

	A (fe)	B	C (fe)	D
LEFTGOV	−1.350	−.081	−.450	.010
	(.870)	(.632)	(.535)	(.345)
LEFTGOV*GOVMAJ	1.647	.160		
	(1.245)	(.929)		
LEFTGOV*OPPCOH	1.663**	.905*	1.763**	.917*
	(.817)	(.527)	(.827)	(.522)
YEARS	.036	.054***	.032	.054***
	(.026)	(.016)	(.026)	(.016)
M2/RES	.006***	.006***	.007***	.006***
	(.002)	(.002)	(.002)	(.002)
RER	−.017**	−.022***	−.016**	−.022***
	(.007)	(.006)	(.007)	(.006)
EMC		.667**		.671**
		(.278)		(.277)
OECD		.453		.452
		(.473)		(.473)
SURVIVAL	.288***	.072***	.285***	.072***
	(.043)	(.026)	(.043)	(.026)
#	1094	1180	1094	1180
Pseudo – R^2	.203	.126	.201	.126
Log Likelihood	−290.43	−412.54	−291.30	−412.56

Note: Probability of erroneous rejection of null-hypothesis (no difference) at the *0.1 percent-level, **0.05 percent-level, and the ***0.01 percent-level.

carries a positive sign in all model specifications, while LEFTGOV becomes insignificant (Table 4.15).

Two explanations would be consistent with this result: either left-leaning governments face a particularly hard time winning the parliamentary support for policy adjustment needed to fend off looming investor doubts in cases where the opposition is strong (and would presumably have much to gain from the fall of the incumbent), or the aversion of left-leaning governments to restrictive monetary policies is particularly strong when they face intense parliamentary opposition, as such a situation forces them to adopt a more polarizing policy agenda to ensure political survival.

5
Conclusion

If an economic policy loses political support, it risks not being policy for much longer. This is, in a nutshell, what the analysis presented in this study suggests. Our capacity to understand the occurrence of currency crises should thus be improved by looking systematically at political factors, in addition to the economic fundamentals on which most of the theoretical and empirical workhorse models of the economics profession currently rely.

First, the evidence contained in the four case studies of Chapter 2 indicates that political factors have indeed played an important role in weakening the ability of economic policy makers to respond effectively to deteriorating economic fundamentals and defend a currency peg amidst growing market pressure. Then, the discussion of various political-economy extensions of a standard currency crisis model has shed some light on the channels through which factors such as a policy maker's time horizon, the electoral calender, intra-governmental conflict, and interest group pressure can affect the stability of exchange rate regimes and, in some cases, trigger speculative attacks. Finally, the econometric analysis has found a variety of political variables to be significant predictors of currency crises in many of the statistical models. The inclusion of political factors in econometric models can thus improve prediction performance compared with specifications that rely exclusively on economic fundamentals, even if the results are not very robust to variations in the empirical strategy.

In the following, I will review the results of the study in more detail before speculating about promising paths for future research and concluding with a thought about the practical relevance of the analysis.

Chapter 2

The experiences of interwar Britain and France, as well as Argentina and Turkey throughout the 1990s and early 2000s, suggest that a variety of political factors can contribute to weakening a government's capacity to respond to growing pressure on foreign exchange markets through adequate policy adjustment. These factors can be grouped into four broad categories: the administration's partisan nature that has a bearing on its economic policy positions; the existence of powerful interest groups with a potential to mobilize a large popular followership in reaction to unfavorable policy proposals; the time horizon of the incumbent administration, which, for example, can be affected by the timing of elections; and the institutional configuration of the political system, which may give rise to important veto players with the capacity of blocking or delaying consensus on policy reforms.

The extent to which these factors weighed on the stability of the exchange rate pegs that the four countries sought to defend varies. In the two interwar cases, a successful defense of the convertibility regime became ultimately impossible when the left-leaning governments proved unwilling to pursue the deep cuts in social entitlement programs that were deemed necessary to deliver the scale of fiscal adjustment that markets expected. But even if the governments had wished to push through the needed expenditure cuts, they might well have proved unable to do so. In both cases, militant labor movements mobilized strong popular support in favor of expansionary policies, and, in the case of Great Britain, the government could not rely on a stable parliamentary basis.

The Turkish experience of 2000–01 provides an example in which politicking within an improbable coalition government gradually weakened the credibility of an exchange rate-based stabilization program, in spite of the fact that the coalition enjoyed a comfortable parliamentary majority and did not face elections. Specifically, after a strong start of the program in early 2000, the authorities began losing the confidence of market participants when frictions among the coalition partners emerged regarding the pace and depth of the restructuring of Turkey's ailing state bank sector, the extent to which fiscal consolidation should be applied to politically difficult areas such as agricultural subsidies, and the pace at which to execute the ambitious program of privatization.[176] In this fragile atmosphere, the last stage of the crisis was triggered by a highly publicized stand-off between the Prime Minister and the President over corruption investigations in the state bank sector, which, within three days, led to the collapse of Turkey's currency peg in February 2001.

Finally, in the case of Argentina, all the factors identified above arguably contributed to some extent to the political deadlock that prevented the formulation of an effective response to the mounting economic challenges over the period 1995–2001. In particular, economic policy makers at the federal level, regardless of their political orientation, lost the ability to organize majorities—within the cabinet, in Congress, and in the provinces—through the dismantling of the initial reform coalition in society, which translated into a series of destabilizing election outcomes and permanent challenges even from inside the ruling party. Interest group behavior has also played an important role: while large businesses became a close ally of the Menem administration in the early years of the convertibility regime and broadly maintained their support through the end, labor unions were increasingly vocal in their criticism of the system. When the various labor organizations launched a two-day national strike in December 2001, the resulting civil unrest undermined the authorities' remaining legitimacy and precipitated the meltdown of the currency peg.

Chapter 3

Inspired by this anecdotal evidence of the link between politics and market turbulence, Chapter 3 presented several extensions to a canonical second-generation currency crisis model, which relate specific political conditions or events to exchange rate outcomes in a formal framework.[177] By using the established methodology of currency crisis theory, and by building upon the same reference model throughout the entire technical exposition, this analysis has lent itself well to deriving several hypotheses regarding the channels through which upcoming elections, veto player activity, and lobbying could affect the stability of an exchange rate regime.

First, the advent of elections—or any other event that renders the outlook for a continued stay in power more uncertain—should reduce the intensity of a policy maker's commitment to defend a currency peg if attacked by market participants.[178] This discomforting finding is due to the fact that many of the benefits associated with a currency peg are confined to the future (increased price stability without a negative effect on mean output), whereas a decision to exit from the regime yields immediate gains. Hence, any event that could reduce the likelihood of retaining office, including elections or a high probability of other forms of government transition such as coups, should work to the detriment of the promise to keep the exchange rate fixed. A country's institutional framework can play a role, too: all else being equal, a shorter anticipated term length for the executive should reduce the incentives for the incumbent to stay on with a currency peg.

Second, the chapter illustrated the potentially harmful impact of veto players on exchange rate stability, with the example of a fiscal policy maker minimizing a policy loss function alongside an independent central bank.[179] Specifically, the analysis has found that, in some situations, the fiscal player would maximize its own utility by setting taxes at a level that is sufficiently high to induce the central bank to exit from the currency peg: a high tax rate causes the output level of the economy to fall, which, in turn, makes it harder for the central bank to continue with the tough monetary stance needed to defend the peg. The scope for such intra-governmental conflict and the veto power for the fiscal authority arises because the level of taxation is determined prior to the central bank's decision on exchange rate policy.[180]

To conclude the theoretical discussion, a model was presented that allows for analyzing the effect of lobbying activity on exchange rate policy through a fiscal channel. Specifically, I used the example of a labor union concerned about real wages and the level of employment to show how the interest group could improve its welfare through making financial contributions to the fiscal policy maker, which would encourage the latter to lower taxes and thus stimulate employment creation.[181] In turn, the positive effect on employment would affect the exchange rate through feeding into the central bank's decision function. Numerical simulations based on this framework revealed how changes in the labor union's policy preferences or the fiscal policy maker's susceptibility to bribes could be expected to change the central bank's decision on the optimal depreciation rate of the home currency vis-à-vis its foreign anchor currency.

Chapter 4

Chapter 4 was dedicated to examining whether the data actually reveal any robust evidence that would support a role for political factors in the explanation of currency crises. To this aim, the study made use of simple descriptive analysis and a variety of logit estimations based on a large sample of 69 countries over 1975–97. The study design distinguished itself from much of the other recent work in the field by using a broad variety of political variables simultaneously in the regressions to minimize omitted variables bias; controlling for temporal dependence and autocorrelation in the data; and careful robustness testing with regard to the choice of dependent variable and the composition of the underlying data sample across countries and time.

Regarding overall model performance, various statistical test procedures revealed that adding political variables slightly increases the efficiency of the models, as the higher explanatory power is not fully offset by additional complexity. However, the Akaide Information Criterion shows that the difference in efficiency between the political-economy models and the baseline specifications that rely solely on economic fundamentals is small. This result was broadly confirmed by a comparison of the various models' forecasting performance, in which the political-economy models fared slightly better than the baseline specifications. In general, these exercises showed that forecasting currency crises, even in an in-sample setting where model parameters are estimated based on the known distribution of crisis events in the sample, is a difficult business; for the various models considered, the share of crises that were not detected ranges between 26 and 31 percent, and false alarms were also quite frequent.[182]

The results pertaining to specific variables also need to be taken with a grain of salt. On the one hand, some of the model specifications have found evidence suggesting that left-leaning governments, election years, the time that the incumbent's party has already spent in power, and a high number of veto players are significant predictors of currency crises. Moreover, a descriptive analysis of the monthly changes in foreign exchange markets around 320 election episodes has produced additional insights into the link between elections and exchange market stability, showing that market volatility typically peaks in the second to fourth post-election month and is particularly high in Latin American countries.

All these findings tend to confirm the hypotheses derived from the preceding theoretical analysis: left-leaning governments are more likely to experience currency crises than others; events such as elections that make the survival of the incumbent policy maker more uncertain tend to increase pressure on foreign exchange markets; the time that an incumbent party already spent in office could increase leader or voter fatigue; and a large number of veto players can impair a government's ability to respond swiftly to growing economic pressure by implementing a strong adjustment package. By contrast, it is difficult to find a satisfactory theoretical interpretation for the observed negative correlation between the degree of polarization in a society and the likelihood of a currency crisis.

On the other hand, most of the results on individual political variables have tended to show limited robustness to variations in research design. In particular, the evidence accumulated in the various regressions suggests that political variables are much more sensitive than economic variables to variation in the operationalization of the dependent variable and the choice of country sample with regard to geography, income level, and time period covered.[183] For example, the link between left-leaning governments and currency crises was found to be statistically significant only for weak crises, and, in the various robustness tests, only for European and Latin American countries in the earlier years covered by the data set. Additional analysis further suggested that left-wing governments are associated only with higher crisis probabilities when the incumbent faces a unified and strong opposition in parliament. By contrast, the election variable retained statistical power as a leading indicator only for strong crises.

Finally, the analysis found that the magnitude of the effect of changes in political variables on crisis probabilities depended crucially on the type of crisis. In the case of strong crises, the effects tended to be small in size, but were comparable to those associated with changes in macroeconomic fundamentals. However, the picture changed dramatically when the weak crisis indicator was used. In that case, the presence of a left-leaning government heightened the likelihood of a currency crisis by 5.3 percent, and thus by much more than a long tenure in office of the ruling party (2.9 percent) or adverse changes in macroeconomic conditions.

Overall, I think that the results of the study do offer some support for the claim that politics affect the vulnerability of a country to currency crises. As the theoretical discussion has shown, it is possible to develop models that draw on well-established frameworks in the economics literature to introduce a richer political dimension to the analysis. In this context, if the work that has recently been produced on the political determinants of fiscal performance is any guide to the future,[184] further advances can also be expected in the field of exchange rate and monetary policy, including with regard to the role of such factors as different electoral rules, various types of veto players, and interest group pressure.

To strengthen this research area, however, more progress is needed on the empirical front. As Eichengreen (1994a, p. 29) says, 'the problem is not to frame hypotheses, of which there are an abundance, but to gauge the explanatory power of the hypotheses against the evidence.' This will not be an easy task to accomplish. As the literature survey in Section 4.2 and the results of this study suggest, researchers probably still have some way to go before a set of political variables can be singled out that are comparable in their explanatory power to the more successful economic indicators used in today's EWS literature.

Several avenues could be taken to improve the design of empirical studies. As the poor reliability of political indicators may partially be caused by the insufficient quality and the low frequency of data, future research should place more emphasis on the problem of data collection. For example, it is hard to find good measures for the lobbying activity of sectoral interest groups; and many political variables show very low variance over time. Moreover, the political indicators seem to be more clearly related to a country's stage of economic development than macroeconomic measures, with the result that it is harder to find statistically significant effects that are independent of a country's per capita income. If more emphasis on data issues means restricting the scope of a panel to a smaller set of countries, then so be it.[185]

Moreover, researchers could dedicate more efforts to replicating previous findings on the link between politics and crises with different empirical strategies and submit the results to rigorous robustness testing. Over time, this should help the discipline to produce a body of well-accepted stylized facts (see also Blaug, 1992). One important challenge in this respect will be the choice of dependent variable, as the explanatory power of political variables is apparently much more sensitive to its particular specification than that of economic measures (see Section 4.5). This said, given the mixed track record of the empirical literature in crisis prediction, we should not be too ambitious in our demands. Most probably, we will have to accept that our knowledge of the multitude of factors that could cause currency crises remains limited.

Finally, I think we can draw one important lesson for policy making from the accumulated evidence: more consideration should be given to the political realities on the ground when designing a framework for exchange rate policy, particularly in countries that are characterized by weak institutions.[186] At present, it appears that such considerations often receive either too little attention among policy makers, or are brushed aside with a dangerous dose of optimism regarding a political system's capacity to adapt to the 'economic necessities.' As organizing majorities in support of sustainable policies becomes increasingly difficult in the face of mounting economic vulnerabilities, it is too late to start looking at these issues when the currency comes under pressure.[187]

Appendix A
Deriving the Supply Function

The various crisis models developed in Chapter 3 of the main text are based on a supply-determined production function. In this appendix, and based on Alesina and Tabellini (1987), we derive the output Equation 3.1 on Page 34.

As the capital stock is fixed in the short run, firms optimize only labor demand N. Short-run aggregate supply Y_s can thus be written as:

$$Y_s = N^{\gamma}, \tag{A.1}$$

with $0 < \gamma < 1$. Labor demand is chosen by differentiating the firms' profit maximization function G with respect to labor demand N, with given price level P and nominal wages W. If $1 - \tau$ is the share of firm revenues that is not taxed by the government, then G can be written as follows:

$$G = (1 - \tau)PY_s - WN. \tag{A.2}$$

Substituting Equation A.1 in A.2 and taking the partial derivative with respect to labor demand N yields

$$\frac{\partial G}{\partial N} = \gamma P(1 - \tau)N^{\gamma - 1} - W = 0. \tag{A.3}$$

Taking natural logarithms ($\ln Y = y$, $\ln P = p$ and $\ln W = w$) and noting that $N = Y^{1/\gamma}$, one obtains:

$$y_s = \frac{\gamma}{\gamma - 1}(w - p - \ln(1 - \tau) - \ln \gamma). \tag{A.4}$$

This aggregate supply function can be further simplified by making use of the approximation $-\tau$ for $\ln(1-\tau)$ and defining $\eta = \gamma/(1-\gamma)$ and $k = \gamma/(1-\gamma)\ln \gamma$:

$$y = \eta(p - w - \tau) + k. \tag{A.5}$$

Next, we set $\eta = 1$ and normalize output to $y = y_s - k$, with y reflecting the equilibrium output level in the presence of structural distortions such as labor market rigidities. A stochastic component μ is also added to the output equation, describing the realization of an exogenous shock with a mathematical expectation of $E(\mu) = 0$:

$$y = (p - w - \tau - \mu). \tag{A.6}$$

As workers aim at protecting real wages against erosion through price level increases, they demand nominal wages in line with the expected period price level p^e:

$$w = p^e. \tag{A.7}$$

Substituting Equation A.7 in the supply function A.6, one obtains the output function for the economy as

$$y = (p - p^e - \tau - \mu). \tag{A.8}$$

After augmentation with p_{-1}, this expression becomes

$$y = (\pi - \pi^e - \tau - \mu), \tag{A.9}$$

with $\pi = p - p_{-1}$ and $\pi^e = p^e - p_{-1}$.

Finally, as is standard for the case of a small open economy, we assume (relative) purchasing power parity to hold and normalize the log of the foreign price level to zero. This implies that the price of the foreign currency is identical with the domestic price level and we can write

$$\epsilon_t == e_t - e_{t-1} = p_t - p_{t-1}. \tag{A.10}$$

Combining Equations A.9 and A.10, one obtains

$$y = (\epsilon - \epsilon^e - \tau - \mu). \tag{A.11}$$

Appendix B
Survey of Econometric Studies

Table B.1 Selected Empirical Political-Economy Studies

Study	Key Design Features	Key Results
Eichengreen, Rose, and Wyplosz (1995)	How much do political variables contribute to explaining the incidence of speculative attacks in 20 industrial countries over the 1959–93 episode after controlling for macroeconomic factors? A multinomial logit model is used to examine, in particular, the impact of elections and partisanship on crisis probability.	Generally, the study fails to generate clear links between political variables and currency crises, with one exception: there is a positive relationship between past government defeats and the occurrence of currency crises.
Blomberg and Hess (1997)	Do political events systematically influence the level of the exchange rate? Several vector autoregression (VAR) models are estimated based on monthly exchange rate data for three major industrialized countries between 1974 and 1994.	An increase in approval ratings tends to depreciate exchange rates, while a shift from a left-leaning to a right-leaning government causes the exchange rate to appreciate. Election periods tend to be associated with stronger exchange rates.

Klein and Marion (1997)	Do political variables increase the likelihood of devaluations in fixed exchange rate regimes? The authors use a logit analysis based on data for 16 Latin American countries over 1956–91. The dependent variable equals zero in any month when the fixed exchange rate spell is in effect and one in the month in which the spell ends.	Both of the political variables included in the study—regular and irregular executive transfer—were found to increase the probability of a devaluation.
Bernhard and Leblang (1999)	How do politicians' incentives influence exchange rate policy? Based on a sample of 20 industrial democracies over the 1974–95 period, the authors use a probit model to examine how the type of government affects the choice of exchange rate regime.	The authors find that coalition governments are more likely to maintain currency pegs than administrations in majoritarian systems.
Bussière and Mulder (2000)	How did political instability impact on economic vulnerability in the context of the 1994 and 1997 crisis episodes? Four political indices (polarization, government cohesion, election uncertainty, and election dates) are added to the data set of Tornell (1998), which covers 23 emerging market countries. The study uses an OLS model with the level of the pressure index as dependent variable.	The volatility index and the election variable are found to be positively related with exchange rate pressure. By contrast, polarization and coalition fragility are not found to be significant.

Table B.1 (continued)

Study	Key Design Features	Key Results
Bernhard and Leblang (2000)	Do political factors affect how markets evaluate the probability of a speculative attack? The authors analyze this issue for 15 OECD countries with parliamentary democracies based on monthly data over the 1970–95 period. First, a discrete-time hazard model is estimated to determine the probability of cabinet termination for each month based on a variety of explanatory variables. The resulting prediction is then used together with a partisan variable in a traditional probit model to predict speculative attacks.	The authors find that a higher probability of cabinet termination and a partisan shift to the left are positively correlated with currency crises.
Frieden, Ghezzi, and Stein (2001)	Can political-economy factors help explain the choice of exchange rate regime? The question is explored by a data set on 26 Latin American countries spanning the 1960–94 period. An ordered logit regression is specified to distinguish between four different regime types that are used as dependent variables.	More flexible exchange rate regimes are associated with a high share of the manufacturing sector in GDP (particularly in the presence of open trade regimes) and higher degrees of political instability as evidenced by regular and irregular government changes. By contrast, fixed exchange rate regimes tend to be associated with nondemocratic governments, administrations with a strong majority in the legislature, and governments facing fragmented opposition.

Bernhard and Leblang (2002)	How do exchange rate regimes affect the duration of cabinets in OECD countries? This question is analyzed in an OLS model using data on 193 cabinets from 16 OECD countries over the 1972–98 period.	The authors find that fixed exchange rates (as well as central bank independence) tend to increase the duration of cabinets.
Leblang (2002)	How do markets react to electoral and partisan changes in 78 developing countries with pegs over the 1975–98 period? The author estimates a logit model with Huber/White robust standard errors.	Using two political factors in addition to a set of economic controls, the author finds that speculative attacks are more likely with left governments. Crisis are also more likely for all government types in the period after elections.
Meon and Rizzo (2002)	How does political uncertainty impact on the choice of exchange rate regimes? This question is tested using data for a panel of 125 countries over the 1980–94 period based on a probit model using various measures of political uncertainty.[188]	The authors find that higher political turnover as measured by various variable specifications is highly correlated with the adoption of flexible exchange rates. Moreover, democracies are more likely to choose flexible exchange rates than autocratic regimes.
Block (2003)	How do structural political conditions impact on the probability of currency crises in emerging markets? The author adds political variables to the EWS model developed in Berg and Patillo (1999) and uses a random-effects probit for 23 emerging market countries over 1975–97.	Right-wing governments as well as administrations with a strong legislative majority or fragmented oppositions are less prone to currency crises. While democracy also tends to reduce crisis probabilities, elections do not have a significant impact.

Appendix C
Data Issues

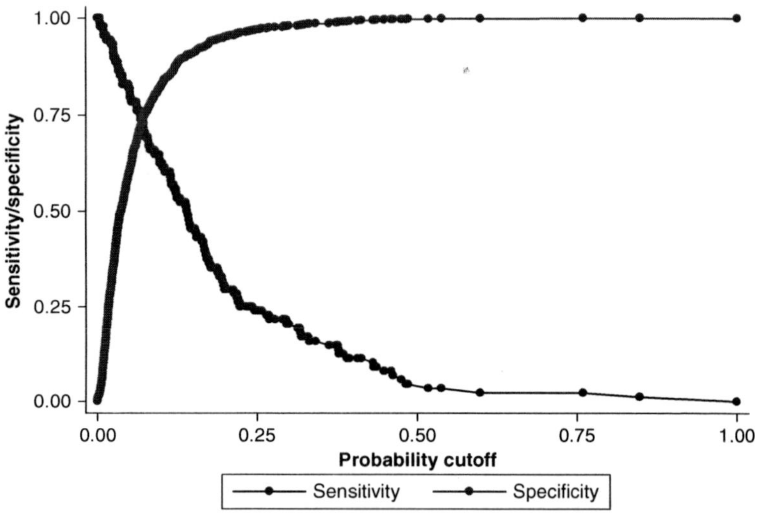

Figure C.1 Strong Crisis Model: Sensitivity and Specificity

Table C.1 Country Sample: Overview

Industrial Countries	Emerging Market Countries	Others
Australia	Argentina	Belize
Austria	Bangladesh	Bolivia
Belgium	Brazil	Ivory Coast
Canada	Botswana	Costa Rica
Denmark	Chile	Cyprus
Finland	Colombia	Dominican Republic
France	Ecuador	El Salvador
Greece	Egypt	Fiji
Iceland	Hungary	Grenada
Ireland	India	Guatemala
Italy	Indonesia	Guyana
Japan	Israel	Honduras
Netherlands	Malaysia	Jamaica
New Zealand	Mauritius	Madagascar
Norway	Mexico	Malta
Portugal	Pakistan	Nepal
Spain	Peru	Panama
Sweden	Philippines	Paraguay
Switzerland	Poland	Zambia
United Kingdom	Romania	
	Singapore	
	South Africa	
	South Korea	
	Sri Lanka	
	Thailand	
	Trinidad and Tobago	
	Turkey	
	Uruguay	
	Venezuela	
	Zimbabwe	

Note: Country classification is based on Glick and Hutchison (1999).

Table C.2 Strong Crises: Robustness of Results Across Regions

	Asia	Europe	Latin America
Years-in-office	.079	.070	.049
	(.050)	(.092)	(.034)
Elections	−1.093	1.901***	1.062*
	(.918)	(.675)	(.611)
Checks	−.020	.217	−.015
	(.226)	(.230)	(.244)
Polarization	.035	−.258	.137
	(.647)	(.421)	(.396)
M2-to-Reserves	.008	.017***	.011***
	(.005)	(.007)	(.004)
Import growth	−.005*	.003	−.003**
	(.004)	(.003)	(.001)
Real exchange rate	−.186***	−.109***	−.053***
	(.052)	(.033)	(.012)
Survival	−.047	−.031	−.081
	(.093)	(.071)	(.063)
#	148	207	292
$Pseudo - R^2$	.391	.274	.340
Log Likelihood	−35.70	−44.42	−66.61

Note: Probability of erroneous rejection of null-hypothesis (no difference) at the *0.1 percent-level, **0.5 percent-level, and the ***0.01 percent-level.

Table C.3 Weak Crises: Robustness of Results Across Regions

	Asia	Europe	Latin America
Years-in-office	.058*	.075*	.056**
	(.032)	(.044)	(.028)
LeftGov	−.248	.583*	.665*
	(.578)	(.315)	(.392)
M2-to-Reserves	.006	.003	.010***
	(.004)	(.003)	(.003)
Real exchange rate	−.109***	−.019	−.021**
	(.027)	(.015)	(.008)
Survival	−.012	.147***	−.026
	(.064)	(.051)	(.051)
#	255	379	350
$Pseudo - R^2$	.266	.143	.215
Log Likelihood	−78.84	−156.69	−105.48

Note: Probability of erroneous rejection of null-hypothesis (no difference) at the *0.1 percent-level, **0.5 percent-level, and the ***0.01 percent-level.

Table C.4 Robustness of Results Over Time

	Strong Crises		Weak Crises	
	Pre-1990s	1990s	Pre-1990s	1990s
Years-in-office	.160**	−.022	.124***	.030
	(.067)	(.039)	(.044)	(.023)
Elections	.292	1.084*		
	(.385)	(.478)		
LeftGov			1.438***	.255
			(.386)	(.285)
Checks	.751***	.096		
	(.289)	(.185)		
Polarization	−.498	−.896**		
	(.557)	(.386)		
M2-to-Reserves	.009***	.006*	.007***	.005***
	(.003)	(.003)	(.002)	(.002)
Import growth	−.001	−.002**		
	(.001)	(.001)		
Real exchange rate	−.037***	−.057***	−.030***	−.006
	(.012)	(.014)	(.009)	(.009)
Survival	.617***	.034	.621***	.015
	(.115)	(.042)	(.083)	(.031)
#	589	438	815	544
Pseudo − R^2	.411	.255	.350	.089
Log Likelihood	−82.95	−77.54	−169.79	−183.16

Note: Probability of erroneous rejection of null-hypothesis (no difference) at the *0.1 percent-level, **0.5 percent-level, and the ***0.01 percent-level.

Table C.5 Robustness of Results to Changes in Data Sample

	Full Democracies		Restricted Sample	
	CRS3	CRS2	CRS3	CRS2
Years-in-office	.134**	.067**	.057	.015
	(.059)	(.033)	(.038)	(.028)
LeftGov		.547**		.389
		(.280)		(.295)
Elections	.756**		.553*	
	(.341)		(.321)	
Checks	.599***		.630***	
	(.225)		(.241)	

Table C.5 (Continued)

	Full Democracies		Restricted Sample	
	CRS3	CRS2	CRS3	CRS2
Polarization	−.785*		−.915**	
	(.447)		(.432)	
M2-to-Reserves	.007**	.006***	.007***	.006***
	(.003)	(.002)	(.002)	(.002)
Import growth	−.003**		−.002**	
	(.001)		(.001)	
Real exchange rate	−.033***	−.012*	−.035***	−.013*
	(.010)	(.007)	(.010)	(.007)
Survival	.255***	.262***	.257***	.282***
	(.061)	(.043)	(.060)	(.047)
#	707	968	752	943
$Pseudo - R^2$	.336	.182	.328	.187
Log Likelihood	−103.74	−268.30	−116.09	−250.74

Note: Probability of erroneous rejection of null-hypothesis (no difference) at the *0.1 percent-level, **0.5 percent-level, and the ***0.01 percent-level. Full democracies include country years associated with a high degree of electoral competition (LIEC = 7). The restricted sample uses only country years without any missing observations in the full model (See Tables 4.9 and 4.10).

Notes

1. Bordo, Eichengreen, Klingebiel, and Soledad Martinez-Peria (2001) find that crisis frequencies in the period since 1973 have been twice as high as under the Bretton Woods system and the classical gold standard.
2. In this context, it is noteworthy that, in spite of the dominance of the bipolar view proclaiming the unsustainability of intermediate regimes such as fixed-but-adjustable currency pegs, many countries continue to maintain such regimes for a variety of reasons. See Eichengreen (1994b) and Fischer (2001) for an exposition of the bipolar view; and Dooley, Folkerts-Landau, and Garber (2003), Hernandez and Montiel (2003), and Calvo and Reinhart (2002) for evidence on the prevalence of continued *de facto* pegging.
3. For example, only one of the papers in the NBER's 2000 conference report on currency crises deals explicitly with political dynamics (see Drazen, 2000b). Specifically, the author develops a model in which a devaluation by one member of a currency union can trigger a reassessment of the costs and benefits of international cooperation through others.
4. Typically, these models assume that the authorities accept domestic credit to grow at a constant rate as the central bank finances a fiscal deficit. This leads to an inevitable and successful attack on the domestic currency as soon as central bank reserves fall under a certain threshold level. Many of the models that were developed in response to the Asian crisis in 1997–98 portray the government's behavior in a similarly simplistic way. See Agénor, Bhandari, and Flood (1992) for a detailed survey of first-generation models, and Marion (1999) for a discussion of the more recent work.
5. See Section 3.2 for a closer look at this family of crisis models, which are intellectually indebted to the work of Kydland and Prescott (1977) and Barro and Gordon (1983), and represent an important part of the standard repertoire of the new political economics literature (see Drazen, 2000c; Persson and Tabellini, 2000).
6. See Hawkins and Klau (2000) and Berg, Borensztein, and Patillo (2005) for good overviews of the mainstream econometric literature.
7. Section 4.2 reviews the small but growing body of studies that are exceptions to this rule and incorporate political factors among the explanatory variables.
8. I follow North (1990) in defining institutions as the humanly devised constraints that shape human interaction in a society. They can be both formal—rules that human beings devise, for example in the form of constitutional law—or informal, such as conventions and codes of behavior.

9. Eichengreen (1998) explains well the differences in approach among economics, history, and political science, while Broz and Frieden (2006) and Willett (2007) offer good introductions to the political-economy literature on exchange rate policy.
10. This pattern differs from the experience of the countries inside the European Exchange Rate Mechanism at the time of the 1992–93 crisis, which typically relied to a much larger extent on monetary policy measures and capital controls for the defense of their currency pegs vis-à-vis the Deutsche Mark.
11. See, for example, Calvo and Végh (1999), Dornbusch (2001), and Eichengreen (2001).
12. The discussion draws heavily on some historical accounts of the classical gold standard era and the interwar years, including Eichengreen (1992), Eichengreen (1996), Simmons (1994), and Wandschneider (2008).
13. According to the traditional interpretation, the classical gold standard worked well because countries used monetary policy in a counter cyclical way to support the adjustment through cross-country flows of gold, maintained reasonably open trade relations to ensure that trade flows could respond to changes in prices, and stood ready to provide exceptional financing to regime members whose currencies came under pressure (see, for example, McKinnon, 1993). While Bayoumi and Eichengreen (1995) find evidence that the adjustment of prices and quantities to economic shocks indeed worked quite well, research has also shown that even in the heyday of the regime, no central bank fully played by the rules. For a recent overview of this debate, see Broz (2000).
14. Great Britain returned to gold in May 1925, followed by Switzerland, France, and Italy. The United States returned to gold convertibility as early as 1919, while Germany linked its Mark to gold in 1924 as part of a strategy to end hyperinflation.
15. Kenwood and Lougheed (1992) present some data on the extraordinary growth of cross-border trade and direct investment flows in the years prior to 1914: for example, per capita international trade grew by an average rate of 33 percent per decade between 1800 and 1913, and the stock of British foreign investment increased from an estimated US$ 3.75 billion in 1870 to US$ 20.0 billion in 1913.
16. For a synopsis of recent research on the causes of the Great Depression, see Eichengreen (2004).
17. The interwar gold-exchange standard was more exposed to confidence issues than the classical gold standard due to a heightened role for the monies of the center countries as currency reserves for the periphery (see Triffin, 1947). At the same time, however, the role of fiat in official reserves declined over time, as countries increasingly sought to exchange their U.S. dollar and sterling holdings for gold.
18. Obstfeld, Shambaugh, and Taylor (2004) find econometric evidence for the existence of such a macroeconomic trilemma: under open capital markets and pegged exchange rates, policy makers could deviate from

the interest rates required for the stability of the gold standard only for short periods of time.

19. Older accounts rely on differences in the structure of the international system in the interwar years compared to the episode of the classical gold standard, emphasizing either the absence of a benevolent hegemon that would willingly bear a disproportionate share of the costs of stabilizing the system (Kindleberger, 1973), or the breakdown of cooperation among central banks (Eichengreen, 1992). Both views are, however, not incompatible with the explanation relying on changes in key polities, as the interests of countries with regard to international cooperation necessarily reflect the political preferences of the key domestic political actors.
20. See, for example, Polanyi (1944), Keynes (1995), and Gallarotti (1995).
21. In a fascinating account of interwar politics in Europe, Luebbert (1991) shows how three political-economy regimes—liberal democracy, social democracy, and fascism—developed as responses in politics and the labor market to the demands of the working class.
22. This was true even before the publication of Keynes' general theory in 1937 (see Blaug, 1985).
23. This has to be seen in the context of an unemployment rate reaching 20 percent of the insured work force in the summer of 1931.
24. In the event, the end of convertibility did not help the Labor Party. Premier Ramsey MacDonald and some of his followers left the party and ran on a platform close to the Conservatives; the latter party won 76.4 percent of the seats in the lower house, while Labor lost dramatically and captured only 8.5 percent of the seats.
25. The call for devaluation did not surface among mainstream politicians before 1934 and remained a minority view even then (see Eichengreen and Temin, 1997).
26. Eichengreen (1992) emphasizes the role of proportional electoral systems for some of the gold countries' inability to adjust to inflationary pressures.
27. Jointly, the three parties united in the coalition government controlled 63 percent of the parliamentary vote over the entire life of the adjustment program.
28. A detailed description of the program's objectives can be found in the authorities' Letter of Intent dated 9 December 1999, which is available at http://www.imf.org.
29. In 1999 and 2000, short-term interbank credit lines from foreign counterparts rose by US$ 2.1 billion and US$4.7 billion, respectively.
30. For example, just before the February crisis broke, the approval ratings for Prime Minister Ecevit's party fell to 11 percent (see Molly Moore and Paul Blustein, 'Financial Woes Grow in Turkey; Crisis Threatens Stability of U.S. Ally,' *The Washington Post*, 22 February 2001.)
31. See http://meria.biu.ac.il/research-g/turkey-elections.html (accessed 10 June 2008), and Onis (2000).

32. For a more detailed discussion of these issues, see Alper and Onis (2002b), Onis (2000), and 'Nervous,' *The Economist*, 1 March 2001.
33. While the authorities succeeded in keeping the spot exchange rate within the floating band, the six-month forward rate shows that investors anticipated a steep depreciation of the Lira within the near future. See Figure 2.1.
34. These concerns were validated *ex post*. For example, the IMF estimated that total public debt arising from the recapitalization of state-owned banks and the takeover of private banks into the Saving Deposit Insurance Fund amounted to 24 percent of GNP at end-April 2001 (see International Monetary Fund, 2001).
35. The perception of not defending agricultural interests would potentially have led to a shift in voter support toward the outright Islamist Virtue Party, which was a strong political competitor in the poorer rural segments of Turkish society.
36. Reportedly, Lira sales on that day alone amounted to US$ 5 billion or about one quarter of the central bank's total foreign exchange reserves. See 'On the Brink Again,' *The Economist*, 22 February 2001.
37. For a more detailed discussion of Argentina's economic performance under the convertibility regime, see Daseking, Ghosh, Lane, and Thomas (2004) and International Monetary Fund, Independent Evaluation Office (2004).
38. Gains in labor productivity in the early years mainly reflected a steep reduction in employment levels rather than improved efficiency in labor market institutions, as the privatized businesses shed large numbers of redundant workers (see Pastor and Wise, 2001).
39. These provinces represented only about 30 percent of the population, but held a majority of seats both in the Senate and in the lower chamber of the Congress. Moreover, most of them were controlled by the Peronist party or political organizations close to it: an average 87 percent of all provincial governors in office during the 1989–95 period were aligned with the Menem administration (see Calvo and Gibson, 2000).
40. In the presidential elections of 1995, President Menem won with nearly 50 percent of the vote. Voter turnout for the Peronist party was highest in the least-developed provinces, while more contested showings were recorded in the major metropolitan areas (see Gibson, 1997).
41. Despite the efforts to implement fiscal adjustment, the real effective exchange rate appreciated, in cumulative terms, by some 20 percent between end-1991 and 1994, and by another 5.0 percent through end-1999.
42. For example, the budget deficit of the Buenos Aires province, which was governed by Eduardo Duhalde, one of Menem's main competitors in the Peronist party for the presidential nomination, increased to 25 percent of current revenues in 1999, from 7 percent in 1996, mostly due to outlays for additional public employment.
43. According to José Luis Machinea, who served as the Minister of Finance in the de la Rua government, the growing dollarization of liabilities on

sectoral balance sheets was a factor in the administration's decision not to consider a devaluation of the Peso in 2000 (see Machinea, 2003).

44. The Allianza coalition, which found its support mainly in the urban middle class, brought together de la Rua's moderate Radical Civic Union (UCR) and the leftist Front for a Country in Solidarity (FREPASO). De la Rua captured 48 percent of the vote in the presidential election and thus clearly defeated Eduardo Duhalde, the Peronist candidate. The Allianza also won the Chamber of Deputies, while the Senate remained under the control of the Peronists (see Sullivan, 2002).
45. The highly unpopular law, which stipulated the decentralization of wage negotiations to the firm level and established a federal mediation agency for labor disputes, passed the Senate with the votes of the Peronist opposition. In this context, allegations surfaced over vote-buying attempts on the part of the de la Rua government (see Pastor and Wise, 2001).
46. The Peronists continued to control the Senate and also became the largest bloc in the Chamber of Deputies. Moreover, 21 percent of the electorate recorded blank or negative votes (compared to a turnout for the Allianza of only 25 percent), clearly showing the extent to which the electorate had lost faith in the country's political institutions (see Pastor and Wise, 2001).
47. By mid-November 2001, the central bank would not even have been in the condition to satisfy the demand of private creditors stemming from foreign-currency deposits; only US$18.8 billion in central bank reserves remained available to back a total of US$49 billion worth of foreign-currency deposits in the banking system. See Martin Wolf, 'Argentina's Agonising Options,' *The Financial Times*, 4 December 2001.
48. When the foreign exchange market reopened for the first time under the new floating exchange rate regime on 11 February 2002, the exchange rate depreciated to 1.8 Pesos to the U.S. dollar.
49. As discussed further in Section 4.2, some of the earlier empirical studies on the political economy of currency crises focused on such extreme events rather than on attributes of democratic political systems in more normal times.
50. A similar pattern is observable for the case of the United States, where the decision to abandon the tie to gold was taken only after the Democrats won a landslide in the presidential and congressional elections of November 1932. Before that date, the Republican Hoover administration withstood all initiatives to reflate the economy, even when faced with a severe banking crisis (see, for example, Eichengreen, 1996; Frieden, 1996).
51. Empirical studies based on a larger set of countries do not even find unequivocal support for the link between left governments and currency crises in the interwar years. While Wandschneider (2008) finds that a high percentage of left-wing representation in parliament has shortened the time a country would stay on gold, Simmons (1994) finds that the likelihood of adhering to gold has increased with left-wing representation in parliament.

52. The French experience at the time of the 1992–93 crisis within the European Exchange Rate Mechanism provides further support for a differentiated view: while the Socialist government maintained a strong commitment to the 'Franc fort' in September 1992, the newly elected conservative coalition was more lukewarm in its support for a continuation of this policy in the summer of 1993, mainly due to the impact of high interest rates on small- and medium-sized businesses.
53. The Argentine case is also instructive because it reveals the difficulties involved in co-opting parts of the more modern and competitive sectors of the labor movement. When economic conditions deteriorated from about 1995, this segment of the reform coalition fell apart and joined the ranks of the convertibility regime's critics (see Starr, 1997).
54. To some extent, the negative impact of missing parliamentary majorities on decision making can be mitigated by recourse to an increased reliance on decree powers, which are typically granted to a president or prime minister. For example, Argentina made extensive use of this method, issuing 336 decrees of 'urgency and necessity' over 1989–1995, compared to a total of only 35 such decrees issued by all its predecessors since 1853 (see Starr, 1997). However, the decree powers would typically have to be periodically renewed through parliament; more fundamentally, this practice is bound to gradually weaken democratic institutions and thus broad political support for the incumbent.
55. See Section 3.4 for a more detailed discussion of the veto player concept.
56. Haque, Mark, and Mathieson (1998) discuss the relative importance of political factors in the credit rating process for selected commercial rating agencies. The weights attached to such factors in the overall rating score range from 15 percent (Euromoney) to 40 percent (Economist Intelligence Unit).
57. For a more extensive discussion of this model, see Obstfeld and Rogoff (1996). It is important to note that enhanced credibility in the fight against inflation is only one of several considerations that could serve as a justification for adopting a currency peg. Such a decision could also be motivated by a desire to maximize benefits from international trade or minimize the impact of currency fluctuation on domestic balance sheets in the presence of substantial liability dollarization. See Mongelli (2002) for a recent survey on the theory of optimum currency areas.
58. This is clearly a simplification, as the responsibility for exchange rate policies typically falls into the realm of the Ministry of Finance. That said, on an operational level, exchange rate policy is typically implemented by a, more or less, independent central bank.
59. I do not discuss whether the initial announcement to establish a fixed exchange rate regime is a welfare-maximizing strategy either for policy makers or society at large. For models of exchange rate choice, see, for example, Obstfeld (1991), Hefeker (1997) and Berger, Jensen, and Schjelderup (2001).
60. The model assumes simplistically that the central bank can directly determine the value of the exchange rate rather than some intermediate policy targets.

61. $\tilde{y} > 0$ is assumed to be chosen on political grounds. Alternatively, it could be interpreted as a summary measure of non tax distortions prevailing in the economy (see Beetsma and Bovenberg, 1998).
62. Recent theoretical developments subsumed under the global games literature deviate from the latter assumption. In these models, the presence of private information potentially leads to a reduction in the number of equilibria in second-generation models (see Morris and Shin, 1998).
63. Credibility-based arguments in favor of fixed exchange rates were often made by the proponents of moving toward European Monetary Union inside the European Communities (see, for example, De Grauwe, 1994; Giavazzi and Pagano, 1988; Giavazzi and Spaventa, 1990), but also in an emerging market context (see, in particular, Edwards, 1993). Hamann (2001) and Willett (2007) offer a critical discussion of the experience with exchange rate-based stabilization programs.
64. Assuming $\epsilon^e = 0$.
65. Devaluation is also the best strategy for the central bank if the private sector anticipates such a move, as the alternative loss under a peg, $1/2[(1+\alpha_c)/(\alpha_c)(\tau+\tilde{y})+\mu]^2$, is strictly higher.
66. Despite the fact that credibility has become a common term in academic circles and among policy makers, it remains difficult to come up with a precise definition. Blackburn and Christensen (1989) offer an early attempt at capturing its meaning, defining credibility as the extent to which beliefs about the current and future course of economic policy are consistent with the program originally announced by the policy makers. Alternatively, and in somewhat simpler words, the term could be understood to mean a policy maker's ability and willingness to actually carry out a pre-announced course of action.
67. See, for example, Obstfeld (1994, 1996) and Velasco (1996). Andersen (1998) develops a model in which the size of the cost term depends on endogenous dynamics.
68. See Obstfeld (1991) for an extensive discussion of escape clause models in the context of exchange rate regime choice.
69. Given that Equation 3.18 is quadratic, there is a second solution for μ. In the case of a sufficiently large *positive* supply shock, the central bank would find it beneficial to revalue the exchange rate rather than keep it fixed.
70. The rule employed in the following is borrowed from Meon and Rizzo (2002) to ensure compatibility with the analysis in Section 3.3.
71. Stein and Streb (2004) show how an opportunistic government may find it attractive to resist devaluation in the pre-election phase as the benefits associated with any extra seigniorage revenue for the budget could well be outweighed by the political costs of an adverse reaction of consumers. The latters' resentment is grounded in the fact that with a cash-in-advance constraint, the interest rate increase associated with a devaluation would act as a tax on their consumption. Ghezzi, Stein, and Streb (2005) develop a similar model focusing on real rather than nominal exchange rate cycles around elections through the addition

of a nontradable goods sector to the framework. In this case, a temporary delay of devaluation leads to an appreciated real exchange rate that stimulates a consumption boom appealing to voters.

72. As in the case of Equation (3.29), $\Phi = (\tau + \mu + \tilde{y})^2/(\tau + \tilde{y})^2$.
73. To facilitate notation, ℓ_i^j represents the present value of the expected losses for the incumbent during one future term lasting M years, when party i is in power ($i = inc, opp$) and the current exchange rate regime is j ($j = fix, flex$). Hence, ℓ_i^j can be written as

$$\ell_i^j = \sum_{s=0}^{M-1} L_i^j = \frac{1-\beta^M}{1-\beta} L_i^j. \tag{C.1}$$

74. $\Phi = (\tau + \mu + \tilde{y})^2/(\tau + \tilde{y})^2$.
75. For good introductions to veto player analysis, see Tsebelis (2002) and Ganghof (2003).
76. Willett (2007) emphasizes this last point when discussing the difficulties of decision making in a crisis context: to reach agreement on a certain course of action, the Minister of Finance must typically convince the chief executive, who in turn may have to convince the legislature, while all through the chain the actors' decisions are likely to be subject to influence by the lobbying and prospective reactions of interest groups and also the general public. Consistent with this view, MacIntyre (2001) argues in his account of the Asian crisis in 1997–98 that the Thai government's slow response to the financial distress was caused by the presence of a large number of veto players. That said, the author also notes that Indonesia and Malaysia suffered from the instability generated by the vacillations of strong leaders who faced only weak political checks.
77. The case for delegating policy authority to an independent central bank with a view to solve the time inconsistency problem plaguing monetary policy and improve society's welfare was forcefully made by Rogoff (1985). For recent surveys on this research program in economic theory, see Drazen (2000c) and Persson and Tabellini (2000).
78. Of course, such arguments are not new to scholars of economic history. See, for example, Holtfrerich (1988) who offers a detailed assessment of the political relations between the central bank and other branches of government for the case of Germany since the nineteenth century.
79. By contrast, the growing literature on fiscal dominance focuses on this relationship, discussing the role of debt sustainability considerations for monetary and exchange rate policy. The structure of these models, however, is very different from that of second-generation currency crisis models, including the use of multi-period time horizons to model debt dynamics. For recent contributions, see, for example, Bank for International Settlements (2003) and Ramos and Tanner (2002).
80. See Drazen (2000a) for a recent model in which fiscal policy rather than monetary policy is the driving force behind partisan cycles. This setup

contrasts with the earlier political business cycle literature pioneered by Nordhaus (1975).

81. For recent studies examining the role of fiscal policy for the European Central Bank's monetary policy decisions, see Beetsma and Bovenberg (1998), Catenaro and Tirelli (2000), and Neugart and Rother (2002).
82. To keep the exposition in this section as simple as possible, I abstract from any stochastic elements in the basic exposition. A stochastic shock on the fiscal policy maker's spending target will be reintroduced to the framework in Section 3.4.3, which focuses on how private sector expectations can interact with the expected shock size to generate multiple equilibria.
83. For comparative studies on countries' fiscal spending preferences and a discussion of the factors that account for the observed heterogeneity, see, for example, Garrett (1998) and Alesina, Perotti, and Tavares (1998).
84. In an effort to keep the model as simple as possible, this rule abstracts from two additional sources of financing for the budget. First, following other authors including Alesina and Tabellini (1987), Catenaro and Tirelli (2000), and Gaertner (2000), I assume that the economy operates without debt, as this allows restricting the analysis to the case of a one-period game. Secondly, I abstract from seigniorage revenue, which is revenue generated by reducing the real value of outstanding domestic currency through printing money. This type of income typically represents only a small share of total government revenue.
85. Scenario C will be introduced on Page 60.
86. In order to reverse this preference ordering, the inflation-aversion of the fiscal branch would have to reach at least the level $\alpha_f = 1 + 2\alpha_c$. This would imply a fiscal authority more than twice as tough on inflation as the central bank.
87. The partial derivatives are

$$\frac{\partial \tilde{g}^*}{\partial \alpha_c} = \frac{\bar{c}(\alpha_c(4+\alpha_c+\alpha_g(2+\alpha_c)) - 3\alpha_f + \alpha_g)}{\alpha_g(1+\alpha_c)^2\sqrt{2\bar{c}(1+\alpha_c)}} > 0,$$

$$\frac{\partial \tilde{g}^*}{\partial \alpha_f} = \frac{\sqrt{2\bar{c}(1+\alpha_c)}}{\alpha_g(1+\alpha_c)^2} > 0$$

and

$$\frac{\partial \tilde{g}^*}{\partial \alpha_g} = -\frac{(\alpha_c^2+\alpha_f)\sqrt{2\bar{c}(1+\alpha_c)}}{\alpha_g(1+\alpha_c)^2} < 0.$$

88. For simplicity, I assume that the central bank would give up the currency peg at exactly this level of taxation rather than at the first feasible tax rate exceeding this threshold.
89. At or above $\tilde{g}^d$, the fiscal authority would minimize its policy loss by implementing a tax rate consistent with Scenario A.
90. $\tilde{g}^*$ responds to changes in underlying policy preferences in a similar way as $\tilde{g}^d$: increases in the inflation-aversion of the two policy makers as well

as a higher political cost term $\bar{c}$ lead to an increase in the threshold. By contrast, increases in the spending preference α_g reduce the level of the spending target $\tilde{g}^*$ necessary to put the fixed exchange rate at risk. A second solution for $\tilde{g}^*$ is located to the right of τ^d and can therefore be ignored for the purpose of this analysis.

91. The role of expectations in the collapse of fixed exchange rates has been highlighted by many analysts since the experience with the 1992–93 crisis in the European Exchange Rate Mechanism. See, for example, Obstfeld (1996), Eichengreen and Jeanne (2000), and Radelet and Sachs (2000). Crisis accounts based on sudden shifts in expectations gained further prominence after the Asian crisis in 1997–98 (see Krugman, 2000), and, according to a recent empirical study by Alvarez-Plata and Schrooten (2003), swings in expectations were also an important factor in the 2001–02 crisis in Argentina.
92. See Velasco (1996) for a similar approach in a second-generation model with one policy maker.
93. The thresholds that render it possible for the fiscal authority to implement its preferred tax rate τ^d rather than τ^* can be derived in a similar way.
94. Typically, economic crisis models do not provide a theory explaining the actual coordination of private sector expectations. Rather, shifts in investor sentiment are attributed to 'sunspot events' such as the French referendum over membership in the European Monetary Union that triggered the 1992–93 crisis inside the European Exchange Rate Mechanism (see, for example, Eichengreen and Wyplosz, 1993).
95. In similar simulation exercises, authors have chosen $\alpha_c = 0.15$ to describe a 'wet' central bank and $\alpha_c = 0.8$ to describe a 'tough' central bank. See, for example, Obstfeld (1994) and Catenaro and Tirelli (2000). Other parameter values underlying the simulations are $\alpha_f = 0.3$, $\tilde{g} = 0.2$, $\tilde{y} = 0.02$ and $\bar{c} = 0.05$. Pessimistic expectations are determined as $\epsilon^e = \epsilon^d$ or $\epsilon^e = \epsilon^*$, depending on the threshold level of the spending target $\tilde{g}$.
96. The framework is based on Obstfeld (1994), who discusses the link between expectations and shocks for the case of a traditional second-generation model. Consistent with Flood and Marion (1996), however, I will show that multiple equilibria do not occur for all parameter specifications, but critically depend on the state of underlying fundamentals.
97. While Kaminsky and Reinhart (1999), and Glick and Hutchison (1999) suggest that there is an empirical link between currency crises and banking crises, theoretical contributions emphasize the role of balance sheet problems in the financial and nonfinancial corporate sector. One strand of the literature including Corsetti (1998); Corsetti, Pesenti, and Roubini (1998); Dooley (2000); Dooley and Shin (2000), and Krugman (1998) emphasizes the role of solvency problems, while other authors stress the importance of liquidity-related vulnerabilities that can give rise to self-fulfilling crises (see, for example, Chang and Velasco, 1999; Diamond and Rajan, 2000; Krugman, 1999; Radelet and Sachs, 2000).

98. Parameter values are chosen with a view to ensure that the economy operates in the gray region of partial credibility. This requires that the peg would survive even the worst possible shock (Z) in case expectations remain optimistic.
99. Parameter values are $\alpha_c = 0.7$, $\alpha_f = 0.3$, $\alpha_g = 1$, $\tilde{y} = 0.02$, $\tilde{g}_0 = 0.2$, $\bar{c} = 0.05$, and $Z = 0.15$. A second equilibrium solution is located outside the permissible shock range and therefore economically insignificant.
100. Similar points were made by Flood and Marion (1996) and Furman and Stiglitz (1998).
101. The analytical literature on interest groups and their impact on economic policy making focused first on the collective action problems inherent in organizing interests. See, for example, Olson (1965) and Hirschman (1970). Studies focusing on the macroeconomic effects of interest groups emerged in the 1980s and often took the form of comparative case studies. Prominent contributions to this strand of literature include Olson (1982), North (1981), North (1990), and Scharpf (1991).
102. For a good survey on the various theories of inflation, see Kirshner (2001).
103. A formal exposition of this approach is offered in the working-paper version of Blomberg, Frieden, and Stein (2005). Specifically, the authors introduce a central bank loss function in which the optimal exchange rate decision depends on the size of the tradable-goods sector. As tradable-goods producers are in favor of a depreciated exchange rate, a rise in their political clout increases the bank's devaluation target and hence the likelihood of a decision to exit the currency peg. A similar two-sector approach underlies the model developed in Hefeker (1997).
104. Focusing on U.S. economic history, Eichengreen (1994a) follows up on earlier work done by Frieden (1991) and examines how distributional conflicts over exchange rate policy affected the 1896 presidential election. His findings from a logit model show that support for the candidate of the Democractic party, William Jennings Bryan, who supported reflationary policies and bimetallism rather than maintaining the prevailing gold standard, increased with employment in agriculture but fell with employment in manufacturing (the latter was seen as an import-substituting industry). For more evidence on the Latin American region, see Wise (2000), Frieden and Stein (2001), and Frieden, Ghezzi, and Stein (2001).
105. Neugart (2003) does not focus on fiscal policy, but examines the impact of interest groups on a government's willingness to engage in labor market reform.
106. Under purchasing power parity ($e = p - p^*$) and assuming that the log foreign price level p^* is zero, e is identical to the domestic price level p.
107. See Grossman and Helpman (2001) for a more detailed discussion of loss functions that incorporate the potential for lobbying.
108. While traditional models of monetary policy typically portray labor unions as being concerned only about real wages, several more recent

papers introduced a richer decision-making framework for unions. See, for example, Hefeker (2001) and Neugart (2003).

109. In other words, Ξ_f would need to be no less than the loss in the economic equilibrium L_f^* weighted by the lobbying-aversion λ.
110. See, for example, Sy (2003) for a discussion of the recent track record of rating agencies, including Moody's and Standard and Poor's, in predicting currency crises. For a recent discussion of the performance of EWS models used within the IMF, see Berg, Borensztein, and Patillo (2005).
111. For similar arguments, see Berg and Patillo (1999), Dumas (1995), Furman and Stiglitz (1998), Kaminsky (2003), and Berg, Borensztein, and Patillo (2005).
112. See Kaminsky, Lisandro, and Reinhart (1998), Hawkins and Klau (2000), Kumar, Moorthy, and Perraudin (2002), and Berg, Borensztein, and Patillo (2005) for good surveys on this strand of literature. See Section 4.3.2.5 for a short review of the key macroeconomic and financial indicators that were often found to be associated with a crisis.
113. Other strategies that have been implemented to improve model performance include broadening the data set both in terms of country and time coverage; and examining the linkage between currency crises, banking crises, and debt defaults (see Rose (2001)). Studies focusing on the more distant past include Simmons (1994), Flandreau, Le Cacheux, and Zumer (1998), and Bordo, Eichengreen, Klingebiel, and Soledad Martinez-Peria (2001). For a typology of crises and the linkages between crisis types, see, for example, Glick and Hutchison (1999), Kaminsky and Reinhart (1999), and Kaminsky (2003).
114. There are, of course, exceptions to this rule. For example, Blomberg and Hess (1997) use a VAR approach for the analysis of exchange rate dynamics for three major advanced countries over 1974–1994, Chang (2004) examines the movement of individual ERM currencies within their fluctuation band, and Willard, Guinnane, and Rosen (1996) examine to what extent the exchange rate between the greenback and gold reacted to major events in the U.S. Civil War. Moreover, in a closely related field, Sussman and Yafeh (2000) investigate the effect of the establishment of modern institutions on the risk premium associated with Japanese government bonds traded in London between 1870 and 1914.
115. In its most recent release (DPI 2008), the Database of Political Institutions contains annual data for 178 countries over the 1975–2006 period (see also Beck, Clarke, Groff, Keefer, and Walsh, 2001). It is available at http://econ.worldbank.org. The Polity IV database comprises annual information on regime and authority characteristics for all independent states in the global state system going back to 1800 (see http://www.systemicpeace.org/polity/polity4.htm).
116. See, for example, Eichengreen, Rose, and Wyplosz (1995); Frieden, Ghezzi, and Stein (2001); Leblang (2002); Ghezzi, Stein, and Streb (2005), and Blomberg, Frieden, and Stein (2005). See also Section 4.6.1.
117. In these studies, the probability of an executive turnover is related to the state of an index that reflects, among other factors, the incumbent's time

in office and the age of the chief executive, in addition to the timing of elections.

118. See Blomberg and Hess (1997); Block (2003); Leblang and Satyanath (2006), and Chiu and Willett (2006).
119. In a study on Latin American countries, Frieden, Ghezzi, and Stein (2001) find that a larger share of manufacturing in the economy leads to the choice of more flexible, procompetitiveness regimes. But the authors are unable to find significant evidence as to the preferences of the mining sector and agriculture. Leblang (2003b) does not find any statistical association between the size of a country's export sector and the probability of currency crises.
120. That said, there seems to be relatively robust evidence on the effect of one particular veto player: the central bank. For example, using the turnover rate of central bank governors as an empirical proxy for the institution's independence from politics, Shortland (2004) shows that more independence is negatively associated with devaluations for a large sample of developing countries; Chang (2004) and Perez-Bermejo and Sosvilla-Rivero (2004) find a similar effect for the case of European countries.
121. The two studies differ in their choice of democracy indicator. Leblang and Satyanath (2006) rely on a dummy variable to capture the presence or absence of a government actually relinquishing office following an election, whereas Block (2003) uses the democracy indicator from the Polity IV database (see Section 4.3.2).
122. Eichengreen and Leblang (2003) suggest that such considerations were relevant for policy makers in the interwar period. Specifically, the study finds a positive correlation between a country's coefficient on the electorate-to-population ratio (reflecting the degree of political integration of the labor movement) and the likelihood of remaining on the gold standard for many advanced countries.
123. Moreover, for the interwar years, Wandschneider (2008) finds that a one percent increase in left-leaning parliamentary representation increases the probability of a country to suspend gold convertibility by 0.05 percent.
124. The underlying models are taken from Frankel and Rose (1996), Kamin, Schindler, and Samuel (2001), and Bussiere and Fratzscher (2002).
125. Block (2003) does not include a forecasting exercise, but bases his claim of superior performance on the improvement in the *Pseudo* – R^2, which, in the best case, increases to 0.40 compared with 0.28 in the control model that relies exclusively on macroeconomic fundamentals. However, the *Pseudo* – R^2 is not a well-suited measure to assess how the estimated crisis probabilities fit the underlying data, given that it merely compares a restricted version of a particular model to an unrestricted version. In addition, it does not punish for the increased model complexity associated with a higher number of regressors.
126. Bussière and Mulder (2000) support this view in arguing that the failure of studies such as Eichengreen, Rose, and Wyplosz (1995) and Haque,

Mark, and Mathieson (1998) to find a strong role for political factors in their crisis accounts may be grounded in the choice of a sample that includes only a limited number of democratically elected governments. A similar problem is identified in Eichengreen and Leblang (2003), who show that the negative correlation between proportional electoral systems and exchange rate stability for the interwar years gives way to a positive association after 1971.

127. Chiu and Willett (2006) implement such an approach by interacting their veto player variable with the type of exchange rate regime. See also Section 4.6.2, focusing in detail on the link between left-wing governments and currency crises.
128. The variable list includes government instability, unified and divided government, the electoral cycle, partisanship, and veto players.
129. See, for example, Edison, Klein, Ricci, and Slok (2004) and Klein (2003) for a similar approach in studies aimed at investigating the link between capital account liberalization and growth for a large panel of countries.
130. Examples of studies using lagged independent variables include Bussière and Mulder (2000), Block (2003), Leblang and Satyanath (2006), and Chiu and Willett (2006), while Leblang (2003a) and Leblang and Satyanath (2006) control for serial correlation.
131. For a list of countries, see Table C.1. The classification of countries into the three income categories follows Glick and Hutchison (1999). Note that due to data constraints, not all of the countries are included in the sample for the full period. Specifically, the Eastern European Transition countries are included only after 1989 (Poland, Hungary) or 1991 (Romania), and missing exchange rate and reserves data have led to the exclusion of Belize for 1975, Brazil over 1976–81, and Botswana for 1976.
132. This approach was pioneered by Girton and Roper (1977) and reached popularity through the work of Eichengreen, Rose, and Wyplosz (1995).
133. The calculations draw on data from the IMF's International Financial Statistics (lines 1.*L*, *af*, and 63 or 64) and use the Deutsche Mark (for European countries) or the U.S. dollar as reference currencies. For periods of hyperinflation, which are defined as episodes in which the consumer price index increases by a minimum of 150 percent over the previous six months, the crisis thresholds are calculated separately based on the hyperinflation means. These episodes include Nicaragua for 03/86-05/92; Peru for 10/88-1/92; Poland for 1/90-2/91; Argentina for 3/76-4/77, 9/83-4/86, and 9/88-7/91; Bolivia for 3/84-11/86; and Brazil for 1/88-6/95.
134. For this conservative assumption, I follow Glick and Hutchison (1999). Other studies including Eichengreen, Rose, and Wyplosz (1995); Kaminsky, Lisandro, and Reinhart (1998); Kaminsky and Reinhart (1999); and Leblang and Satyanath (2006) use an exclusion window of only six months.
135. See Frankel and Rose (1996) and Kumar, Moorthy, and Perraudin (2002) for approaches that rely on large nominal exchange rate devaluations to identify crisis episodes. Some studies that focus on advanced countries

also include in the pressure index a measure of policy interest rates to accommodate situations in which the central bank stages an interest rate defense of the peg. However, this approach is precluded in the case of broad country samples due to data limitations.

136. Given that we are only interested in events in one tail of the normal distribution, a two-standard deviation measure would imply that crises would only be called if the index exceeds 97.73 percent of the assumed normal distribution, whereas the three-standard deviation index would be called in case the pressure index exceeds 99.9 percent of the theoretical distribution. Studies typically use numerical values for Ω ranging between 1.5 and 3.

137. Edison (2000) reports similar findings in a survey of various EWS models.

138. The POLITY indicator differs from the democracy indicator in the Polity IV database in that it subtracts the subindicator of a country's authoritarian state characteristics from its score on the democracy dimension. The results reported below are not sensitive to this manipulation.

139. Following standard practice, openness is defined as the joint share of exports and imports in GDP.

140. For a presidential system, the key decision makers comprise the president, the largest party in the legislature, and the largest party in the Senate (second chamber). For a parliamentary system, the prime minister and the parties in the government coalition are identified as the relevant veto players.

141. The veto player approach could offer an alternative interpretation for the effect of this variable: the longer a party stays in power and consolidates its base within the bureaucracy, the more likely it is to limit the scope for independent decision-making by the chief executive.

142. GOVCOH and OPPCOH are based on the DPI's Herfgov and Herfopp indicators, which are defined as Herfindahl indices to measure the political concentration of both the ruling coalition and the opposition based on the seat distribution in parliament. Specifically, the indices are calculated as $GOVCOH(OPPCOH) = \sum_{i=1}^{N} p_i^2 = \left(\left(\sum_{i=1}^{N} a_i^2\right) / \left(\sum_{i=1}^{N} a_i\right)^2\right)$, with a_i being the number of seats of party p_i that is a coalition (opposition) member. The more the index converges toward its maximum value of 1, the more concentrated is the political power: for example, a value of 1 would indicate a one-party government or opposition.

143. The indicator is based on the DPI's Checks3 variable, whose use has been pioneered in Keefer and Stasavage (2003). Its value increases with the number of veto players that are capable of blocking the executive's decisions. For presidential systems, the indicator captures (i) whether the opposition controls the legislature; (ii) whether the polity has one or more legislative chambers; and (iii) whether the ideological position of the biggest party in government is closer to the largest opposition party than to the other members of the executive on economic issues. In parliamentary systems, the value of this variable is increased when (i) a legislature is controlled by the opposition; (ii) several parties form a

coalition government; and (iii) any of the governing parties are closer to the largest opposition party than to the executive on economic issues.

144. In their study on debt crises, Van Rijckeghem and Weder (2004) interpret polarization as a measure for government cohesion.
145. Shortland (2004) argues that this indicator may not be particularly informative, as de jure independence does not necessarily imply actual independence. As an alternative, she proposes a measure for actual independence based on the average turnover of central bank governors in a given period.
146. In this context, Kaminsky (2003) argues against the prevailing 'one-size-fits-all' approach that is typically followed in the empirical literature, emphasizing the need to distinguish among six different types of currency crises.
147. See, for example, Berg and Patillo (1999); Glick and Hutchison (1999); Kaminsky and Reinhart (1999); Edison (2000); Hawkins and Klau (2000); Bussiere and Fratzscher (2002); Frankel and Wei (2004), and Berg, Borensztein, and Patillo (2005).
148. An indicator relating reserves to maturing short-term debt would also be a promising indicator, particularly in cases where deposit dollarization is less prevalent or capital control restrictions remain significant. However, data on short-term debt is not readily available for many countries.
149. Dornbusch, Goldfajn, and Valdés (1995) emphasize this risk factor, arguing that overvalued real exchange rates tend to emerge in the presence of fixed exchange rate regimes as residual inflation differentials vis-à-vis the anchor country cannot be neutralized by nominal depreciation, and thus lead to competitiveness losses. Large capital inflows attracted by structural reforms and a liberalization of the domestic financial sector could further reinforce these pressures. For an excellent and timely case study on Mexico, see Dornbusch and Werner (1994).
150. For European countries, I focus on the three-month policy rate of the German Bundesbank. For all others, the analysis uses the rate for three-month U.S. treasury bills.
151. The twin-crisis literature examines the empirical link between banking crises and currency crises. Often, banking crises are found to lead currency crises (see, for example, Glick and Hutchison, 1999; Kaminsky and Reinhart, 1999).
152. For the binary dependent currency crisis variable CRS, the predicted logit, or log odds, L, can be calculated as

$$L = \ln\left(\frac{P(\text{CRS}=1)}{1-P(\text{CRS}=1)}\right) = \alpha + \sum_{i=1}^{n} \beta_i * x_i,$$

where each coefficient β_i describes the effect of the independent variable x_i on the logit of a currency crisis. As the predicted logit is difficult to interpret, the model can be transformed into an odds ratio model

$$\frac{P(\text{CRS}=1)}{1-P(\text{CRS}=1)} = e^{\alpha *} \prod_{i=1}^{i=n} e^{(b_i * x_i)},$$

in which the coefficient β_i represents the amounts by which the odds favoring CRS = 1 over CRS = 0 are multiplied with each one-unit increase in the independent variable x_i.

To obtain crisis probabilities rather than odd ratios, the logit obtained from the first estimation can be transformed to read

$$P(\text{CRS} = 1) = \frac{1}{1 + e^{-L}}.$$

153. A random-effects model could be an alternative to the fixed effects model without facing the same set of restrictions. However, it assumes that the country-specific component in the error term is random and thus not correlated with the independent variables specified in the model. This may be a reasonable assumption if a small number of units were drawn randomly from a large population, and the inference pertained to the population from which this sample was drawn (household surveys would be an obvious example). But such an approach is typically not appropriate for cross-country analysis where the data covers the entire population. For a more detailed discussion of these issues, see Baltagi (2001).
154. As the sample starts with the year 1975, the analysis could potentially face a problem because the data are left-censored—crisis events prior to that year would not be considered in the estimated probabilities. However, this issue should not cause severe problems, as 1975 roughly marks the beginning of the post-Bretton Woods regime, and hence represents a structural break in the international monetary system.
155. The differentiation between fully developed democracies and other political regimes can make a significant difference for results. For example, the link between strong crises and election periods is found to be highly significant for the case of the former, but loses statistical power when the threshold is lowered to LIEC = 5. This result is consistent with the interpretation that, in order to be a meaningful constraint on policy makers' behavior, elections would need to be competitive.
156. In particular, many Latin American countries were not fully developed democracies in the 1970s and 1980s, but were under military rule. By contrast, some countries, including Bangladesh, Egypt, Grenada, Jamaica, Mexico, Pakistan, the Philippines, Thailand, and Zimbabwe, experienced cycling between full democracy status and less competitive forms of political representation throughout the sample period.
157. This may be a particularly serious shortcoming in the case of political variables, as they often show high degrees of pair-wise correlations. In our data set, these statistical linkages are strongest among the various measures of institutional constraints, with a correlation coefficient of 0.65 between VETO and POLARIZ and of −0.59 between VETO and GOVCOH.
158. See, for example, Kamin, Schindler, and Samuel (2001) and Nsouli, Atoyan, and Mourmouras (2004) for other examples of implementing

such an approach. By contrast, Haque, Mark, and Mathieson (1998) follow a reversed process in their model selection strategy, adding, at each step, the regressor with the highest significance to move from a very narrow specification to a more encompassing one.

159. The time-invariant indicator of central bank independence, however, was dropped from the estimations, as it is not compatible with the fixed-effects estimator.
160. As the significance disappears when the EMC and OCED dummies are used, the link between POLARIZ and crises may be caused by the distribution of crisis cases along the countries' income position, given that the statistical mean of this indicator is very sensitive to a country's income level (see Table 4.4), even if the regressions seek to control for this effect through the use of the per capita terms.
161. The per capita terms are significant in all fixed-effects specifications for the strong crisis indicator and, in all models, show the expected signs (given the clustering of strong crises in middle-income countries, the sign is positive for the squared term, and negative for the others). A likelihood-ratio test based on the two reduced models rejects the null hypotheses that the time dummies would have no effect on the likelihood of crises at the five percent level.
162. This test departs from the null hypothesis that the additional variables in the political-economy model are jointly insignificant at the 99 or 95 percent level, with the likelihood ratio statistic being computed as $LR = -2\log(LO/L1) = 2(\log L0 - \log L1)$, where $L1$ is the value of the likelihood function for the political-economy model and $L0$ is the maximum value of the likelihood function if all of the additional coefficients in the augmented model relative to that of the economic benchmark specification were zero (see Aldrich and Nelson, 1984).
163. The Akaike Information Criteria can be computed as $AIC = -2 * LL_{UR} + 2k$, with LL_{UR} being the log likelihood of the unrestricted model and k being the number of independent variables. It decreases with the log likelihood of the model, but at the same time punishes each log likelihood for model complexity to reflect the number of parameters being estimated (see, for example, Perez-Bermejo and Sosvilla-Rivero, 2004).
164. See Footnote 152 for a description of how the logit model can be transformed to calculate crisis probabilities.
165. The probability of a currency crisis increases by 0.64 percent through a one-standard deviation increase in the M2-to-reserves ratio and decreases by 0.98 percent through an improvement in the real exchange rate of the same magnitude.
166. A one-standard deviation increase in the M2-to-reserves ratio raises the probability of a crisis by 2.6 percent, while a similar change in the real exchange rate decreases crisis risk by 4.8 percent.
167. This is different from ordinary least square regressions, in which the r^2 reports the share of the total variance in the data explained by a model's estimates.

168. Figure C.1 shows the tradeoff between model sensitivity and specificity for the case of the strong crisis indicator.
169. This is an observation that is often made in the EWS literature; see, for example, Berg and Patillo (1999), Berg, Borensztein, and Patillo (2005), and, for the case of a political-economy model, Leblang and Satyanath (2006).
170. For example, when repeating the forecasting exercise with an arbitrarily chosen threshold of 50 percent, the various models reduce the number of false alarms to a maximum of four cases, but at the same time fail to identify more than six (in the best case) of the true crisis cases.
171. By contrast, resticting the data set to countries with full democracies (LIEC = 7) does not alter the findings in a qualitative way. Moreover, missing data do not affect the results for the reduced strong crisis model, but cause both YEARS and LEFTGOV to lose explanatory power in the weak crisis specification (see Table C.5).
172. The results are shown for the reduced models that include fixed effects, time dummies, and the per capita income controls.
173. The estimations were implemented on pooled data, but control for temporal dependence; other developing countries were dropped from the data sample. See Fontaine (2005) for a similar methodological approach.
174. Using a similar methodology, Frieden, Ghezzi, and Stein (2001) find that the rate of nominal exchange rate depreciation is two percentage points higher than normal, on average, in the second to fourth month following an election in 26 Latin American countries, with the largest effect observable in the second post-election month. Their findings are broadly supported by evidence presented in a number of follow-up papers on the Latin American region (see Cermeno, Grier, and Grier, 2005; Ghezzi, Stein, and Streb, 2005; Stein and Streb, 2004).
175. Block (2003) finds that strong governments (those with larger legislative majorities and those which face more fragmented legislative opposition) are less vulnerable to crises, whereas Frieden, Ghezzi, and Stein (2001) produce evidence that Latin American countries are more likely to adopt fixed exchange rates when an administration enjoys solid support in the legislature or faces fragmented opposition.
176. Interestingly, in the Turkish case, the strongest opposition to fiscal adjustment and structural reforms came from the extreme right of the political spectrum rather than the left, as it sought to protect its strong agricultural constituency.
177. The model that serves as a common basis for the discussion in this chapter is borrowed from Obstfeld (1994), but features a slightly modified production function for the economy as described in Appendix Appendix A.
178. The election model is based on methodology developed by Meon and Rizzo (2002).
179. This analysis draws on the literature on fiscal and monetary policy coordination, and in particular on a model developed in Alesina and

Tabellini (1987). This said, the methodology has not yet been used to analyze the stability of currency pegs.

180. The veto player model also offers two other interesting results that have, however, little to do with the political dimension of currency crises. By incorporating a stochastic shock to the fiscal authority's spending target, the model provides a simple way of introducing a key dimension of third-generation crisis models into a second-generation framework: the harmful effect on exchange rate stability of realizing contingent liabilities on the government's balance sheet. The model also confirms the finding from many second-generation models that there is scope for multiple equilibria and thus self-fulfilling currency crises.
181. The model is inspired by Neugart (2003), who, however, focuses on labor market reform rather than tax policy.
182. These problems, which are compounded in the case of out-of-sample forecasting, are well known among researchers specializing in the EWS literature (see Berg, Borensztein, and Patillo, 2005).
183. Great care was taken in the study to examine the impact of methodological changes in the determination of crisis episodes that served as dependent variables in the regressions (see Section 4.3.1). In particular, based on a pressure index developed by Girton and Roper (1977), the study distinguished between weak crises and strong crises, which differ regarding the extent to which pressure on the foreign exchange markets needs to build before the index calls a crisis.
184. See Alesina, Ardagna, and Trebbi (2006) for a recent survey of this literature.
185. As emerging market countries are particularly vulnerable to currency crises, more research could focus on the political dynamics within this particular country grouping.
186. This claim is supported by the evidence presented in Alesina and Wagner (2006), finding that countries with poor institutional quality find it particularly difficult to maintain fixed exchange rate regimes.
187. For example, while observers have pointed to the difficulties of the Argentine and Turkish political systems to sustain the required adjustment *after* the collapse occurred, such analysis remained largely absent prior to the event. See, for example, 'Turkey's Real Crisis,' *The Economist*, 16 May 2001; Allan Meltzer, 'New Loan Will Not Solve Argentine Crisis,' *The Financial Times*, 12 January 2003.
188. Specifically, the authors use the frequency of legislative elections, and the turnover of the chief executive—both in each year and as a variable averaged over the sample period to measure structural uncertainty.
189. Based on time spent in office, leader age, regime type, and election timing. The multinomial set-up is chosen to account for the possibility of both constitutional and unconstitutional leadership changes.

Bibliography

AGÉNOR, P.-R., J. S. BHANDARI, AND R. P. FLOOD (1992): "Speculative Attacks and Models of Balance-of-Payments Crises," *IMF Staff Papers*, 39(2), 357–394.

ALDRICH, J. H., AND F. D. NELSON (1984): *Linear Probability, Logit, and Probit Models*, Sage University Paper 45. Sage Publications, Newbury Park, C.A.

ALESINA, A., S. ARDAGNA, AND F. TREBBI (2006): "Who Adjusts and When? The Political Economy of Reforms," *IMF Staff Papers*, 53(Special Issue), 1–29.

ALESINA, A., R. PEROTTI, AND J. TAVARES (1998): "The Political Economy of Fiscal Adjustments," *Brookings Papers on Economic Activity*, 29(1), 197–248.

ALESINA, A., AND G. TABELLINI (1987): "Rules and Discretion with Uncoordinated Monetary and Fiscal Policies," *Economic Inquiry*, 25(4), 619–630.

ALESINA, A., AND A. WAGNER (2006): "Choosing (and Reneging on) Exchange Rate Regimes," *Journal of the European Economic Association*, 4(4), 770–799.

ALPER, C. E. (2001): "The Turkish Liquidity Crisis of 2000: What Went Wrong...," *Russian and East European Finance and Trade*, 37(6), 51–71.

ALPER, C. E., AND Z. ONIS (2002a): *Emerging Market Crises and the IMF: Rethinking the Role of the IMF in the Light of Turkey's 2000–01 Financial Crisis*, Department of Economics Working Paper 02–03. Bogaziçi University, Istanbul.

—— (2002b): *Soft Budget Constraints, Government Ownership of Banks and Regulatory Failure: The Political Economy of the Turkish Banking System in the Post-Capital Account Liberalization Era*, Department of Economics Working Paper 02–02. Bogaziçi University, Istanbul.

ALVAREZ-PLATA, P., AND M. SCHROOTEN (2003): *The Argentinean Currency Crisis: A Markov-Switching Model Estimation*, Discussion Paper 348. German Institute for Economic Research, Berlin.

ANDERSEN, T. (1998): "Shocks and the Viability of a Fixed Exchange Rate Commitment," *Open Economies Review*, 9(2), 139–156.

BALTAGI, B. H. (2001): *Econometric Analysis of Panel Data*. John Wiley and Sons, Chichester, 2nd edn.

BANK FOR INTERNATIONAL SETTLEMENTS (2003): *Fiscal Issues and Central Banking in Emerging Economies*, BIS Papers No. 20. Bank for International Settlements, Basel.

BARRO, R. J., AND D. B. GORDON (1983): "Rules, Discretion and Reputation in a Model of Monetary Policy," *Journal of Monetary Economics*, 12(1), 101–121.

BAYOUMI, T., AND B. EICHENGREEN (1995): *The Stability of the Gold Standard and the Evolution of the International Monetary System*, CEPR Discussion Paper 1248. Centre for Economic Policy Research, London.

BECK, N., J. N. KATZ, AND R. TUCKER (1998): "Taking Time Seriously: Time-Series-Cross-Section Analysis with a Binary Dependent Variable," *American Journal of Political Science*, 42(4), 1260–1288.

BECK, T., G. CLARKE, A. GROFF, P. KEEFER, AND P. WALSH (2001): "New Tools in Comparative Political Economy: The Database of Political Institutions," *World Bank Economic Review*, 15(1), 165–176.

BEETSMA, R. M., AND A. L. BOVENBERG (1998): "Monetary Union without Fiscal Coordination may Discipline Policymakers," *Journal of International Economics*, 45(2), 239–258.

BERG, A., E. BORENSZTEIN, AND C. PATILLO (2005): "Assessing Early Warning Systems: How Have They Worked in Practice?," *IMF Staff Papers*, 52(3), 462–502.

BERG, A., AND C. PATILLO (1999): "Are Currency Crises Predictable? A Test," *IMF Staff Papers*, 46(2), 107–138.

BERGER, H., H. JENSEN, AND G. SCHJELDERUP (2001): *To Peg or Not to Peg? A Simple Model of Exchange Rate Regime Choice in Small Economies*, CESifo Working Paper 468. CESifo, Munich.

BERNHARD, W., AND D. LEBLANG (1999): "Democratic Institutions and Exchange-Rate Commitments," *International Organization*, 53(1), 71–97.

—— (2000): "The Politics of Speculative Attacks in Industrial Democracies," *International Organization*, 54(2), 291–324.

—— (2002): "Political Parties and Monetary Commitments," *International Organization*, 56(4), 803–831.

BLACKBURN, K., AND M. CHRISTENSEN (1989): "Monetary Policy and Policy Credibility: Theory and Evidence," *Journal of Economic Literature*, 27(1), 1–45.

BLAUG, M. (1985): *Economic Theory in Retrospect*. Cambridge University Press, Cambridge and New York, 4 edn.

—— (1992): *The Methodology of Economics. Or How Economists Explain*. Cambridge University Press, Cambridge, 2 edn.

BLOCK, S. A. (2003): "Political Conditions and Currency Crises in Emerging Markets," *Emerging Markets Review*, 3(4), 287–309.

BLOMBERG, S. B., J. A. FRIEDEN, AND E. STEIN (2005): "Sustaining Fixed Rates: The Political Economy of Currency Pegs in Latin America," *Journal of Applied Economics*, 8(2), 203–225.

BLOMBERG, S. B., AND G. D. HESS (1997): "Politics and Exchange Rate Forecasts," *Journal of International Economics*, 43(1–2), 189–205.

BORDO, M. D., B. EICHENGREEN, D. KLINGEBIEL, AND M. SOLEDAD MARTINEZ-PERIA (2001): "Financial Crises. Lessons From the Last 120 Years," *Economic Policy*, 16(32), 51–82.

BREMMER, I. (2006): *The J Curve. A New Way to Understand Why Nations Rise and Fall*. Simon & Schuster, New York.

BROZ, J. L., AND J. A. FRIEDEN (2006): "The Political Economy of Exchange Rates," in *The Oxford Handbook of Political Economy*, ed. by B. R. Weingast, and D. Wittman, pp. 587–597. Oxford University Press, Oxford and New York.

BROZ, L. (2000): "The Domestic Politics of International Monetary Order: The Gold Standard," in *International Political Economy. Perspectives on Global Power and Wealth*, ed. by J. A. Frieden, and D. A. Lake, pp. 199–219. Routledge, London and New York.

BUSSIERE, M., AND M. FRATZSCHER (2002): *Towards a New Early Warning System of Financial Crises*, ECB Working Paper 145. European Central Bank, Frankfurt.

BUSSIÈRE, M., AND C. MULDER (2000): "Political Instability and Economic Vulnerability," *International Journal of Finance and Economics*, 5(4), 309–330.

CALVO, E., AND E. L. GIBSON (2000): "Federalism and Low-Maintenance Constituencies: Territorial Dimensions of Economic Reform in Argentina," *Studies in Comparative International Development*, 35(3), 32–55.

CALVO, G. A., AND C. M. REINHART (2002): "Fear of Floating," *Quarterly Journal of Economics*, 107(2), 379–408.

CALVO, G. A., AND C. A. VÉGH (1999): *Inflation Stabilization and BOP Crises in Developing Countries*, NBER Working Paper 6925. National Bureau of Economic Research, Cambridge, M.A.

CATENARO, M., AND P. TIRELLI (2000): *Reconsidering the Pros and Cons of Fiscal Policy Co-ordination in a Monetary Union: Should We Set Public Expenditure Targets?*, Working Paper 30. University of Milano-Bicocca, Milan.

CERMENO, R., R. GRIER, AND K. GRIER (2005): *Elections, Exchange Rates and Central Bank Reform in Latin America*, Working Paper. Department of Economics, University of Oklahoma, Norman, O.K.

CHANG, M. (2004): "Domestic Politics and Currency Crises: The European Experience," Unpublished, Colgate University, Hamilton, N.Y.

CHANG, R., AND A. VELASCO (1999): "Liquidity Crises in Emerging Markets: Theory and Policy," *NBER Macroeconomics Annual 1999*, 14(1), 11–58.

CHIU, E. M. P., AND T. D. WILLETT (2006): "The Interactions of Strength of Governments and Alternative Exchange Rate Regimes in Avoiding Currency Crises," Prepared for the Annual Meeting of the International Political Economy Society, Princeton University, November 2006.

COLE, H. L., AND T. J. KEHOE (1996): "A Self-Fulfilling Model of Mexico's 1994–1995 Debt Crisis," *Journal of International Economics*, 41(3–4), 309–330.

COOPER, R. N. (1971): *Currency Devaluations in Developing Countries*, Princeton Essays in International Finance 86. International Finance Section, Department of Economics, Princeton University, Princeton, N.J.

CORRALES, J. (2002): "The Politics of Argentina's Meltdown," *World Policy Journal*, 19(3), 29–42.

CORSETTI, G. (1998): "Interpreting the Asian Financial Crisis: Open Issues in Theory and Policy," *Asian Development Review*, 16(2), 1–45.

CORSETTI, G., P. PESENTI, AND N. ROUBINI (1998): *Paper Tigers? A Model of the Asian Crisis*, NBER Working Paper 6783. National Bureau of Economic Research, Cambridge, M.A.

CUKIERMAN, A. (1992): *Central Bank Strategy, Credibility, and Independence: Theory and Evidence*. MIT Press, Cambridge, M.A.

DASEKING, C., A. GHOSH, T. LANE, AND A. THOMAS (2004): *Lessons From the Crisis in Argentina*, Occasional Paper 236. International Monetary Fund, Washington, D.C.

DE GRAUWE, P. (1994): *The Economics of Monetary Integration*. Oxford University Press, Oxford and New York, 2 edn.

DIAMOND, D. W., AND R. G. RAJAN (2000): *Banks, Short Term Debt And Financial Crises: Theory, Policy Implications, and Applications*, NBER Working Paper 7764. National Bureau of Economic Research, Cambridge, M.A.

DOOLEY, M. P. (2000): "A Model of Crises in Emerging Markets," *Economic Journal*, 110(460), 256–272.

DOOLEY, M. P., D. FOLKERTS-LANDAU, AND P. GARBER (2003): *An Essay on the Revised Bretton Woods System*, NBER Working Paper 9971. National Bureau of Economic Research, Cambridge, M.A.

DOOLEY, M. P., AND I. SHIN (2000): *Private Inflows when Crises are Anticipated: a Case Study of Korea*, NBER Working Paper 6380. National Bureau of Economic Research, Cambridge, M.A.

DORNBUSCH, R. (2001): *A Primer on Emerging Market Crises*, NBER Working Paper 8326. National Bureau of Economic Research, Cambridge, M.A.

DORNBUSCH, R., I. GOLDFAJN, AND R. O. VALDÉS (1995): "Currency Crises and Collapses," *Brookings Papers on Economic Activity*, 26(1), 219–293.

DORNBUSCH, R., AND A. WERNER (1994): "Mexico: Stabilization, Reform, and No Growth," *Brookings Papers on Economic Activity*, 25(1), 253–315.

DRAZEN, A. (2000a): "The Political Business Cycle after 25 Years," *NBER Macroeconomics Annual 2000*, 15(1), 75–117.

—— (2000b): "Political Contagion in Currency Crises," in *Currency Crises*, ed. by P. R. Krugman, pp. 47–67. NBER and University of Chicago Press, Chicago, I.L.

—— (2000c): *Political Economy in Macroeconomics*. Princeton University Press, Princeton, N.J.

DUMAS, B. (1995): "Discussion," *Economic Policy*, 10(21), 297–300.

EDISON, H. J. (2000): *Do Indicators of Financial Crises work? An Evaluation of Early Warning Systems*, International Finance Discussion Paper 675. Board of Governors of the Federal Reserve System, Washington, D.C.

EDISON, H. J., M. W. KLEIN, L. A. RICCI, AND T. SLOK (2004): "Capital Account Liberalization and Economic Performance: Survey and Synthesis," *IMF Staff Papers*, 51(2), 220–256.

EDWARDS, S. (1993): *Exchange Rates as Nominal Anchors*, NBER Working Paper 4246. National Bureau of Economic Research, Cambridge, M.A.

EDWARDS, S., AND J. A. SANTAELLA (1993): "Devaluation Controversies in the Developing Countries: Lessons from the Bretton Woods Era," in *A Retrospective on Bretton Woods*, ed. by M. D. Bordo, and B. Eichengreen, pp. 405–455. University of Chicago Press, Chicago, I.L.

EICHENGREEN, B. (1985): "International Policy Coordination in Historical Perspective: A View From the Interwar Years," in *International Economic Policy Coordination*, ed. by W. H. Buiter, and R. C. Marston, pp. 139–178. Cambridge University Press, Cambridge.

—— (1992): *Golden Fetters. The Gold Standard and the Great Depression, 1919–1939*. Oxford University Press, Oxford and New York.

—— (1994a): "The Endogeneity of Exchange-Rate Regimes," in *Managing the World Economy*, ed. by P. B. Kenen, pp. 3–33. Institute for International Economics, Washington D.C.

—— (1994b): *International Monetary Arrangements for the 21st Century*. The Brookings Institution, Washington, D.C.

—— (1996): *Globalizing Capital. A History of the International Monetary System*. Princeton University Press, Princetown, N.J.

—— (1998): "Dental Hygiene and Nuclear War: How International Relations Looks from Economics," *International Organization*, 52(4), 993–1012.

—— (2001): "Crisis Prevention and Management: Any New Lessons from Argentina and Turkey?," Unpublished, www.econ.berkeley.edu/~eichengr/policy.html (accessed 10 March 2006).

—— (2003): "Three Generations of Crises, Three Generations of Crisis Models," *Journal of International Money and Finance*, 22(7), 1089–1094.

—— (2004): "Viewpoint: Understanding the Great Depression," *Canadian Journal of Economics*, 37(1), 1–27.

EICHENGREEN, B., AND O. JEANNE (2000): "Currency Crisis and Employment: Sterling in 1931," in *Currency Crises*, ed. by P. R. Krugman, pp. 7–43. NBER and University of Chicago Press, Chicago, I.L.

EICHENGREEN, B., AND D. LEBLANG (2003): "Exchange Rates and Cohesion: Historical Perspectives and Political-Economy Considerations," *Journal of Common Market Studies*, 41(5), 797–822.

EICHENGREEN, B., A. K. ROSE, AND C. WYPLOSZ (1995): "Exchange Market Mayhem: The Antecedents and Aftermath of Speculative Attacks," *Economic Policy*, 10(21), 251–312.

EICHENGREEN, B., AND P. TEMIN (1997): *The Gold Standard and the Great Depression*, NBER Working Paper 6060. National Bureau of Economic Research, Cambridge, M.A.

EICHENGREEN, B., AND C. WYPLOSZ (1993): "The Unstable EMS," *Brookings Papers on Economic Activity*, 24(1), 51–143.

FISCHER, S. (2001): "Exchange Rate Regimes: Is the Bipolar View Correct?," *Journal of Economic Perspectives*, 15(2), 3–24.

FLANDREAU, M., J. LE CACHEUX, AND F. ZUMER (1998): "Stability Without A Pact? Lessons From the European Gold Standard, 1880–1914," *Economic Policy*, 13(26), 115–162.

FLOOD, R. P., AND P. M. GARBER (1984): "Collapsing Exchange-Rate Regimes. Some Linear Examples," *Journal of International Economics*, 17(1–2), 1–13.

FLOOD, R. P., AND N. P. MARION (1996): *Policy Implications of "Second-Generation" Crisis Models*, Working Paper 97/16. International Monetary Fund, Washington, D.C.

FONTAINE, T. (2005): *Currency Crises in Developed and Emerging Market Economies: A Comparative Empirical Treatment*, Working Paper 05/13. International Monetary Fund, Washington, D.C.

FRANKEL, J. A. (2005): "Mundell-Fleming Lecture: Contractionary Currency Crashes in Developing Countries," *IMF Staff Papers*, 52(2), 149–192.

FRANKEL, J. A., AND A. K. ROSE (1996): *Currency Crashes in Emerging Markets: Empirical Indicators*, NBER Working Paper 5437. National Bureau of Economic Research, Cambridge, M.A.

FRANKEL, J. A., AND S.-J. WEI (2004): *Managing Macroeconomic Crises*, NBER Working Paper 10907. National Bureau of Economic Research, Cambridge, M.A.

FRIEDEN, J. A. (1991): *Greenbacks, Gold and Silver: The Politics of American Exchange Rate Policy, 1870–1973*, CIBER Working Paper 91-04. University of California, Los Angeles, Anderson School of Management, Los Angeles, C.A.

—— (1996): "Economic Integration and the Politics of Monetary Policy in the United States," in *Internationalization and Domestic Politics*, ed. by R. O. Keohane, and H. V. Milner, pp. 108–136. Cambridge University Press, Cambridge and New York.

—— (1997): "The Politics of Exchange Rates," in *Mexico 1994. Anatomy of an Emerging-Market Crash*, ed. by S. Edwards, and M. Naim, pp. 81–124. Carnegie Endowment for International Peace, Washington, D.C.

—— (2002): "Real Sources of European Currency Policy: Sectoral Interests and European Monetary Integration," *International Organization*, 56(4), 831–860.

FRIEDEN, J. A., P. GHEZZI, AND E. STEIN (2001): "Politics and Exchange Rates: A Cross-Country Approach to Latin America," in *The Currency Game. Exchange Rate Politics in Latin America*, ed. by J. A. Frieden, and E. Stein, pp. 21–63. Johns Hopkins University Press, Washington, D.C.

FRIEDEN, J. A., AND E. STEIN (2001): "The Political Economy of Exchange Rate Policy in Latin America: An Analytical Overview," in *The Currency Game. Exchange Rate Politics in Latin America*, ed. by J. A. Frieden, and E. Stein, pp. 1–19. Johns Hopkins University Press, Washington, D.C.

FURMAN, J., AND J. STIGLITZ (1998): "Economic Crises: Evidence and Insights from East Asia," *Brookings Papers on Economic Activity*, 29(2), 1–119.

GAERTNER, M. (2000): "Political Macroeconomics: A Survey of Recent Developments," *Journal of Economic Surveys*, 14(5), 527–561.

GALLAROTTI, G. M. (1995): *The Anatomy of an International Monetary Regime. The Classical Gold Standard, 1880–1914*. Oxford University Press, Oxford and New York.

GANGHOF, S. (2003): "Promises and Pitfalls of Veto Player Analysis," *Swiss Political Science Review*, 9(2), 1–25.

GARRETT, G. (1998): *Partisan Politics in the Global Economy*. Cambridge University Press, Cambridge.

GHEZZI, P., E. STEIN, AND J. STREB (2005): "Real Exchange Rate Cycles Around Elections," *Economics and Politics*, 17(3), 297–330.

GIAVAZZI, F., AND M. PAGANO (1988): "The Advantage of Tying One's Hands: EMS Discipline and Central Bank Credibility," *European Economic Review*, 32(5), 1055–1082.

GIAVAZZI, F., AND L. SPAVENTA (1990): *The "New" EMS*, CEPR Discussion Paper 369. Centre for Economic Policy Research, London.

GIBSON, E. (1997): "The Populist Road to Market Reform. Policy and Electoral Coalitions in Mexico and Argentina," *World Politics*, 49(3), 339–370.

GIRTON, L., AND D. ROPER (1977): "A Monetary Model of Exchange Market Pressure Applied to Postwar Canadian Experience," *American Economic Review*, 67(4), 537–548.

GLICK, R., AND M. HUTCHISON (1999): *Banking and Currency Crises: How Common are the Twins?*, Working Paper PB99-07. Federal Reserve Bank of San Francisco, San Francisco, C.A.

GOUREVITCH, P. A. (1996): "Squaring the Circle: The Domestic Sources of International Cooperation," *International Organization*, 50(2), 349–373.

GROSSMAN, G., AND E. HELPMAN (2001): *Special Interest Politics*. MIT Press, Cambridge, M.A. and London.

HAMANN, A. J. (2001): "Exchange-Rate-Based Stabilization: A Critical Look at the Stylized Facts," *IMF Staff Papers*, 48(1), 111–138.

HAQUE, N. U., N. MARK, AND D. J. MATHIESON (1998): *The Relative Importance of Political and Economic Variables in Creditworthiness Ratings*, Working Paper 98/46. International Monetary Fund, Washington, D.C.

HAWKINS, J., AND M. KLAU (2000): *Measuring Potential Vulnerabilities in Emerging Market Economies*, Working Paper 91. Bank for International Settlements, Basel.

HEFEKER, C. (1997): *Interest Groups and Monetary Integration. The Political Economy of Exchange Rate Choice*. Westview Press, Boulder, C.O.

—— (2001): "Labor Market Rigidities and EMU," *Journal of Economic Integration*, 16(2), 229–244.

HERNANDEZ, L., AND P. J. MONTIEL (2003): "Post-Crisis Exchange Rate Policy in Five Asian Countries: Filling in the Hollow Middle?," *Journal of the Japanese and International Economies*, 17(3), 336–369.

HIRSCHMAN, A. O. (1970): *Exit, Voice, and Loyalty. Responses to Decline in Firms, Organizations, and States*. Harvard University Press, Cambridge, M.A.

HOLTFRERICH, C.-L. (1988): "Relations Between Monetary Authorities and Governmental Institutions: The Case of Germany From the 19th Century to the Present," in *Central Banks' Independence in Historical Perspective*, ed. by G. Toniolo, pp. 105–159. Walter de Gruyter, Berlin and New York.

INTERNATIONAL MONETARY FUND (2001): *Turkey: Sixth and Seventh Reviews under the Stand-By Arrangement; Staff Supplement; and Press Release on the Executive Board Decision*, IMF Country Report No. 01/89. Washington, D.C.

—— (2002): *Turkey: 2002 Article IV Consultation and First Review under the Stand-By Arrangement—Staff Report, Staff Statement, Public Information Notice and News Brief on the Executive Board Decision*, IMF Country Report No. 02/137. Washington, D.C.

—— (2005): *Turkey: 2004 Article IV Consultation and Eighth Review under the Stand-By Arrangement and Request for Waiver of Nonobservance of Performance Criterion—Staff Reports, Staff Supplements, Public Information Notice and Press Release on the Executive Board Decision; and Statement by the Executive Director of Turkey*, IMF Country Report No. 05/163. Washington, D.C.

INTERNATIONAL MONETARY FUND, INDEPENDENT EVALUATION OFFICE (2004): *The IMF and Argentina, 1991–2001*, Evaluation Report. Washington, D.C.

KAMIN, S. M., J. SCHINDLER, AND S. SAMUEL (2001): *The Contribution of Domestic and External Factors to Emerging Market Devaluation Crises*, International Finance Discussion Paper 711. The Federal Reserve System, Washington, D.C.

KAMINSKY, G. L. (2003): *Varieties of Currency Crises*, NBER Working Paper 10193. National Bureau of Economic Research, Cambridge, M.A.

KAMINSKY, G. L., S. LISANDRO, AND C. M. REINHART (1998): "Leading Indicators of Currency Crises," *IMF Staff Papers*, 45(1), 1–48.

KAMINSKY, G. L., AND C. M. REINHART (1999): "The Twin Crises: The Causes of Banking and Balance-of-Payments Problems," *American Economic Review*, 89(3), 473–500.

KEEFER, P., AND D. STASAVAGE (2000): *Bureaucratic Delegation and Political Institutions: When are Independent Central Banks Irrelevant*, World Bank Policy Research Working Paper 2356. World Bank, Washington, D.C.

—— (2002): "Checks and Balances, Private Information, and the Credibility of Monetary Commitments," *International Organization*, 56(4), 751–774.

—— (2003): "The Limits of Delegation, Veto Players, Central Bank Independence, and the Credibility of Monetary Policy," *American Political Science Review*, 47(3), 389–403.

KENWOOD, A. G., AND A. J. LOUGHEED (1992): *The Growth of the International Economy, 1820–1990*. Routledge, London and New York, 3 edn.

KEYNES, J. M. (1995): *The Economic Consequences of the Peace*. Penguin Books, New York.

KINDLEBERGER, C. P. (1973): *The World in Depression 1929–1939*. Allen Lane The Penguin Press, London.

—— (1989): *Maniacs, Panics, and Crashes. A History of Financial Crises*. MacMillan, Houndmills and London, 2 edn.

KIRSHNER, J. (2001): "The Political Economy of Low Inflation," *Journal of Economic Surveys*, 15(1), 41–70.

KLEIN, M., AND N. MARION (1997): "Explaining the Duration of Exchange Rate Pegs," *Journal of Development Economics*, 54(2), 387–404.

KLEIN, M. W. (2003): *Capital Account Openness and the Varieties of Growth Experience*, NBER Working Paper 9500. National Bureau of Economic Research, Cambridge, M.A.

KRUGMAN, P. R. (1979): "A Model of Balance-of-Payments Crises," *Journal of Money, Credit, and Banking*, 11(3), 311–325.

—— (1998): "What Happened to Asia," Unpublished, www.web.mit.edu \ Krugman (accessed 16 June 2008).

—— (1999): "Balance Sheets, the Transfer Problem, and Financial Crises," in *International Finance and Financial Crises. Essays in Honor of Robert P. Flood*, ed. by P. Isard, A. Razin, and A. K. Rose, pp. 31–44. Kluwer and International Monetary Fund, Dortrecht.

—— (2000): "Introduction," in *Currency Crises*, ed. by P. R. Krugman, pp. 1–6. NBER and University of Chicago Press, Chicago, I.L.

KUMAR, M., U. MOORTHY, AND W. PERRAUDIN (2002): *Predicting Emerging Market Currency Crashes,* Working Paper 02/7. International Monetary Fund, Washington, D.C.

KYDLAND, F. E., AND E. C. PRESCOTT (1977): "Rules Rather than Discretion: The Inconsistency of Optimal Plans," *Journal of Political Economy,* 85(3), 473–491.

LEBLANG, D. (2002): "The Political Economy of Speculative Attacks in the Developing World," *International Studies Quarterly,* 46(1), 69–91.

—— (2003a): "Political Uncertainty and Speculative Attacks," in *Coping With Globalization: Cross-National Patterns in Domestic Governance and Policy Performance,* ed. by S. Chan, and J. Scarritt, pp. 171–206. Frank Cass, Portland, O.R.

—— (2003b): "To Devalue or to Defend? The Political Economy of Exchange Rate Policy," *International Studies Quarterly,* 47(4), 533–559.

—— (2005): "Pegs and Politics," Presented at the Annual Meeting of the American Political Science Association, Washington, D.C., September 2005, www.allacademic.com \ meta \ p40123 index.html (accessed 16 June 2008).

LEBLANG, D., AND S. SATYANATH (2006): "Institutions, Expectations, and Currency Crises," *International Organization,* 60(1), 245–262.

LIPSET, S. M., AND S. ROKKAN (1967): "Cleavage Structures, Party Systems, and Voter Alignments: An Introduction," in *Party Systems and Voter Alignments: Cross-National Perspectives,* ed. by S. M. Lipset, and S. Rokkan, pp. 1–64. The Free Press, New York.

LUEBBERT, G. M. (1991): *Liberalism, Fascism, or Social Democracy. Social Classes and the Political Origins of Regimes in Interwar Europe.* Oxford University Press, Oxford and New York.

MACHINEA, J. L. (2003): "Currency Crises: A Practitioner's View," in *Brookings Trade Forum 2002,* ed. by S. M. Collins, and D. Rodrik, pp. 183–209. Brookings Institution Press, Washington, D.C.

MACINTYRE, A. (2001): "Institutions and Investors: The Politics of the Economic Crisis in Southeast Asia," *International Organization,* 55(1), 81–122.

MARION, N. P. (1999): "Some Parallels between Currency and Banking Crises," in *International Finance and Financial Crises. Essays in Honor of Robert P. Flood,* ed. by P. Isard, A. Razin, and A. K. Rose, pp. 1–18. Kluwer and International Monetary Fund, Dortrecht.

MCKINNON, R. I. (1993): "The Rules of the Game: International Money in Historical Perspective," *Journal of Economic Literature,* 31(1), 1–44.

MEON, P.-G. (2001): "A Model of Exchange Rate Crises With Partisan Governments," *Journal of Macroeconomics,* 23(4), 517–535.

—— (2004): "Why Are Realignments Postponed? A Model of Exchange Rate Revisions with Opportunistic Governments," *The Manchester School,* 72(3).

MEON, P.-G., AND J.-M. RIZZO (2002): "The Viability of Fixed Exchange Rate Commitments: Does Politics Matter? A Theoretical and Empirical Investigation," *Open Economies Review,* 13(2), 111–132.

MONGELLI, F. P. (2002): *"New" Views on the Optimum Currency Area Theory: What is EMU Telling US?*, Working Paper No. 138. European Central Bank, Frankfurt.

MORRIS, S., AND H. S. SHIN (1998): "Unique Equilibrium in a Model of Self-Fulfilling Currency Attacks," *American Economic Review*, 88(3), 587–597.

NEUGART, M. (2003): "Interest Groups, Enlargement of the EMU, and Labor Market Reform," in *Institutional Conflicts and Complementarities. Monetary Policy and Wage Bargaining Institutions in EMU*, ed. by R. Franzese, P. Mooslechner, and M. Schuerz, pp. 147–164. Kluwer, Dortrecht.

NEUGART, M., AND B. ROTHER (2002): "A Remedy for Fiscal Externalities in a Monetary Union," in *Jahrbuch für Handlungs- und Entscheidungstheorie 2/2002*, ed. by H.-P. Barth, and T. Plümper, pp. 91–111. VS-Verlag, Wiesbaden.

NORDHAUS, W. (1975): "The Political Business Cycle," *Review of Economic Studies*, 42(2), 169–190.

NORTH, D. C. (1981): *Structure and Change in Economic History*. Norton, New York.

—— (1990): *Institutions, Institutional Change and Economic Performance*. Cambridge University Press, Cambrige.

NSOULI, S. M., R. ATOYAN, AND A. MOURMOURAS (2004): *Institutions, Program Implementation, and Macroeconomic Performance*, Working Paper 04/184. International Monetary Fund, Washington, D.C.

NURKSE, R. (1944): *International Currency Experience. Lessons of the Inter-War Period*. League of Nations, Geneva.

OBSTFELD, M. (1991): *Destabilizing Effects of Exchange-Rate Escape Clauses*, CEPR Discussion Paper 518. Centre for Economic Policy Research, London.

—— (1994): *The Logic of Currency Crises*, NBER Working Paper 4640. National Bureau of Economic Research, Cambridge, M.A.

—— (1996): "Models of Currency Crises with Self-Fulfilling Features," *European Economic Review*, 40(3–5), 1037–1047.

OBSTFELD, M., AND K. ROGOFF (1995): "The Mirage of Fixed Exchange Rates," *Journal of Economic Perspectives*, 9(4), 73–96.

—— (1996): *Foundations of International Macroeconomics*. MIT Press, Cambridge, M.A.

OBSTFELD, M., J. C. SHAMBAUGH, AND A. M. TAYLOR (2004): "Monetary Sovereignty, Exchange Rates, and Capital Controls: The Trilemma in the Interwar Period," *IMF Staff Papers*, 51(Special Issue), 75–108.

OLSON, M. (1965): *The Logic of Collective Action. Public Goods and the Theory of Groups*. Harvard University Press, Cambridge, M.A.

—— (1982): *The Rise and Decline of Nations: Economic Growth, Stagflation, and Social Rigidities*. Yale University Press, New Haven, N. J.

ONIS, Z. (2000): "Neoliberal Globalization and the Democracy Paradox: Interpreting the Turkish General Elections of 1999," Unpublished, www.home.ku.edu.tr/~zonis/ (accessed 16 June 2008).

—— (2003): "Globalization, Democratization and the Far Right: Turkey's Nationalist Action Party in Critical Perspective," *Democratization*, 10(1), 27–52.

—— (2007): "Beyond the 2001 Crisis: The Political Economy of the New Phase of Neo-Liberal Restructuring in Turkey," Unpublished, www.home.ku.edu.tr/~zonis/ (accessed 16 June 2008).

OYE, K. A. (1985): "The Sterling–Dollar–Franc Triangle: Monetary Diplomacy 1929–1937," *World Politics*, 38(1), 173–199.

PASTOR, M., AND C. WISE (2001): "From Poster Child to Basket Case," *Foreign Affairs*, 80(6), 60–72.

PEREZ-BERMEJO, F., AND S. SOSVILLA-RIVERO (2004): *Currency Crises and Political Factors: Drawing Lessons from the EMS Experience*, FEDEA Documento de Tabajo 2004-04. Fundacion de Estudios de Economia Aplicada, Madrid.

PERSSON, T., AND G. TABELLINI (2000): *Political Economics. Explaining Economic Policy*. MIT Press, Cambridge, M.A.

POLANYI, K. (1944): *The Great Transformation: the Political and Economic Origins of Our Time*. Beacon Press, Boston, M.A.

PUTNAM, R. D. (1988): "The Logic of Two Level Games," *International Organization*, 42(3), 427–460.

RADELET, S., AND J. A. SACHS (2000): "The Onset of the East Asian Financial Crisis," in *Currency Crises*, ed. by P. R. Krugman, pp. 105–153. NBER and University of Chicago Press, Chicago, I.L.

RAMOS, A. M., AND E. TANNER (2002): *Fiscal Sustainability and Fiscal Versus Monetary Dominance: Evidence from Brazil, 1991–2000*, Working Paper 02/5. International Monetary Fund, Washington, D.C.

ROGOFF, K. (1985): "The Optimal Degree of Commitment to an Intermediate Monetary Target," *Quarterly Journal of Economics*, 100(4), 1169–1190.

ROSE, A. K. (2001): "Discussion," *Economic Policy*, 16(32), 75–77.

ROSE, A. K., AND L. E. O. SVENSSON (1994): "European Exchange Rate Credibility Before the Fall," *European Economic Review*, 38(6), 1185–1216.

SCHARPF, F. (1991): *Crisis and Choice in European Social Democracy*. Cornell University Press, Ithaca, N.Y. and London.

SCHNATZ, B. (1998): *Makroökonomische Bestimmungsgründe von Währungsturbulenzen in "Emerging Markets"*, Discussion Paper 03/98. Deutsche Bundesbank, Frankfurt.

SHORTLAND, A. (2004): *The Role of Politics and Institutions in LDC Currency Devaluations*, Department of Economics Working Paper 04/30. University of Leicester, Leicester.

SIMMONS, B. (1994): *Who Adjusts? Domestic Sources of Foreign Economic Policy During the Interwar Years*. Princeton University Press, Princeton, N.J.

STARR, P. K. (1997): "Government Coalitions and the Viability of Currency Boards: Argentina under the Cavallo Plan," *Journal of Interamerican Studies and World Affairs*, 39(2), 83–134.

STEIN, E., AND J. STREB (2004): "Elections and the Timing of Devaluations," *Journal of International Economics*, 63(1), 119–145.

SULLIVAN, M. P. (2002): *Argentina's Political Upheaval.* The Library of Congress, Congressional Research Service, Washington, D.C.

SUSSMAN, N., AND Y. YAFEH (2000): "Institutions, Reforms, and Country Risk: Lessons from Japanese Government Debt in the Meiji Era," *Journal of Economic History*, 60(2), 442–467.

SY, A. (2003): *Rating the Ratings Agencies: Anticipating Currency Crises or Debt Crises*, Working Paper 03/122. International Monetary Fund, Washington, D.C.

TORNELL, A. (1998): *Common Fundamentals in the Tequila and Asian Crises*, Working Paper 7139. National Bureau of Economic Research, Cambridge, M.A.

TRIFFIN, R. (1947): "National Central Banking and the International Economy," *The Review of Economic Studies*, 14(2), 53–75.

TSEBELIS, G. (2002): *Veto Players: How Political Institutions Work.* Princeton University Press, Princeton, N.J.

VAN RIJCKEGHEM, C., AND B. WEDER (2004): *The Politics of Debt Crises*, CEPR Discussion Paper 4683. Centre for Economic Policy Research, London.

VELASCO, A. (1996): "Fixed Exchange Rates: Credibility, flexibility and multiplicity," *European Economic Review*, 40(3–5), 1023–1035.

WANDSCHNEIDER, K. (2008): "The Stability of the Inter-war Gold Exchange Standard: Did Politics Matter?," *Journal of Economic History*, 68(1), 151–181.

WILLARD, K. L., T. W. GUINNANE, AND H. S. ROSEN (1996): "Turning Points in the Civil War: Views from the Greenback Market," *American Economic Review*, 86(4), 1001–1018.

WILLETT, T. D. (2007): "The Political Economy of Exchange Rate Regimes and Currency Crises," *World Economy*, 30(5), 709–732.

WISE, C. (2000): "Argentina's Currency Board," in *Exchange Rate Politics in Latin America*, ed. by C. Wise, and R. Roett, pp. 93–122. Brookings Institution Press, Washington, D.C.

Index